We shall call any business event which alters the amount of assets, liabilities, or capital a *transaction*. In Example 1, the net changes in asset groups were discussed; in Example 2, we show how the accountant makes a meaningful record of a series of transactions, reconciling them step by step with the accounting equation.

EXAMPLE 2.

During the month of January, Mr. Alan Bagon, Lawyer,

(1) Invested $5,000 to open his law practice.

(2) Bought supplies (stationery, forms, pencils, etc.) for cash, $300.

(3) Bought office equipment from Altway Furniture Company on account, $2,500.

(4) Received $2,000 in fees earned during the month.

(5) Paid office rent for January, $500.

(6) Paid salary for part-time help, $200.

(7) Paid $1,000 to Altway Furniture Company on account.

(8) After taking an inventory at the end of the month, found he had used $200 worth of supplies.

(9) Withdrew $300 for personal use.

These transactions might be analyzed and recorded as follows.

Transaction (1). Mr. Bagon invested $5,000 to open his law practice. There are two accounts that are affected: the asset Cash is increased, and the capital of the firm is increased by the same amount.

	ASSETS	=	LIABILITIES	+	CAPITAL
	Cash				A. Bagon, Capital
(1)	+ $5,000	=			+ $5,000

Transaction (2). Bought supplies for cash, $300. In this case, Mr. Bagon is substituting one asset for another: he is receiving (+) the asset Supplies and paying out (−) the asset Cash. Note that the capital of $5,000 remains unchanged.

	ASSETS		=	LIABILITIES	+	CAPITAL
	Cash	+ Supplies				A. Bagon, Capital
	$5,000					$5,000
(2)	− 300	+ $300				
	$4,700 +	$300	=			$5,000

Transaction (3). Bought office equipment from Altway Furniture Company on account, $2,500. He is receiving the asset Equipment but is not paying for it with the asset Cash. Instead, he will *owe* the money to the Altway Furniture Company. Therefore, he is *liable* for this amount in the future, thus creating the liability Accounts Payable.

	ASSETS			=	LIABILITIES	+	CAPITAL
	Cash	+ Supplies +	Equipment		Accounts Payable		A. Bagon, Capital
	$4,700	$300					$5,000
(3)			$2,500		+ $2,500		
	$4,700 +	$300 +	$2,500	=	$2,500	+	$5,000

Transaction (4). Received $2,000 in fees earned during the month. Because he received $2,000, the asset Cash increased and also his capital increased. It is important to note that he labels the $2,000 *fees income* to show its origin.

	ASSETS			=	LIABILITIES	+	CAPITAL	
	Cash	+ Supplies +	Equipment		Accounts Payable		A. Bagon, Capital	
	$4,700	$300	$2,500		$2,500		$5,000	
(4)	+ 2,000						+ 2,000	Fees Income
	$6,700 +	$300 +	$2,500	=	$2,500	+	$7,000	

Transaction (5). **Paid office rent for January, $500.** When the word "paid" is stated, you know it means a deduction from Cash, since he is paying *out* his asset Cash. Payment of expense is a reduction of capital. It is termed *rent expense*.

	ASSETS			=	LIABILITIES	+	CAPITAL
	Cash	+ Supplies +	Equipment		Accounts Payable		A. Bagon, Capital
	$6,700	$300	$2,500		$2,500		$7,000
(5)	− 500						− 500 Rent Expense
	$6,200 +	$300 +	$2,500	=	$2,500	+	$6,500

Transaction (6). **Paid salary for part-time help, $200.** Again the word "paid" means a deduction of cash and a reduction in capital. This time it refers to *salaries expense*.

	ASSETS			=	LIABILITIES	+	CAPITAL
	Cash	+ Supplies +	Equipment		Accounts Payable		A. Bagon, Capital
	$6,200	$300	$2,500		$2,500		$6,500
(6)	− 200						− 200 Salaries Expense
	$6,000 +	$300 +	$2,500	=	$2,500	+	$6,300

Transaction (7). **Paid $1,000 to Altway Furniture Company on account.** Here he is reducing the asset Cash because he is paying $1,000, and reducing the liability Accounts Payable. He will now owe $1,000 less.

	ASSETS			=	LIABILITIES	+	CAPITAL
	Cash	+ Supplies +	Equipment		Accounts Payable		A. Bagon, Capital
	$6,000	$300	$2,500		$2,500		$6,300
(7)	− 1,000				− 1,000		
	$5,000 +	$300 +	$2,500	=	$1,500	+	$6,300

Transaction (8). **After taking an inventory at the end of the month, Mr. Bagon found he had used $200 worth of supplies.** The original amount of supplies purchased has been reduced to the amount that was found to be left at the end of the month. Therefore, the difference was the amount used ($300 − $100 = $200). This reduces the asset Supplies by $200, and reduces capital by the same amount. It is termed *supplies expense*.

	ASSETS			=	LIABILITIES	+	CAPITAL
	Cash	+ Supplies +	Equipment		Accounts Payable		A. Bagon, Capital
	$5,000	$300	$2,500		$1,500		$6,300
(8)		− 200					− 200 Supplies Expense
	$5,000 +	$100 +	$2,500	=	$1,500	+	$6,100

Transaction (9). **Withdrew $300 for personal use.** The withdrawal of cash is a reduction not only in Mr. Bagon's cash position but also in his capital. This is not an expense but a personal withdrawal, a reduction of the amount invested.

	ASSETS			=	LIABILITIES	+	CAPITAL
	Cash	+ Supplies +	Equipment		Accounts Payable		A. Bagon, Capital
	$5,000	$100	$2,500		$1,500		$6,100
(9)	− 300						− 300 Drawing
	$4,700 +	$100 +	$2,500	=	$1,500	+	$5,800

Summary of Transactions
Month of January, 197—

	ASSETS			=	LIABILITIES	+	CAPITAL	
	Cash +	Supplies +	Equipment		Accounts Payable		A. Bagon, Capital	
(1)	$5,000						$5,000	
(2)	− 300 +	$300						
	$4,700 +	$300		=			$5,000	
(3)			$2,500		$2,500			
	$4,700 +	$300 +	$2,500	=	$2,500	+	$5,000	
(4)	+ 2,000						+ 2,000	Fees Income
	$6,700 +	$300 +	$2,500	=	$2,500	+	$7,000	
(5)	− 500						− 500	Rent Expense
	$6,200 +	$300 +	$2,500	=	$2,500	+	$6,500	
(6)	− 200						− 200	Salaries Expense
	$6,000 +	$300 +	$2,500	=	$2,500	+	$6,300	
(7)	− 1,000				− 1,000			
	$5,000 +	$300 +	$2,500	=	$1,500	+	$6,300	
(8)		− 200					− 200	Supplies Expense
	$5,000 +	$100 +	$2,500	=	$1,500	+	$6,100	
(9)	− 300						− 300	Drawing
	$4,700 +	$100 +	$2,500	=	$1,500	+	$5,800	

Summary

(1)   The four phases of accounting are _____, _____, _____, and _____.

(2)   The accounting equation is _____ = _____ + _____.

(3)   Items owned by a business that have money value are known as _____.

(4)   _____ is the interest of the owners in a business.

(5)   Money owed to an outsider is a _____.

(6)   The difference between assets and liabilities is _____.

(7)   Financial events that occur in a business are termed _____.

(8)   An investment in the business increases _____ and _____.

(9)   To purchase "on account" is to create a _____.

(10) When the word "paid" occurs, it means a deduction of _____.

(11) Income increases net assets and also _____.

(12) A withdrawal of cash reduces cash and _____.

Answers: (1) recording, classifying, summarizing, reporting; (2) ASSETS, LIABILITIES, CAPITAL; (3) assets; (4) capital; (5) liability; (6) capital; (7) transactions; (8) assets, capital; (9) liability; (10) cash; (11) capital; (12) capital

Solved Problems

1.1. What effect do the transactions below have on the owner's equity (capital)?

(a) The owner invested $5,000 in the business. _____

(b) He bought equipment on account, $2,400. _____

(c) He paid 1/2 of the bill owed to the creditor. _____

(d) He received $2,000 in fees. _____

(e) He paid salaries for the week, $800. _____

(f) He withdrew $400 from the business. _____

(g) He paid rent for the month, $320. _____

(h) Inventory of supplies decreased $350 during the month. _____

SOLUTION

(a) increase	(c) no effect	(e) decrease	(g) decrease
(b) no effect	(d) increase	(f) decrease	(h) decrease

1.2. Compute the amount of the missing element:

	ASSETS	LIABILITIES	CAPITAL
(a)	$24,000	$19,000	?
(b)	16,500	?	12,300
(c)	?	2,700	14,000
(d)	15,665	9,406	?

SOLUTION

(a)	$ 5,000	($24,000 − $19,000)
(b)	$ 4,200	(16,500 − 12,300)
(c)	$16,700	(2,700 + 14,000)
(d)	$ 6,259	(15,665 − 9,406)

1.3. Transactions completed by J. Epstein, M.D., appear below. Indicate the increase (+), decrease (−), or no change (0) in the accompanying table.

		ASSETS =	LIABILITIES +	CAPITAL
(a)	Paid rent expense for month.			
(b)	Paid bi-weekly salary for lab assistant.			
(c)	Cash fees collected for the week.			
(d)	Bought medical equipment, paying cash.			
(e)	Bought equipment on account.			
(f)	Paid a creditor (liability) money owed.			

SOLUTION

		ASSETS =	LIABILITIES +	CAPITAL
(a)	(reduction of cash and capital)	−	0	−
(b)	(reduction of cash and capital)	−	0	−
(c)	(increase in cash and capital)	+	0	+
(d)	(increase in equipment, reduction in cash)	+ −	0	0
(e)	(increase in equipment and in accounts payable)	+	+	0
(f)	(decrease in cash and in accounts payable)	−	−	0

1.4.   Mr. Allen begins business, investing $4,000 in cash, equipment valued at $12,000, and $1,000 worth of supplies.   What is the capital of the firm?

SOLUTION

ASSETS	=	LIABILITIES	+	CAPITAL
$ 4,000				
12,000				
1,000				
$17,000	=	0	+	$17,000

Mr. Allen's capital is $17,000, as it is the total of all his assets, less his liabilities (0).

1.5.   If in Problem 1.4, Mr. Allen had included a $6,000 note payable (written liability), what would his capital then have been?

SOLUTION

ASSETS	=	LIABILITIES	+	CAPITAL
$17,000	=	$6,000	+	$11,000

The total assets of $17,000, reduced by liabilities of $6,000, results in $11,000 capital. Stated a different way:

$$\text{ASSETS (\$17,000)} = \text{LIABILITIES (\$6,000)} + \text{CAPITAL (?)}$$
$$17,000 = 6,000 + ?$$
$$17,000 = 6,000 + 11,000$$

1.6.   Supplies had a balance of $2,400 at the beginning of the year.   At the end of the period, its inventory showed $1,400.   How is this decrease recorded?

SOLUTION

ASSETS	=	LIABILITIES	+	CAPITAL	
Supplies					
Balance $2,400				$2,400	
Decrease − 1,000				− 1,000	Supplies Expense
Balance $1,400				$1,400	

1.7.   Illustrate the difference between *supplies* and *supplies expense*.

SOLUTION

Supplies is an asset and represents the value of supplies owned (supplies on hand).   *Supplies expense* is the value of supplies *used* during the period and is a reduction of capital.

Supplies (Asset)	$2,400 (beginning)
Supplies Expense	1,000 (used during year)
Supplies (Asset)	1,400 (end)

The value of supplies at the end of the period is the difference between the beginning balance and the amount that has been used.

1.8. Record the following transaction in the space provided: Bought equipment for $22,000, paying $6,000 in cash and owing the balance.

	ASSETS	=	LIABILITIES	+	CAPITAL
	Cash + Equipment		Accounts Payable		
Balance	$30,000				$30,000
Entry (?)					
Balance (?)					

SOLUTION

Step 1. Reduce the cash account by the amount paid, $6,000.

Step 2. Record the purchase of the equipment at its cost, $22,000.

Step 3. Increase Accounts Payable for the amount owed, $16,000.

	ASSETS	=	LIABILITIES	+	CAPITAL
	Cash + Equipment		Accounts Payable		
Balance	$30,000				$30,000
Entry	− 6,000 + $22,000		+ $16,000*		
Balance	$24,000 + $22,000	=	$16,000	+	$30,000

*$22,000 (equipment)
 6,000 (paid in cash)
$16,000 (balance owed)

1.9. In Problem 1.8 what effect does the purchase of the equipment on account have on capital?

SOLUTION

No effect.

ASSETS				LIABILITIES
Equipment	−	Cash	=	Accounts Payable
$22,000	−	$6,000	=	$16,000

1.10. In Problem 1.8 what effect does the payment of the liability in full have on the capital account?

SOLUTION

No effect.

	ASSETS	=	LIABILITIES	+	CAPITAL
	Cash + Equipment		Accounts Payable		
Balance	$24,000 $22,000		$16,000		$30,000
Entry	− 16,000		− 16,000		
Balance	$ 8,000 + $22,000	=			$30,000

The reduction of cash is accompanied by an equal reduction of the accounts payable.

1.11. The summary data of the Boyd Taxi Company for May are presented below in equation form. Describe each of the transactions that occurred during the month.

	Cash	+	Supplies	+	Equipment	=	Liabilities	+	Capital	
(1)	+ $6,600								+ $6,000	
(2)	− 3,200				+ $3,200					
(3)	− 500		+ $500							
(4)					+ 2,000		+ $2,000			
(5)	+ 2,500								+ 2,500	Fares Income
(6)	− 1,100								+ 1,100	Salaries Expense
(7)	− 500						− 500			
(8)	− 300								− 300	Drawing
	$3,500	+	$500	+	$5,200	=	$1,500	+	$7,700	

SOLUTION

(1) An investment was made by the owner.

(2) Equipment was bought and *paid* for.

(3) Supplies were bought and paid for.

(4) Additional equipment was bought *on account*, thus creating the liability.

(5) Income from taxi fares is recorded.

(6) Salaries were paid to the company's drivers.

(7) Cash was paid, reducing a liability.

(8) Owner *withdrew* funds for his personal use.

1.12. The following transactions occurred during the year for the Ken Stanton Musical Band. **(1)** Invested $2,000 in the formation of a band. **(2)** Bought instruments costing $1,200, on account. **(3)** Bought musical supplies for cash, $300. **(4)** Received $600 for services rendered. **(5)** Paid salaries of $250. **(6)** Paid in full the money owed on instruments. **(7)** Travel expenses of $150 were paid. **(8)** Withdrew $200 for personal use.

Record the effect of each transaction in the table below. (*Note*: The term *element* refers to assets, liabilities, or capital; *account* refers to the individual item within an element.)

	Increase		Decrease	
	Element	Account	Element	Account
(1)	Assets	Cash $2,000		
	Capital	K. Stanton, Capital $2,000		
(2)				
(3)				
(4)				
(5)				
(6)				
(7)				
(8)				

SOLUTION

	Increase			Decrease		
	Element	Account		Element	Account	
(1)	Assets	Cash	$2,000			
	Capital	K. Stanton, Capital	2,000			
(2)	Assets	Equipment	1,200			
	Liabilities	Accounts Payable	1,200			
(3)	Assets	Supplies	300	Assets	Cash	$ 300
(4)	Assets	Cash	600			
	Capital	Music Income	600			
(5)				Capital	Salaries Expense	250
				Assets	Cash	250
(6)				Liabilities	Accounts Payable	1,200
				Assets	Cash	1,200
(7)				Capital	Travel Expense	150
				Assets	Cash	150
(8)				Capital	K. Stanton, Drawing	200
				Assets	Cash	200

1.13. The following transactions were engaged in during the month of March by Dr. M. Levy, Physician.

(1) Opened his practice by investing $10,000 in the business.

(2) Bought office equipment for $7,000 on account from Medical Products, Inc.

(3) Paid $2,000 for various medical supplies for the office.

(4) Received $1,600 in fees earned during the first month of operations.

(5) Paid office rent for the month, $200.

(6) Paid medical assistant salary for the month, $400.

(7) Paid Medical Products, Inc., $3,000.

(8) Withdrew $500 for personal use.

Enter each transaction in the following form.

Cash + Supplies + Equipment   =   Liabilities + Capital

(1)

(2)

(3)
Balance _____   _____   _____   _____   _____

(4)
Balance _____   _____   _____   _____   _____

(5)
Balance _____   _____   _____   _____   _____

(6)
Balance _____   _____   _____   _____   _____

(7)
Balance _____   _____   _____   _____   _____

(8)
Balance _____   _____   _____   _____   _____

SOLUTION

	Cash	+ Supplies	+ Equipment	=	Liabilities	+ Capital	
(1)	$10,000					$10,000	
(2)			+ $7,000		+ $7,000		
(3)	− 2,000	+ + $2,000					
Balance	$ 8,000 +	$2,000 +	$7,000	=	$7,000 +	$10,000	
(4)	+ 1,600					+ 1,600	Fees Income
Balance	$ 9,600 +	$2,000 +	$7,000	=	$7,000 +	$11,600	
(5)	− 200					− 200	Rent Expense
Balance	$ 9,400 +	$2,000 +	$7,000	=	$7,000 +	$11,400	
(6)	− 400					− 400	Salaries Expense
Balance	$ 9,000 +	$2,000 +	$7,000	=	$7,000 +	$11,000	
(7)	− 3,000				− 3,000		
Balance	$ 6,000 +	$2,000 +	$7,000	=	$4,000 +	$11,000	
(8)	− 500					− 500	Drawing
Balance	$ 5,500 +	$2,000 +	$7,000	=	$4,000 +	$10,500	

1.14. Summary financial data of the Nu-Look Dry Cleaning Company for November are presented below in transaction form.

(1) Opened a business bank account, depositing $12,000.

(2) Purchased supplies for cash, $220.

(3) Purchased dry cleaning equipment for $3,500, paying $1,500 in cash with the balance on account.

(4) Paid rent for the month, $425.

(5) Cash sales for the month totaled $1,850.

(6) Paid salaries of $375.

(7) Paid $500 on account.

(8) The cost of supplies used was determined to be $60.

Record the transactions and running balances in the form below.

	ASSETS			**=**	**LIABILITIES**	**+**	**CAPITAL**
	Cash	+ Supplies	+ Equipment		Accounts Payable		Nu-Look Company
(1)							
(2)	____	____	____		____		____
Balance							
(3)	____	____	____		____		____
Balance							
(4)	____	____	____		____		____
Balance							
(5)	____	____	____		____		____
Balance							
(6)	____	____	____		____		____
Balance							
(7)	____	____	____		____		____
Balance							
(8)	____	____	____		____		____
Balance							

SOLUTION

	ASSETS			=	LIABILITIES	+	CAPITAL
	Cash +	Supplies +	Equipment		Accounts Payable		Nu-Look Dry Cleaning Company
(1)	$12,000						$12,000
(2)	− 220 +	+ $220					
Balance	$11,780 +	$220					$12,000
(3)	− 1,500		+ $3,500		+ $2,000		
Balance	$10,280 +	$220 +	$3,500	=	$2,000	+	$12,000
(4)	− 425						− 425 Rent Expense
Balance	$ 9,855 +	$220 +	$3,500	=	$2,000	+	$11,575
(5)	+ 1,850						+ 1,850 Cleaning Income
Balance	$11,705 +	$220 +	$3,500	=	$2,000	+	$13,425
(6)	− 375						− 375 Salaries Expense
Balance	$11,330 +	$220 +	$3,500	=	$2,000	+	$13,050
(7)	− 500				− 500		
Balance	$10,830 +	$220 +	$3,500	=	$1,500	+	$13,050
(8)		− 60					− 60 Supplies Expense
Balance	$10,830 +	$160 +	$3,500	=	$1,500	+	$12,990

1.15. Mike Jameson operates a shoe repair shop known as the Repair Center. The balances of his accounts on June 1 of the current year are as follows: Cash, $5,400; Supplies, $600; Equipment, $3,200; Accounts Payable, $3,000; Capital, $6,200. The transactions during the month of June appear below.

(1) Paid salaries of $350.

(2) Paid creditors on account $2,000.

(3) Bought additional equipment on account for $3,100.

(4) Received cash from customers for repair service, $3,600.

(5) Paid delivery expense, $140.

(6) Inventory of supplies at the end of the month was $275.

(7) Mr. Jameson withdrew for his personal use $250.

Record the transactions below in the form provided.

	ASSETS			=	LIABILITIES	+	CAPITAL
	Cash +	Supplies +	Equipment		Accounts Payable		M. Jameson, Capital
	$5,400	$600	$3,200		$3,000		$6,200
(1)	———	———	———		———		———
Balance							
(2)	———	———	———		———		———
Balance							
(3)	———	———	———		———		———
Balance							
(4)	———	———	———		———		———
Balance							
(5)	———	———	———		———		———
Balance							
(6)	———	———	———		———		———
Balance							
(7)	———	———	———		———		———
Balance							

SOLUTION

		ASSETS			=	LIABILITIES	+	CAPITAL
	Cash	+ Supplies	+ Equipment		=	Accounts Payable	+	M. Jameson, Capital
Balance	$5,400 +	$600 +	$3,200		=	$3,000	+	$6,200
(1)	− 350							− 350 Salaries Expense
Balance	$5,050 +	$600 +	$3,200		=	$3,000	+	$5,850
(2)	− 2,000					− 2,000		
Balance	$3,050 +	$600 +	$3,200		=	$1,000	+	$5,850
(3)			+ 3,100			+ 3,100		
Balance	$3,050 +	$600 +	$6,300		=	$4,100	+	$5,850
(4)	+ 3,600							+ 3,600 Repair Income
Balance	$6,650 +	$600 +	$6,300		=	$4,100	+	$9,450
(5)	− 140							− 140 Delivery Expense
Balance	$6,510 +	$600 +	$6,300		=	$4,100	+	$9,310
(6)		− 325*						− 325 Supplies Expense
Balance	$6,510 +	$275 +	$6,300		=	$4,100	+	$8,985
(7)	− 250							− 250 Drawing
Balance	$6,260 +	$275 +	$6,300		=	$4,100	+	$8,735

*$600   (beginning inventory)
− 275   (ending inventory)
$325   (amount used, or supplies expense)

Chapter 2

Financial Statements

2.1 INTRODUCTION

The two principal questions that the owner of a business asks periodically are:

(1) What is my net income (profit)?

(2) What is my capital?

The simple balance of assets against liabilities and capital, provided by the accounting equation, is insufficient to give complete answers. For (1) we must know the type and amount of income and the type and amount of each expense for the period in question. For (2) it is necessary to obtain the type and amount of each asset, liability, and capital account at the end of the period. This information is provided by (1) the *income statement* and (2) the *balance sheet*.

EXAMPLE 1.

After the transactions for the month of January have been recorded in the books of Mr. Alan Bagon, the accounts show the following balances (see page 5).

ACCOUNTS	ASSETS	LIABILITIES AND CAPITAL
Cash	*$4,700*	
Supplies	*100*	
Equipment	*2,500*	
Accounts Payable		*$1,500*
A. Bagon, Capital		*5,800*
Total	*$7,300*	*$7,300*

It is seen that the assets of the business changed from the original $5,000 invested by Mr. Bagon at the beginning of January to $7,300 at the end of January. Does that represent the amount of profit earned? It does not, because (1) liabilities have changed and (2) some of the transactions affecting capital were those relating to his investment; that is, he withdrew some of his original investment. It is apparent that his liabilities increased: they are now $1,500 more than the beginning liabilities (the balance due on the equipment).

His net assets or his capital is now $5,800, an increase of $800 over the beginning amount. That would represent his profit if he had not withdrawn some of his investment.

2.2 INCOME STATEMENT

The income statement may be defined as *a summary of the revenue, expenses, and net income of a business entity for a specific period of time.* This may also be called a Profit & Loss Statement, Operating Statement, or Statement of Operations. Let us review the meanings of the elements entering into the income statement.

14

Revenue. The increase in capital resulting from the delivery of goods or rendering of services by the business. In amount, the revenue is equal to the cash and receivables gained in compensation for the goods delivered or services rendered.

Expenses. The decrease in capital caused by the business's revenue-producing operations. In amount, the expense is equal to the value of goods and services used up or consumed in obtaining revenue.

Net Income. The increase in capital resulting from profitable operation of a business; it is the excess of revenues over expenses for the accounting period.

It is important to note that a cash receipt qualifies as revenue only if it serves to increase capital. Similarly, a cash payment is an expense only if it decreases capital. Thus, for instance, borrowing cash from a bank does not contribute to revenue.

EXAMPLE 2.

Mr. A. Bagon's total January income and the totals for his various expenses can be obtained by analyzing the transactions shown under the heading "Capital" on page 5. The income from fees amounted to $2,000 and the expenses incurred to produce this income were: rent, $500; salaries, $200; and supplies, $200. The formal Income Statement can now be prepared.

Alan Bagon
Income Statement
month of January, 197–

Income from Fees		*$2,000*
Operating Expenses		
Rent	*$500*	
Salaries	*200*	
Supplies	*200*	
Total Operating Expenses		*900*
Net Income		*$1,100*

In many companies there are hundreds and perhaps thousands of income and expense transactions in one month. To lump all these transactions under one account would be very cumbersome and would, in addition, make it impossible to show relationships among the various items. For example, we might wish to know the relationship of selling expenses to sales and whether the ratio is higher or lower than in previous periods. To solve this problem we leave the investment or permanent entries in the capital account and then set up a *temporary* set of income and expense accounts. The net difference of these accounts, the net profit or net loss, is then transferred in one figure to the capital account.

2.3 ACCRUAL BASIS AND CASH BASIS OF ACCOUNTING

Because an income statement pertains to a definite period of time, it becomes necessary to determine just *when* an item of revenue or expense is to be accounted for. Under the *accrual basis of accounting,* revenue is recognized only when earned and expense recognized only when incurred. This differs significantly from the *cash basis of accounting,* which recognizes revenue and expense generally with the receipt and payment of cash. Essential to the accrual basis is the *matching* of expenses with the revenue that they helped produce. Under the accrual system the accounts are adjusted at the end of the accounting period to properly reflect the revenue earned and the cost and expenses applicable to the period.

Most business firms use the accrual basis, while individuals and professional people generally use the cash basis. Ordinarily the cash basis is not suitable when there are significant amounts of inventories, receivables, and payables.

2.4 BALANCE SHEET

The information needed for the balance sheet items are the net balances at the end of the period, rather than the total for the period as in the income statement. Thus, management wants to know the balance of cash in the bank, the balance of inventory, equipment, etc., on hand at the end of the period.

The balance sheet may then be defined as *a statement showing the assets, liabilities, and capital of a business entity at a specific date.* This statement is also called a Statement of Financial Position or Statement of Financial Condition.

In preparing the balance sheet, it is not necessary to make any further analysis of the data. The needed data — that is, the balances of the asset, liability, and capital accounts — are already available.

EXAMPLE 3.

Alan Bagon
Balance Sheet
January 31, 197–

ASSETS

Cash	$4,700
Supplies	100
Equipment	2,500
Total Assets	$7,300

LIABILITIES AND CAPITAL

Liabilities			
Accounts Payable			$1,500
Capital			
Balance, January 1, 197–		$5,000	
Net Income for January	$1,100		
Less: Withdrawals	300		
Increase in Capital		800	
Total Capital			5,800
Total Liabilities and Capital			$7,300

The close relationship of the income statement and the balance sheet is apparent. The net income of $1,100 for January, shown as the final figure on the income statement of Example 2, is also shown as a separate figure on the balance sheet of Example 3. The income statement is thus the connecting link between two balance sheets. As discussed earlier, the income and expense items are actually a further analysis of the capital account.

The balance sheet of Example 3 is arranged in *report form*, with the liabilities and capital sections shown below the asset section. It may also be arranged in *account form*, with the liabilities and capital sections to the right of, rather than below, the asset section, as shown in Example 4.

EXAMPLE 4.

Alan Bagon
Balance Sheet
January 31, 197–

ASSETS

Cash	$4,700
Supplies	100
Equipment	2,500

LIABILITIES AND CAPITAL

Liabilities			
Accounts Payable			$1,500
Capital			
Balance, January 31, 197–		$5,000	
Net Income for January	$1,100		
Less: Withdrawals	300		
Increase in Capital		800	
Total Capital			$5,800

Total Assets	$7,300	

Total Liabilities and Capital		$7,300

Instead of showing the details of the capital account in the balance sheet, we may show the changes in a separate form called the Capital Statement. In that case, we have three interrelated statements, as shown in Example 5.

EXAMPLE 5.

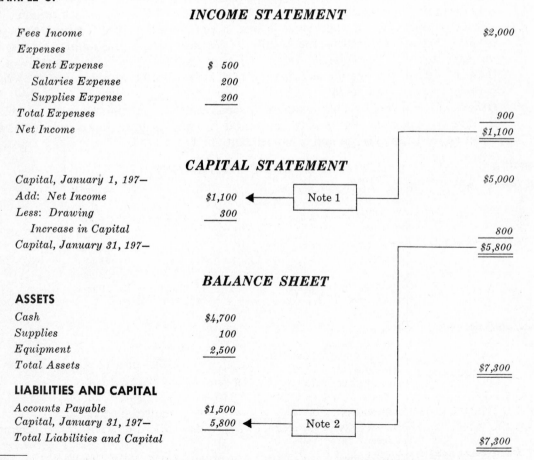

INCOME STATEMENT

Fees Income		$2,000
Expenses		
Rent Expense	$ 500	
Salaries Expense	200	
Supplies Expense	200	
Total Expenses		900
Net Income		$1,100

CAPITAL STATEMENT

Capital, January 1, 197–		$5,000
Add: Net Income	$1,100	
Less: Drawing	300	
Increase in Capital		800
Capital, January 31, 197–		$5,800

Note 1

BALANCE SHEET

ASSETS

Cash	$4,700
Supplies	100
Equipment	2,500
Total Assets	$7,300

LIABILITIES AND CAPITAL

Accounts Payable	$1,500
Capital, January 31, 197–	5,800
Total Liabilities and Capital	$7,300

Note 2

Note 1. The net income of the income statement, $1,100, is transferred to the capital statement.

Note 2. The capital is summarized in the capital statement and the final balance included in the balance sheet.

2.5 CLASSIFIED FINANCIAL STATEMENTS

Financial statements become more useful when the individual items are classified into significant groups for comparison and financial analysis. The classifications relating to the primary statements, the income statement and the balance sheet, will be discussed in this section.

THE INCOME STATEMENT

The classified income statement sets out the amount of each function and enables management, stockholders, analysts, and others to study the changes in function costs over successive accounting periods. There are four functional classifications of the income statement.

(1) *Revenue.* This includes gross income from the sale of products or services. It may be designated as Sales, Income from Fees, etc., to indicate gross income. The gross amount is reduced by Sales Returns and Allowances and by Sales Discounts to arrive at Net Sales.

(2) *Cost of goods sold.* This includes the costs related to the products or services sold. It would be relatively simple to compute for a firm that retails furniture; it would be more complex for a manufacturing firm that changes raw materials into finished products.

(3) *Operating expenses.* This includes all expenses or resources consumed in obtaining revenue. Operating expenses are further divided into two groups. *Selling expenses* are those related to the promotion and sale of the company's product or service. Generally, one individual is held accountable for this function and his performance is measured by the results in increasing sales and maintaining selling expenses at an established level. *General and administrative expenses* are those related to the overall activities of the business, such as the salaries of the president and other officers.

(4) *Other expenses (net).* This includes nonoperating and incidental expenses such as interest expense. Often any incidental income, such as interest income, is offset against the expense and a net amount shown.

EXAMPLE 6.   *CLASSIFIED INCOME STATEMENT*

Gross Sales	Sales of Goods or Services		$25,000	
	Less: Sales Returns and Allowances	$1,250		
	Sales Discounts	750	2,000	
	Net Sales			$23,000
Cost of Goods Sold	Inventory, January 1		$ 2,500	
	Purchases		16,500	
			19,000	
	Inventory, December 31		3,000	
	Cost of Goods Sold			16,000
	Gross Profit			$ 7,000
Operating Expenses	Selling Expenses			
	Sales Salaries	$1,200		
	Travel Expense	200		
	Advertising	600	$ 2,000	
	General Expenses			
	Officers' Salaries	1,000		
	Insurance	600	1,600	
	Total Operating Expenses			3,600
	Net Income from Operations			$ 3,400
Other Expenses (net)	Interest Expense		$ 500	
	Less: Interest Income		100	
	Other Expenses (net)			400
	Net Income			$ 3,000

THE BALANCE SHEET

The balance sheet becomes a more useful statement for comparison and financial analysis if the asset and liability groups are classified. For example, an important index of the financial state of business, derivable from the classified balance sheet, is the ratio of current assets to current liabilities. This *current ratio* ought generally to be at least 2 to 1; that is, current assets should be twice current liabilities. For our purposes we will designate the following classifications.

ASSETS	LIABILITIES
Current	Current
Property, plant, and equipment	Long-term
Other	

Current assets. Assets reasonably expected to be converted into cash or used in the current operation of the business. (The current period is generally taken as one year.) Examples are cash, notes receivable, accounts receivable, inventory, and prepaid expenses (prepaid insurance, prepaid rent, etc.).

Property, plant, and equipment. Long-lived assets used in the production of goods or services. These assets, sometimes called *fixed assets* or *plant assets*, are used in the operation of the business rather than being held for sale, as are inventory items.

Other assets. Various assets other than current assets, fixed assets, or assets to which specific captions are given. For instance, the caption Investments would be used if significant sums were invested. Often companies show a caption for intangible assets such as patents or goodwill. In other cases, there may be a separate caption for deferred charges. If, however, the amounts are not large in relation to total assets, the various items may be grouped under one caption, Other Assets.

Current liabilities. Debts which must be satisfied from current assets within the next operating period, usually one year. Examples are accounts payable, notes payable, the current portion of long-term debt, and various accrued items such as salaries payable and taxes payable.

Long-term liabilities. Liabilities which are payable beyond the next year. The most common examples are bonds payable and mortgages payable.

Example 7, on the following page, shows a classified balance sheet of typical form.

EXAMPLE 7.

CLASSIFIED BALANCE SHEET

ASSETS

Current Assets			
Cash		$5,400	
Accounts Receivable		1,600	
Supplies		500	
Total Current Assets			$ 7,500
Fixed Assets			
Land		$4,000	
Building		8,000	
Equipment		2,000	
Total Fixed Assets			14,000
Total Assets			$21,500

LIABILITIES AND CAPITAL

Current Liabilities			
Accounts Payable		$2,000	
Notes Payable		1,750	
Total Current Liabilities			$ 3,750
Long-Term Liabilities			
Mortgage Payable			12,000
Total Liabilities			$15,750
Capital			
J. Ales, Capital, January 1		$4,750	
Net Income for the Year	$3,000		
Less: Withdrawals	2,000		
Increase in Capital		1,000	
J. Ales, Capital, December 31			5,750
Total Liabilities and Capital			$21,500

Summary

(1)   Another term for an accounting report is an _____.

(2)   The statement that shows net income for the period is known as the _____ statement.

(3)   The statement that shows net loss for the period is known as the _____ statement.

(4)   Two groups of items comprising the income statement are _____ and _____.

(5)   The difference between income and expense is known as _____.

SCHAUM'S OUTLINE OF

THEORY AND PROBLEMS

of

ACCOUNTING I

•

by

JAMES A. CASHIN, M.S., CPA

Professor of Accounting
Hofstra University

and

JOEL J. LERNER, M.S.

Chairman, Faculty of Business
Sullivan County Community College

SCHAUM'S OUTLINE SERIES

McGRAW-HILL BOOK COMPANY

New York, St. Louis, San Francisco, Düsseldorf, Johannesburg, Kuala Lumpur, London, Mexico,
Montreal, New Delhi, Panama, São Paulo, Singapore, Sydney, and Toronto

07-010211-2

3 4 5 6 7 8 9   SH SH   7 9 8 7 6 5 4

Library of Congress Cataloging in Publication Data

Cashin, James A
   Schaum's outline of theory and problems of accounting
I-

   (Schaum's outline series)
    1. Accounting — Problems, exercises, etc.
I. Lerner, Joel J., joint author.   II. Title.
III. Title: Theory and problems of accounting I.

[HF5661.C38]   657'.076   73-5890
ISBN 0-07-010211-2

Preface

This volume is the first in a series of Schaum's Outlines that bring to the study of Accounting the same *solved-problems approach* which has proved so successful in the disciplines of Engineering and Mathematics. In contrast to previous supplementary materials, which have been little more than summary textbooks, the new Accounting Series is organized around the *practical application* of basic accounting concepts. By providing the student with:

1. concise definitions and explanations, in easily understood terms

2. fully worked-out solutions to a large range of problems (against which the student can check his own solutions)

3. review questions

4. sample examinations typical of those used by two-year and four-year colleges

these books help him to develop the all-important know-how for solving problems — on the CPA examination and in his professional practice.

Accounting I and its sequel, *Accounting II,* parallel the full-year introductory course offered in most colleges and universities. Subject matter has been carefully coordinated with the leading textbooks, so that any topic can easily be found from the Table of Contents or the Index. In addition, this book should prove a valuable supplement to other accounting courses and to individual study. Today, there are an increasing number of programs offering college credit by examination, such as the College Level Examination Program (CLEP) and the New York College Proficiency Examination. Advanced placement, too, is now possible. Returning veterans and others who may have taken Introductory Accounting some years ago will find much-needed aid in brushing up for the next course.

Among the many individuals the authors have to thank for contributions to *Accounting I,* they would like to single out the members of a student panel who offered suggestions and helped in designing the problems. They are: Richard S. Clarke, Louis Lucido, Vi Messerli, Herman J. Ortmann, Jane Hickman, and Gary Weller.

JAMES A. CASHIN
JOEL J. LERNER

Hofstra University
Sullivan County Community College
March 1973

CONTENTS

CONTENTS

CONTENTS

Chapter 1

Accounting Concepts

1.1 NATURE OF ACCOUNTING

Every element of society — from the individual to an entire industry or government branch — has to make decisions on how to allocate its resources. *Accounting is the process which aids these decisions by (1) recording, (2) classifying, (3) summarizing, and (4) reporting business transactions and interpreting their effects on the affairs of the business entity.* This definition makes it clear that the recording of data, or *bookkeeping*, is only the first and simplest step in the accounting process.

The financial information provided by accounting is used both directly and indirectly, as summarized in the following table.

DIRECT USERS	INDIRECT USERS
Owners	Labor unions
Managers	Financial analysts
Creditors	Stock exchanges
Suppliers	Lawyers
Taxing authorities	Regulatory authorities
Employees	Financial press
Customers	Trade associations

1.2 BRANCHES AND SPECIALIZATIONS

Like many professions, the field of accounting has expanded into separate branches and further into many different specializations.

BRANCHES

(1) *Private accounting.* Accountants employed by a company to work on its own affairs are engaged in *private accounting.* Some private accountants become controllers (the chief accounting officer), vice presidents of finance, or even presidents of companies.

(2) *Public accounting.* Accountants who offer their professional services to the public for a fee, as does a doctor or lawyer, are engaged in *public accounting.* These are Certified Public Accountants, or CPAs, who have passed a very rigorous examination.

(3) *Governmental accounting.* Accountants working in the large number of federal, state, and local government units are engaged in *governmental accounting.* Sometimes this group is broadened to include accountants employed by hospitals, colleges, etc.

(4) *Teaching.* Accountants teach accounting courses in colleges and universities, junior colleges, and some high schools. Most high school courses are really oriented to bookkeeping rather than accounting.

SPECIALIZATIONS

The six principal specializations of private accounting are indicated in Fig. 1-1. These same specializations may be performed in other branches of accounting. For example, auditing is performed by public accountants, by private accountants who are called internal auditors, and by governmental auditors.

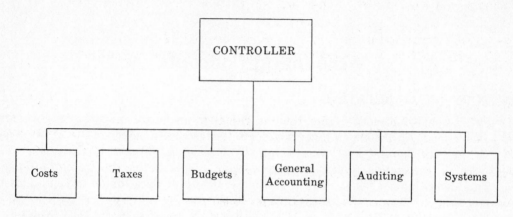

Fig. 1-1

1.3 BASIC ELEMENTS OF FINANCIAL POSITION: THE ACCOUNTING EQUATION

The financial condition or position of a business enterprise is represented by the relationship of assets to liabilities and capital.

Assets. Properties that are owned and have monetary value; for instance, cash, inventory, buildings, equipment.

Liabilities. Amounts owed to outsiders, such as notes payable, accounts payable, bonds payable. Liabilities may also include certain deferred items, such as income taxes to be allocated.

Capital. The interest of the owners in an enterprise.

These three basic elements are connected by a fundamental relationship called the *accounting equation*. This equation expresses the equality of the assets on one side with the claims of the creditors and owners on the other side:

$$\textbf{ASSETS} \quad = \quad \textbf{LIABILITIES} \quad + \quad \textbf{CAPITAL}$$

According to the accounting equation, a firm is assumed to possess its assets subject to the rights of the creditors and owners.

EXAMPLE 1.

Assume that a business *owned* assets of $100,000, *owed* creditors $70,000, and *owed* the owner $30,000. The accounting equation would be:

$$\textbf{ASSETS} \quad = \quad \textbf{LIABILITIES} \quad + \quad \textbf{CAPITAL}$$
$$\$100,000 \qquad\qquad \$70,000 \qquad\qquad \$30,000$$

If over a certain period the firm had a net income of $10,000, representing an increase of net assets, the change may be reflected as increased cash, increased inventory or other assets, or as a decrease in liabilities. Suppose that $6,000 was used to reduce liabilities and the balance remained in assets. The equation would then be:

$$\textbf{ASSETS} \quad = \quad \textbf{LIABILITIES} \quad + \quad \textbf{CAPITAL}$$
$$\$104,000 \qquad\qquad \$64,000 \qquad\qquad \$40,000$$

(6)   Withdrawal of money by the owner is not an expense but a reduction of _____.

(7)   To show the change in capital of a business, the _____ statement is used.

(8)   The balance sheet contains _____ , _____ , and _____.

(9)   Assets must equal _____.

(10)   Expense and income must be matched in the same _____.

Answers: (1) accounting statement   (6) capital
                  (2) income   (7) capital
                  (3) income   (8) assets, liabilities, capital
                  (4) income, expense   (9) liabilities and capital
                  (5) net income   (10) year or period

Solved Problems

2.1. Discuss the underlying rules which govern the preparation of the income statement and the balance sheet.

SOLUTION

Clearly, there must exist such rules; for otherwise it would be necessary to state for each financial statement the specific assumptions used in preparing it. Over the years, certain principles have been developed on the basis of experience, reason, custom, and practical necessity. We may call these "generally accepted accounting principles."

Business entity. Accounts are kept for business entities rather than for the persons who own or are associated with the business.

Continuity. Unless there is strong evidence to the contrary, it is assumed that the business will continue to operate as a going concern. If it were not to continue, then liquidation values, generally much lower, would apply.

Unit of measure. It is assumed that the most practical unit of measure is money and that changes in investment and income will be measured in money. So far, no better unit of measure has been found.

Time period. An essential function of accounting is to provide information for decision making. To accomplish this it is necessary to establish accounting periods, or systematic time intervals, so that timely accounting data can be developed.

Cost. The properties and services acquired by an enterprise are generally recorded at cost (the cash or its equivalent given to acquire the property or service). The cost is spread over the accounting periods which benefit from the expenditure.

Revenue. Revenue relates to the output of goods and services. In most cases revenue is recognized when goods are delivered or services rendered. In some cases revenue is recognized (1) during production, (2) when production is completed, or (3) when cash is collected.

Matching. In determining the proper periodic income, it is necessary to match related costs and expenses to revenue for the period. The cost of the product sold and all expenses incurred in producing the sale should be matched against the revenue.

Objectivity. Accounting entries should be based on objective evidence to the fullest possible extent. Business documents originating outside the firm provide the best evidence. Estimates should be supported by verifiable objective data.

Consistency. A standard method of treatment is necessary if periodic financial statements are to be compared with one another. Where a different method will state results and financial position more fairly, the change may be made if the effect upon the statements is clearly disclosed.

Disclosure. Financial statements and notes to financial statements should contain all relevant data of a material nature. They should disclose such things as a change in accounting methods, contingent liabilities, etc.

Materiality. The accountant must be practical and must consider the relative importance of data. The decision as to what is material and what is unimportant requires judgment rather than inflexible rules.

Conservatism. Accountants necessarily make many value judgments which affect financial statements. In these judgments it is desirable that they provide for all possible losses and not anticipate profits as yet unrealized.

2.2. Based on the following information, determine the capital as of December 31, 1972: Net Income for period, $18,000; Drawing, $6,000; Capital (January 1, 1972), $20,000.

SOLUTION

Capital, January 1, 1972		$20,000
Net Income	$18,000	
Less: Drawing	6,000	
Increase in Capital		12,000
Capital, December 31, 1972		$32,000

2.3. The following information was taken from an income statement: Fees Income, $14,000; Rent Expense, $2,000; Salaries Expense, $5,000; Miscellaneous Expense, $1,000. If the owner withdrew $2,000 from the firm, what is the increase or decrease in capital?

SOLUTION

Step 1. Prepare an income statement.

Fees Income		$14,000
Expenses		
Rent	$2,000	
Salaries	5,000	
Miscellaneous	1,000	
Total Expenses		8,000
Net Income		$ 6,000

Step 2. Increases or decreases in capital are determined by subtracting the drawing (withdrawal) from the net income.

Net Income	$6,000	
Drawing	2,000	
Increase in Capital	$4,000	

2.4. Based on the information in Problem 2.3, if the withdrawal were $9,000 instead of $2,000, what would his increase (decrease) become?

SOLUTION

If the withdrawal is larger than the net income, a decrease in capital will result.

Net Income	$6,000
Drawing	9,000
Decrease in Capital	$3,000

2.5. If the capital account has a balance, January 1, of $32,000, what will be the balance, December 31, (a) based on Problem 2.3? (b) based on Problem 2.4?

SOLUTION

(a)	Capital, January 1		$32,000
	Net Income	$6,000	
	Drawing	2,000	
	Increase in Capital		4,000
	Capital, December 31		$36,000
(b)	Capital, January 1		$32,000
	Net Income	$6,000	
	Drawing	9,000	
	Decrease in Capital		3,000
	Capital, December 31		$29,000

2.6. Based on the following information, determine the capital on December 31.

Cash	$6,000
Supplies	400
Equipment	8,000
Accounts Payable	4,500
Notes Payable	2,500

SOLUTION

ASSETS		LIABILITIES AND CAPITAL	
Cash	$ 6,000	Accounts Payable	$ 4,500
Supplies	400	Notes Payable	2,500
Equipment	8,000	Total Liabilities	7,000
	$14,400	Capital	7,400*
		Total Liabilities and Capital	$14,400

*$14,400	Assets
7,000	Liabilities
$ 7,400	Capital

2.7.   Prepare a balance sheet as of December 31, 1973 from the data below.

Accounts Payable	$ 3,000
Cash	4,000
Equipment	16,000
Notes Payable	12,000
Supplies	200
Net Income	11,400
Drawing	10,200
Capital, January 1, 1973	4,000

ASSETS		
Cash		
Equipment		
Supplies		
Total Assets		
LIABILITIES AND CAPITAL		
Accounts Payable		
Notes Payable		
Total Liabilities		
Capital, December 31, 1973		
Total Liabilities and Capital		
CAPITAL STATEMENT		

SOLUTION

ASSETS		
Cash		$ 4,000
Equipment		16,000
Supplies		200
Total Assets		$20,200
LIABILITIES AND CAPITAL		
Accounts Payable		$ 3,000
Notes Payable		12,000
Total Liabilities		$15,000
Capital, December 31, 1973		5,200
Total Liabilities and Capital		$20,200
CAPITAL STATEMENT		
Capital, January 1, 1973		$ 4,000
Net Income	$11,400	
Drawing	10,200	
Increase in Capital		1,200
Capital, December 31, 1973		$ 5,200

2.8. Classify the following accounts by placing a check in the appropriate column.

		Current Asset	Fixed Asset	Current Liability	Long-Term Liability
(1)	Accounts Receivable				
(2)	Accounts Payable				
(3)	Notes Payable				
(4)	Mortgage Payable				
(5)	Cash				
(6)	Supplies Inventory				
(7)	Salaries Payable				
(8)	Bonds Payable				
(9)	Equipment				
(10)	Land				

SOLUTION

		Current Asset	Fixed Asset	Current Liability	Long-Term Liability
(1)	Accounts Receivable	√			
(2)	Accounts Payable			√	
(3)	Notes Payable			√	
(4)	Mortgage Payable				√
(5)	Cash	√			
(6)	Supplies Inventory	√			
(7)	Salaries Payable			√	
(8)	Bonds Payable				√
(9)	Equipment		√		
(10)	Land		√		

2.9. From the information that follows, prepare a classified balance sheet as of December 31: Cash, $6,000; Accounts Receivable, $3,000; Supplies Inventory, $1,000; Equipment, $14,000; Accounts Payable, $2,500; Notes Payable, $1,500; Mortgage Payable, $12,000; Capital, December 31, $8,000.

ASSETS		
Current Assets		
Total Current Assets		
Fixed Assets		
Total Assets		
LIABILITIES AND CAPITAL		
Current Liabilities		
Total Current Liabilities		
Long-Term Liabilities		
Total Liabilities		
Capital		
Total Liabilities and Capital		

SOLUTION

ASSETS		
Current Assets		
Cash	$6,000	
Accounts Receivable	3,000	
Supplies Inventory	1,000	
Total Current Assets		$10,000
Fixed Assets		
Equipment		14,000
Total Assets		$24,000
LIABILITIES AND CAPITAL		
Current Liabilities		
Accounts Payable	$2,500	
Notes Payable	1,500	
Total Current Liabilities		$ 4,000
Long-Term Liabilities		
Mortgage Payable		12,000
Total Liabilities		$16,000
Capital		8,000
Total Liabilities and Capital		$24,000

2.10. What is the current ratio in Problem 2.9?

SOLUTION

$$\text{Total Current Assets} \quad \$10,000$$
$$\text{Total Current Liabilities} \quad 4,000$$

$$\frac{10,000}{4,000} = 2.5 : 1$$

The firm has $2.50 in current assets for every $1 in current liabilities.

2.11. Complete the chart by writing in the appropriate column the name of the account group in which the particular account belongs.

	Income Statement	Balance Sheet
Accounts Payable		
Accounts Receivable		
Advertising Expense		
Cash		
Capital		
Equipment		
Fees Income		
Machinery		
Notes Payable		
Notes Receivable		
Other Income		
Salaries Expense		
Supplies Inventory		
Supplies Expense		

SOLUTION

	Income Statement	Balance Sheet
Accounts Payable		Liability
Accounts Receivable		Asset
Advertising Expense	Expense	
Cash		Asset
Capital		Capital
Equipment		Asset
Fees Income	Income	
Machinery		Asset
Notes Payable		Liability
Notes Receivable		Asset
Other Income	Income	
Salaries Expense	Expense	
Supplies Inventory		Asset
Supplies Expense	Expense	

2.12. Prepare (a) an income statement and (b) a balance sheet, using the data of Problem 1.13, page 10.

(a)

Dr. M. Levy		
Income Statement		
month of March		

(b)

Dr. M. Levy		
Balance Sheet		
March 31		
ASSETS		
LIABILITIES AND CAPITAL		

SOLUTION

(a)

Dr. M. Levy		
Income Statement		
month of March		
Fees Income		$1,600
Expenses		
Rent Expense	$200	
Salaries Expense	400	
Total Expenses		600
Net Income		$1,000

(b)

Dr. M. Levy		
Balance Sheet		
March 31		
ASSETS		
Cash	$ 5,500	
Supplies	2,000	
Equipment	7,000	
Total Assets		$14,500
LIABILITIES AND CAPITAL		
Accounts Payable	$ 4,000	
Capital	10,500*	
Total Liabilities and Capital		$14,500

*If capital statement is not required, capital is computed as follows:

Capital (beginning)		$10,000
Add: Net Income	$1,000	
Less: Drawing	500	
Increase in Capital		500
Capital (end)		$10,500

2.13. Below are the account balances as of December 31, 1975, of Mr. R. Gregg, owner of a movie theater.

Accounts Payable	$11,400
Admissions Income	34,200
Capital, January 1, 1975	16,000
Cash	7,500
Drawing	5,400
Equipment	18,500
Film Rental Expense	6,000
Miscellaneous Expense	4,000
Notes Payable	1,000
Rent Expense	10,000
Salaries Expense	7,000
Supplies Inventory	4,200

Prepare (a) an income statement, (b) a capital statement, (c) a balance sheet.

(a)

R. Gregg		
Income Statement		
year ended December 31, 1975		

(b)

R. Gregg		
Capital Statement		
year ended December 31, 1975		

(c)

R. Gregg		
Balance Sheet		
December 31, 1975		

SOLUTION

(a)

R. Gregg		
Income Statement		
year ended December 31, 1975		
Income		$34,200
Expenses		
Film Rental Expense	$ 6,000	
Rent Expense	10,000	
Salaries Expense	7,000	
Miscellaneous Expense	4,000	
Total Expenses		27,000
Net Income		$ 7,200

(b) The capital statement is needed to show the capital balance at the *end* of the year. Mr. Gregg's capital balance above is at the beginning. Net income increases capital and drawing reduces capital.

R. Gregg		
Capital Statement		
year ended December 31, 1975		
Capital, January 1, 1975		$16,000
Add: Net Income	$ 7,200	
Less: Drawing	5,400	
Increase in Capital		1,800
Capital, December 31, 1975		$17,800

(c)

R. Gregg		
Balance Sheet		
December 31, 1975		
ASSETS		
Cash	$ 7,500	
Supplies Inventory	4,200	
Equipment	18,500	
Total Assets		$30,200
LIABILITIES AND CAPITAL		
Accounts Payable	$11,400	
Notes Payable	1,000	
Total Liabilities		$12,400
Capital		17,800
Total Liabilities and Capital		$30,200

2.14. The balances of the accounts of Dr. R. Tames, Dentist, appear as follows:

Accounts Payable	$ 2,800
Accounts Receivable	3,600
Building	12,000
Capital, January 1, 1969	19,000
Cash	12,200
Dental Income	38,000
Drawing	6,000
Equipment	15,000
Furniture	3,000
Mortgage Payable	10,000
Miscellaneous Expense	2,000
Notes Payable	2,000
Supplies Inventory	6,000
Salaries Expense	8,000
Supplies Expense	4,000

Using the forms provided below, prepare (*a*) an income statement, (*b*) a capital statement, and (*c*) a classified balance sheet.

(a)

Dr. R. Tames		
Income Statement		
year ended December 31, 1969		
Income from Fees		
Expenses		
Total Expenses		
Net Income		

(b)

Dr. R. Tames		
Capital Statement		
year ended December 31, 1969		
Capital, January 1, 1969		
Add: Net Income		
Less: Drawing		
Increase in Capital		
Capital, December 31, 1969		

(c)

Dr. R. Tames		
Balance Sheet		
December 31, 1969		
ASSETS		
Current Assets		
Total Current Assets		
Fixed Assets		
Total Fixed Assets		
Total Assets		
LIABILITIES AND CAPITAL		
Current Liabilities		
Total Current Liabilities		
Long-Term Liabilities		
Total Liabilities		
Capital		
Total Liabilities and Capital		

SOLUTION

(a)

Dr. R. Tames		
Income Statement		
year ended December 31, 1969		
Income from Fees		$38,000
Expenses		
Salaries Expense	$ 8,000	
Supplies Expense	4,000	
Miscellaneous Expense	2,000	
Total Expenses		14,000
Net Income		$24,000

(b)

Dr. R. Tames		
Capital Statement		
year ended December 31, 1969		
Capital, January 1, 1969		$19,000
Add: Net Income	$24,000	
Less: Drawing	6,000	
Increase in Capital		18,000
Capital, December 31, 1969		$37,000

(c)

Dr. R. Tames		
Balance Sheet		
December 31, 1969		
ASSETS		
Current Assets		
Cash	$12,200	
Accounts Receivable	3,600	
Supplies Inventory	6,000	
Total Current Assets		$21,800
Fixed Assets		
Building	$12,000	
Equipment	15,000	
Furniture	3,000	
Total Fixed Assets		30,000
Total Assets		$51,800
LIABILITIES AND CAPITAL		
Current Liabilities		
Accounts Payable	$ 2,800	
Notes Payable	2,000	
Total Current Liabilities		$ 4,800
Long-Term Liabilities		
Mortgage Payable		10,000
Total Liabilities		$14,800
Capital (see Capital Statement)		37,000
Total Liabilities and Capital		$51,800

Chapter 3

Analyzing and Classifying Transactions

3.1 INTRODUCTION

Preparing a new equation $A = L + C$ after each transaction would be cumbersome and costly, especially when there are a great many transactions in an accounting period. Also, information for a specific item such as cash would be lost as successive transactions were recorded. This information could be obtained by going back and summarizing the transactions but that would be very time-consuming.

A much more efficient way is to classify the transactions according to items on the balance sheet and income statement. The increases and decreases are then recorded according to type of item by means of a summary called an *account*.

3.2 THE ACCOUNT

A separate account is maintained for each item that appears on the balance sheet (assets, liabilities, and capital) and on the income statement (revenue and expense). Thus an account may be defined as *a record of the increases, decreases, and balances in an individual item of asset, liability, capital, revenue, or expense.*

The simplest form of the account is known as the "T" account because it resembles the letter "T". The account has three parts: (1) the name of the account and the account number, (2) the debit side (left side), and (3) the credit side (right side). The increases are entered on one side, the decreases on the other. Which change goes on which side will be discussed in Section 3.3. The balance (the excess of the total of one side over the total of the other) is inserted near the last figure on the side with the larger amount.

3.3 DEBITS AND CREDITS. THE DOUBLE-ENTRY SYSTEM

When an amount is entered on the left side of an account, it is a *debit* and the account is said to be *debited*. When an amount is entered on the right side, it is a *credit* and the account is said to be *credited*. The abbreviations for debit and credit are Dr. and Cr., respectively.

Whether an increase in a given item is credited or debited depends on the category of the item. By convention, asset and expense increases are recorded as debits, while liability, capital, and income increases are recorded as credits. Asset and expense decreases are recorded as credits, while liability, capital, and income decreases are recorded as debits. The following tables summarize the rule.

ASSETS AND EXPENSES		LIABILITIES, CAPITAL, AND INCOME	
Dr.	Cr.	Dr.	Cr.
+	−	−	+
(Increases)	(Decreases)	(Decreases)	(Increases)

EXAMPLE 1.

Let us re-examine the transactions that occurred in Mr. A. Bagon's law firm during the first month of operation. These are the same as in Chapter 1, except that accounts are now used to record the transactions.

Transaction (1). **Mr. Bagon opened his law practice, investing $5,000 in cash.** The two accounts affected are Cash and Capital. Remember that an increase in an asset (cash) is debited, whereas an increase in capital is credited.

Cash			Capital	
Dr. +	Cr. −		Dr. −	Cr. +
(1) 5,000				5,000 (1)

Transaction (2). **Bought supplies for cash, $300.** Here we are substituting one asset (cash) for another asset (supplies). We debit Supplies, because we are receiving more supplies. We credit Cash, because we are paying out cash.

Cash			Supplies on Hand	
Dr. +	Cr. −		Dr. +	Cr. −
5,000	300 (2)		(2) 300	

Transaction (3). **Bought equipment from Altway Furniture Company on account, $2,500.** We are receiving an asset (equipment), and therefore debit Equipment to show the increase. We are not paying cash, but creating a new liability, thereby increasing the liability account (Accounts Payable).

Equipment			Accounts Payable	
Dr. +	Cr. −		Dr. −	Cr. +
(3) 2,500				2,500 (3)

Transaction (4). **Received $2,000 in fees earned during the month.** In this case, we are increasing the asset account Cash, as we have received $2,000. Therefore, we debit it. We are increasing the capital, yet we do not credit Capital. It is better temporarily to separate the income from the owner's equity (capital) and create a new account, Fees Income.

Cash			Fees Income	
Dr. +	Cr. −		Dr. −	Cr. +
5,000	300			2,000 (4)
(4) 2,000				

Transaction (5). **Paid office rent for January, $500.** We must decrease the asset account Cash, because we are paying out money. Therefore, we credit it. It is preferable to keep expenses separated from the owners' equity. Therefore, we open a new account for the expense involved, Rent Expense. The $500 is entered on the left side, as expenses decrease owner's equity.

Cash			Rent Expense	
Dr. +	Cr. −		Dr. +	Cr. −
5,000	300		(5) 500	
2,000	500 (5)			

Transaction (6).   **Paid salary for part-time help, $200.**   Again, we must reduce our asset account (Cash), because we are paying out money. Therefore, we credit the account. Bagon's capital was reduced by an expense and we open another account, Salary Expense. A debit to this account shows the decrease in capital.

Cash			Salary Expense	
Dr. +	Cr. −		Dr. +	Cr. −
(1) 5,000	300 (2)		(6) 200	
(4) 2,000	500 (5)			
	200 (6)			

Transaction (7).   **Paid $1,000 to Altway Furniture Company, on account.**   This transaction reduced our asset account (Cash), since we are paying out money. We therefore credit Cash. We also reduce our liability account (Accounts Payable) by $1,000; we now owe that much less. Thus, we debit Accounts Payable.

Cash			Accounts Payable	
Dr. +	Cr. −		Dr. −	Cr. +
(1) 5,000	300 (2)		(7) 1,000	2,500 (3)
(4) 2,000	500 (5)			
	200 (6)			
	1,000 (7)			

Transaction (8).   **After taking inventory at the end of the month, Mr. Bagon found he had used $200 worth of supplies.**   We must reduce the asset account Supplies by crediting it for $200. Supplies Expense is debited for the decrease in capital. This is computed as follows: beginning inventory of $300, less supplies on hand at the end of the month ($100), indicates $200 must have been used during the month.

Supplies			Supplies Expense	
Dr. +	Cr. −		Dr. +	Cr. −
(2) 300	200 (8)		(8) 200	

Transaction (9).   **Withdrew $300 for personal use.**   The withdrawal of cash means there is a reduction in the asset account Cash. Therefore, it is credited. The amount invested by the owner is also $300 less. We must open the account Drawing, which is debited to show the decrease in capital.

Cash			Drawing	
Dr. +	Cr. −		Dr. +	Cr. −
(1) 5,000	300 (2)		(9) 300	
(2) 2,000	500 (5)			
	200 (6)			
	1,000 (7)			
	300 (9)			

An account has a debit balance when the sum of its debits exceeds the sum of its credits; it has a credit balance when the sum of the credits is the greater. In *double-entry accounting,* which is in almost universal use, there are equal debit and credit entries for every transaction. Where there are only two accounts affected, the debit and credit amounts are equal. If more than two accounts are affected, the total of the debit entries must equal the total of the credit entries.

3.4 THE LEDGER

The complete set of accounts for a business entity is called a ledger. It is the "reference book" of the accounting system and is used to classify and summarize transactions and to prepare data for financial statements. It is also a valuable source of information for managerial purposes, giving, for example, the amount of sales for the period or the cash balance at the end of the period. Depending on what method of data processing is used, the ledger may take the form of a bound book with a page for each account, punched cards, or magnetic tapes or disks. In any case, the accounting principles are the same. Further information on data processing methods is given in the Appendix.

3.5 THE CHART OF ACCOUNTS

It is desirable to establish a systematic method of identifying and locating each account in the ledger. The *chart of accounts*, sometimes called the *code of accounts*, is a listing of the accounts by title and numerical designation. In some companies the chart of accounts may run to hundreds of items.

In designing a numbering structure for the accounts it is important to provide adequate flexibility to permit expansion without having to revise the basic system. Generally, blocks of numbers are assigned to various groups of accounts, such as assets, liabilities, etc. There are various systems of coding, depending on the needs and desires of the company.

EXAMPLE 2.

A simple chart structure is to have the first digit represent the major group in which the account is located. Thus accounts which have numbers beginning with 1 are assets; 2, liabilities; 3, capital; 4, income; and 5, expenses. The second or third digit designates the position of the account in the group.

In the two-digital system, assets are assigned the block of numbers 11–19, and liabilities 21–29. In larger firms a three-digital (or higher) system may be used, with assets assigned 100–199 and liabilities 200–299. Following are the numerical designations for the account groups under both methods.

ACCOUNT GROUP	TWO-DIGITAL	THREE-DIGITAL
1. Assets	10–19	100–199
2. Liabilities	20–29	200–299
3. Capital	30–39	300–399
4. Income	40–49	400–499
5. Expense	50–59	500–599

Thus Cash may be account 11 under the first system and 101 under the second system. The cash account may be further broken down as: 101, Cash – First National Bank; 102, Cash – Second National Bank; etc.

3.6 THE TRIAL BALANCE

As every transaction results in an equal amount of debits and credits in the ledger, the total of all debit entries in the ledger ought to equal the total of all credit entries. At the end of the accounting period we check this equality by preparing a two-column schedule called a *trial balance*, which compares the total of all debit *balances* with the total of all credit *balances*. The procedure is as follows:

1. List account titles in numerical order in two columns of a worksheet.
2. Record balances of each account, entering debit balances in the left column and credit balances in the right column. (*Note*: Asset and expense accounts are debited for increases and would normally have debit balances. Liabilities, capital, and income accounts are credited for increases and would normally have credit balances.)
3. Add the columns and record the totals.
4. Compare the totals.

If the totals agree, the trial balance is in balance, indicating the equality of the debits and credits for the hundreds or thousands of transactions entered in the ledger. While the trial balance provides *arithmetic* proof of the accuracy of the records, it does not provide *theoretical* proof. For example, if the purchase of a machine was incorrectly charged to Expense, the trial balance columns may agree, but theoretically the accounts would be wrong, as Expense would be overstated and Machinery understated. In addition to providing proof of arithmetic accuracy in accounts, the trial balance facilitates the preparation of the periodic financial statements. Generally the trial balance comprises the first two columns of a worksheet, from which financial statements are prepared. The worksheet procedure is discussed in Chapter 7.

EXAMPLE 3.

The summary of the transactions for Mr. Bagon (see Example 1), and their effect on the accounts, is shown below. The trial balance is then taken.

ASSETS	LIABILITIES	CAPITAL

Cash 11

(1) 5,000	300 (2)
(4) 2,000	500 (5)
	200 (6)
	1,000 (7)
	300 (9)

Accounts Payable 21

(7) 1,000	2,500 (3)

A. Bagon, Capital 31

	5,000 (1)

Drawing 32

(9) 300	

Supplies 12

(2) 300	200 (8)

Fees Income 41

	2,000 (4)

Equipment 13

(3) 2,500	

Rent Expense 51

(5) 500	

Salaries Expense 52

(6) 200	

Salaries Expense 53

(8) 200	

A. Bagon, Lawyer
Trial Balance
January 31, 197–

	Dr.	Cr.
Cash	$4,700	
Supplies	100	
Equipment	2,500	
Accounts Payable		$1,500
A. Bagon, Capital		5,000
Drawing	300	
Fees Income		2,000
Rent Expense	500	
Salaries Expense	200	
Supplies Expense	200	
	$8,500	$8,500

Summary

(1) To classify and summarize a single item of an account group, we use a form called an _____.

(2) The accounts comprise a record called a _____.

(3) The left side of the account is known as the _____, while the right side is the _____.

(4) Increases in all asset accounts are _____.

(5) Increases in all liability accounts are _____.

(6) Increases in all capital accounts are _____.

(7) Increases in all income accounts are _____.

(8) Increases in all expense accounts are _____.

(9) Expenses are debited because they decrease _____.

(10) The schedule showing the balance of each account at the end of the period is known as the _____.

Answers: (1) account; (2) ledger; (3) debit side, credit side; (4) debited; (5) credited; (6) credited; (7) credited; (8) debited; (9) capital; (10) trial balance

Solved Problems

3.1. Revenue and expense accounts are designated as *temporary* or *nominal* accounts (accounts in name only). Explain.

SOLUTION

The increase in capital resulting from revenue is temporary, since capital will be reduced by expenses in the same period. These accounts are closed out at the end of the accounting period and the net balance (for example, the excess of revenue over expenses for the period) is then transferred to the capital account.

The *permanent* or *real account* balances—assets, liabilities, and capital—are not closed out at the end of the accounting period. For example, the cash or inventory balance at the end of one period becomes the beginning balance in the following period.

3.2. Interpret the balance in the supplies account at the end of the period.

SOLUTION

The book figure before adjustment is the amount on hand at the beginning of the period plus the amount purchased during the period. The sum is the total amount that was available during the period and was either used up or is still on hand. When an inventory count is made at the end of the period, the amount still on hand is determined, and the difference between that amount and the available amount above represents what was used during the period, which is an expense (supplies expense). The balance on hand is an asset (supplies on hand).

3.3. In each of the following types of "T" accounts, enter an increase (by writing +) and a decrease (by writing −).

ASSETS		LIABILITIES		CAPITAL
Dr.	Cr.	Dr.	Cr.	Dr.	Cr.

INCOME		EXPENSES
Dr.	Cr.	Dr.	Cr.

SOLUTION

	ASSETS			LIABILITIES			CAPITAL	
Dr. +		Cr. −	Dr. −		Cr. +	Dr. −		Cr. +

	INCOME			EXPENSES	
Dr. −		Cr. +	Dr. +		Cr. −

3.4. Indicate in the columns below the increases and decreases in each account by placing a check in the appropriate column.

	Debit	Credit
(a) Capital is increased		
(b) Cash is decreased		
(c) Accounts Payable is increased		
(d) Rent Expense is increased		
(e) Equipment is increased		
(f) Fees Income is increased		
(g) Capital is decreased (through drawing)		

SOLUTION

(a) Cr.   (b) Cr.   (c) Cr.   (d) Dr.   (e) Dr.   (f) Cr.   (g) Dr.

3.5. For each transaction in the table below, indicate the account to be debited and the account to be credited by placing the letter representing the account in the appropriate column.

Name of Account
(a) Accounts Payable
(b) Capital
(c) Cash
(d) Drawing
(e) Equipment
(f) Fees Income
(g) Notes Payable
(h) Rent Expense
(i) Salaries Expense
(j) Supplies
(k) Supplies Expense

Transaction	Dr.	Cr.
1. Invested cash in the firm		
2. Paid rent for month		
3. Received cash fees for services		
4. Paid salaries		
5. Bought equipment on account		
6. Paid 1/2 balance on equipment		
7. Bought supplies on account		
8. Borrowed money from bank, giving a note in exchange		
9. Supplies inventory showed 1/3 used during the month		
10. Withdrew cash for personal use		

SOLUTION

	Dr.	Cr.
1.	(c)	(b)
2.	(h)	(c)
3.	(c)	(f)
4.	(i)	(c)
5.	(e)	(a)
6.	(a)	(c)
7.	(j)	(a)
8.	(c)	(g)
9.	(k)	(j)
10.	(d)	(c)

3.6.   Record each transaction in the accompanying accounts.

(a) Bought equipment for cash for $600.

(b) Bought additional equipment for $2,700, paying 1/3 down and owing the balance.

(c) Gave a note in settlement of transaction (b).

(d) Received $500 in plumbing fees.

Equipment

Cash
Bal. 2,000

Equipment

Cash
Bal. 1,000

Accounts Payable

Accounts Payable
Bal. 1,800

Notes Payable

Cash

Fees Income

SOLUTION

(a)

Equipment		Cash	
600		Bal. 2,000	600

(b)

Equipment		Cash		Accounts Payable	
2,700		Bal. 1,000	900		1,800

(c)

Accounts Payable		Notes Payable	
1,800	Bal. 1,800		1,800

(d)

Cash		Fees Income	
500			500

3.7.   The ten accounts which follow summarize the first week's transactions of the Willis Taxi Company.

Cash				Equipment		Drawing	
(a) 14,000	10,000 (b)			(b) 10,000		(h) 100	
(e) 1,000	200 (d)			(c) 6,000			
	300 (f)					**Fees Income**	
	500 (g)			**Accounts Payable**			1,000 (e)
	100 (h)			(i) 2,000	6,000 (c)		
	2,000 (i)					**Salaries Expense**	
	300 (j)			**Capital**		(f) 300	
					14,000 (a)		
Supplies						**Rent Expense**	
(d) 200						(g) 500	
						Gasoline Expense	
						(j) 300	

Complete the form below.   (The analysis of the first transaction is given as a sample.)

Transaction	Account Debited	Effect of Debit	Account Credited	Effect of Credit
(a) Invested $14,000 in firm	Cash	Increased asset	Capital	Increased capital
(b)				
(c)				
(d)				
(e)				
(f)				
(g)				
(h)				
(i)				
(j)				

SOLUTION

	Transaction	Account Debited	Effect of Debit	Account Credited	Effect of Credit
(a)	Invested $14,000 in firm	Cash	Increased asset	Capital	Increased capital
(b)	Bought equipment for cash	Equipment	Increased asset	Cash	Decreased asset
(c)	Bought additional equipment on account	Equipment	Increased asset	Accts. Payable	Increased liability
(d)	Paid $200 for supplies	Supplies	Increased asset	Cash	Decreased asset
(e)	Received $1,000 in fees	Cash	Increased asset	Fees Income	Increased income
(f)	Paid $300 for salaries	Salaries Expense	Increased expense	Cash	Decreased asset
(g)	Paid $500 for rent	Rent Expense	Increased expense	Cash	Decreased asset
(h)	Withdrew $100 for personal use	Drawing	Decreased capital	Cash	Decreased asset
(i)	Paid $2,000 on account	Accounts Payable	Decreased liability	Cash	Decreased asset
(j)	Paid $300 for gasoline	Gasoline Expense	Increased expense	Cash	Decreased asset

3.8. Using the information of Problem 1.13, record the entries in the accounts below for Dr. M. Levy, labeling each item by number as in Problem 1.13. Then prepare a trial balance.

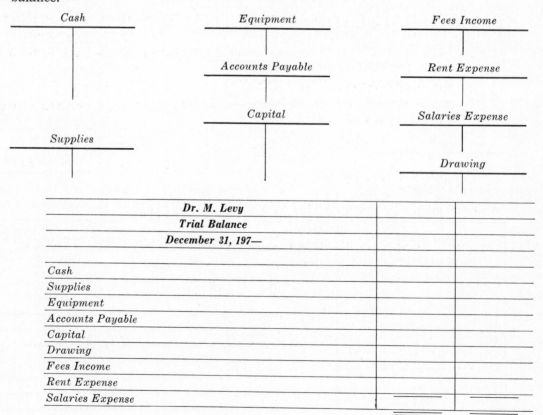

Dr. M. Levy		
Trial Balance		
December 31, 197—		
Cash		
Supplies		
Equipment		
Accounts Payable		
Capital		
Drawing		
Fees Income		
Rent Expense		
Salaries Expense		

SOLUTION

Cash		Equipment		Fees Income	
(1) 10,000	2,000 (3)	(2) 7,000			1,600 (4)
(4) 1,600	200 (5)				
	400 (6)	**Accounts Payable**		**Rent Expense**	
	3,000 (7)	(7) 3,000	7,000 (2)	(5) 200	
	500 (8)				
		Capital		**Salaries Expense**	
Supplies			10,000 (1)	(6) 400	
(3) 2,000					
				Drawing	
				(8) 500	

Dr. M. Levy		
Trial Balance		
December 31, 197—		
Cash	$ 5,500	
Supplies	2,000	
Equipment	7,000	
Accounts Payable		$ 4,000
Capital		10,000
Drawing	500	
Fees Income		1,600
Rent Expense	200	
Salaries Expense	400	
	$15,600	$15,600

3.9. For the transactions below, record each entry in the "T" accounts furnished. (*Note*: The transactions are those of Problem 1.14, which may be used in reference.)

(1) The Nu-Look Dry Cleaning Company opened a business bank account by depositing $12,000 on November 1.

(2) Purchased supplies for cash, $220.

(3) Purchased dry cleaning equipment for $3,500, paying $1,500 in cash with the balance on account.

(4) Paid rent for the month, $425.

(5) Cash sales for the month totaled $1,850.

(6) Paid salaries of $375.

(7) Paid $500 on account.

(8) The cost of supplies used was determined to be $60.

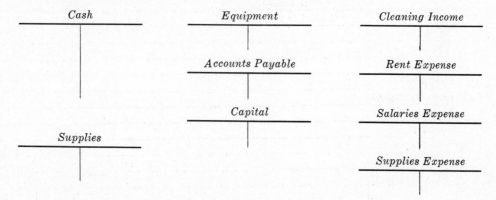

SOLUTION

Cash				Equipment			Cleaning Income	
(1) 12,000	220 (2)		(3) 3,500				1,850 (5)
(5) 1,850	1,500 (3)						
	425 (4)		**Accounts Payable**			**Rent Expense**	
	375 (6)						
	500 (7)		(7) 500	2,000 (3)		(4) 425	

Supplies			Capital			Salaries Expense	
(2) 220	60 (8)			12,000 (1)		(6) 375	

Supplies Expense

(8) 60

3.10. Prepare a trial balance as of November 30 for the Nu-Look Dry Cleaning Company, using the account balances in Problem 3.9.

Nu-Look Dry Cleaning Company		
Trial Balance		
November 30		
Cash		
Supplies Inventory		
Equipment		
Accounts Payable		
Nu-Look Dry Cleaning Company, Capital		
Cleaning Income		
Rent Expense		
Salaries Expense		
Supplies Expense		

SOLUTION

Nu-Look Dry Cleaning Company		
Trial Balance		
November 30		
Cash	$10,830	
Supplies Inventory	160	
Equipment	3,500	
Accounts Payable		$ 1,500
Nu-Look Dry Cleaning Company, Capital		12,000
Cleaning Income		1,850
Rent Expense	425	
Salaries Expense	375	
Supplies Expense	60	
	$15,350	$15,350

Examination I

Chapters 1-3

1. What is meant by the accounting cycle?

2. Define the following terms and give an example of each: (*a*) assets, (*b*) liabilities, (*c*) capital.

3. Define (*a*) revenue, (*b*) expense, (*c*) net income.

4. (*a*) What is an account? (*b*) What is a chart of accounts?

5. Distinguish between temporary and permanent accounts.

6. What is meant by the double-entry system of accounting?

7. What does the balance in the supplies account at the end of the period represent?

8. Prepare the capital statement as of December 31 of the Grant Company, given:

Capital, January 1	$72,400
Income for the period	27,600
Withdrawals by the proprietor for the year	1,000 per month

9. On January 1, William Accord began business by investing $5,000 in his firm. During the month, he had the following income and expenditures:

Income from Services	$12,600
Rent Expense	200
Salaries Expense	150
Commission Expense	100
Supplies Expense	75
Utilities Expense	125
Repairs and Maintenance	400
Miscellaneous Expense	225

Present the income statement for January.

10. Below are the account balances of the State-Rite Cleaning Company as of December 31, 197–. Prepare (*a*) an income statement, (*b*) a capital statement, (*c*) a balance sheet.

Accounts Payable	$11,600	Miscellaneous Expense	$ 3,000
Cleaning Income	39,500	Notes Payable	2,800
Capital (beginning)	14,300	Rent Expense	12,600
Cash	9,300	Salaries Expense	9,200
Drawing	4,800	Supplies Expense	2,400
Equipment	19,200	Supplies Inventory	5,300
Equipment Repairs and Maintenance	2,400		

11. For each numbered transaction below, indicate the account to be debited and the account to be credited by placing the letter representing the account in the appropriate column. Accounts Payable (*a*); Capital (*b*); Cash (*c*); Drawing (*d*); Equipment (*e*); Fees Income (*f*); Notes Payable (*g*); Rent Expense (*h*); Salaries Expense (*i*); Supplies (*j*); Supplies Expense (*k*).

		Debit	Credit
(1)	Invested cash in the firm.	(*c*)	(*b*)
(2)	Received cash for services rendered.		
(3)	Paid salaries for the week.		
(4)	Bought equipment on account.		
(5)	Bought supplies on account.		
(6)	Gave a note in settlement of the equipment on account.		
(7)	Borrowed money from the bank.		
(8)	Withdrew cash for personal use.		
(9)	A count showed that approximately 3/4 of the supplies inventory had been used during the year.		
(10)	Paid rent for the month.		

12. The Sullivan Residence Club established business on January 1, 197–, and invested $15,000 cash and a $22,000 building in their club. A summary of transactions for January follows.

(1)	Collected rents for the month of January	$ 2,400
(2)	Check was written for a one-year insurance policy	850
(3)	Paid the electric bill	240
(4)	Paid the utility man his January salary	350
(5)	Bought supplies on account	800
(6)	Borrowed $15,000 from the bank for additions to the building	15,000
(7)	Withdrew $300 for personal use	300
(8)	Supplies on hand at the end of the month	500

Prepare the appropriate "T" accounts.

13. The "T" accounts below were taken from the ledger of the Utility Service Company. Prepare a trial balance from these accounts.

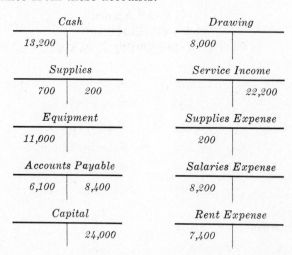

Cash		Drawing	
13,200		8,000	

Supplies		Service Income	
700	200		22,200

Equipment		Supplies Expense	
11,000		200	

Accounts Payable		Salaries Expense	
6,100	8,400	8,200	

Capital		Rent Expense	
	24,000	7,400	

Answers to Examination I

1. The accounting cycle is the sequence of procedures repeated each accounting period. The steps are: (1) recording transactions in journals; (2) classifying data by posting to ledger; (3) summarizing data by classification; (4) adjusting and correcting recorded data; (5) preparing statements.

2. (a) Property of value owned by a business; Cash.

   (b) Amounts owed by the business to outsiders; Accounts Payable.

   (c) The investment by the owner(s) and the earnings retained in the business (also called *proprietorship* or *owners' equity*); J. Smith, Capital.

3. (a) The inflow of cash and receivables for an accounting period, resulting from the delivery of goods or the rendering of services.

   (b) The cost of goods and services used up or consumed in the process of obtaining revenue.

   (c) The increase in capital resulting from profitable operation of a business. Alternatively, the excess of revenues over expenses for the particular period.

4. (a) The account is a form used to record changes in a particular asset, liabiltiy, or item of capital, revenue, or expense. It is used to classify and summarize transactions.

   (b) The chart of accounts is a listing of the account titles showing the sequence of the accounts in the ledger and the number assigned to each account. It is a systematic method of identifying and locating each account.

5. Revenue and expense accounts are designated as temporary or nominal accounts because the increase in capital resulting from revenue is subject to reduction by expenses in the same period. These accounts are closed out at the end of the accounting period and the net balance transferred to the capital account. Permanent or real account balances — assets, liabilities, and capital — are not closed out at the end of the accounting period.

6. In the double-entry system, the recording of each transaction must be such that the total debits equal the total credits. In most cases, there will be only one debit and one credit account affected, and thus the dollar amounts will be equal.

7. Amount on hand at the beginning of the period, plus purchases during the period, minus consumption during the period.

8.

Grant Company
Capital Statement
December 31

Capital, January 1		$72,400
Income	$27,600	
Less: Drawing	12,000	
Increase in Capital		15,600
Capital, December 31		$88,000

9.

William Accord
Income Statement
for the period ending January 31

Income from Services		$12,600
Expenses		
Rent Expense	$200	
Salaries Expense	150	
Commission Expense	100	
Supplies Expense	75	
Utilities Expense	125	
Repairs and Maintenance	400	
Miscellaneous Expense	225	
Total Expenses		1,275
Net Income		$11,325

10. **(a)**

State-Rite Cleaning Company
Income Statement
for the period ending December 31, 197–

Cleaning Income		$39,500
Expenses		
Equipment Repairs and Maintenance	$ 2,400	
Rent Expense	12,600	
Salaries Expense	9,200	
Supplies Expense	2,400	
Miscellaneous Expense	3,000	
Total Expenses		29,600
Net Income		$ 9,900

(b)

State-Rite Cleaning Company
Capital Statement
December 31, 197–

Capital, January 1, 197–		$14,300
Net Income	$9,900	
Less: Drawing	4,800	
Increase in Capital		5,100
Capital, December 31, 197–		$19,400

(c)

State-Rite Cleaning Company
Balance Sheet
December 31, 197–

ASSETS

Cash	$ 9,300	
Supplies Inventory	5,300	
Equipment	19,200	
Total Assets		$33,800

LIABILITIES AND CAPITAL

Accounts Payable	$11,600	
Notes Payable	2,800	
Total Liabilities		$14,400
Capital, December 31, 197–		19,400
Total Liabilities and Capital		$33,800

11.

	Debit	Credit
(1)	(c)	(b)
(2)	(c)	(f)
(3)	(i)	(c)
(4)	(e)	(a)
(5)	(j)	(a)
(6)	(a)	(g)
(7)	(c)	(g) or (a)
(8)	(d)	(c)
(9)	(k)	(j)
(10)	(h)	(c)

12.

Cash

Bal. 15,000	850 (2)
(1) 2,400	240 (3)
(6) 15,000	350 (4)
	300 (7)

Supplies

(5) 800	300 (8)

Drawing

(7) 300	

Capital

	Bal. 37,000

Supplies Expense

(8) 300	

Salaries Expense

(4) 350	

Building

Bal. 22,000	

Prepaid Insurance

(2) 850	

Accounts Payable

	800 (5)

Rent Income

	2,400 (1)

Utilities Expense

(3) 240	

Loans Payable

	15,000 (6)

13.

Utility Service Company
Trial Balance

Cash	$13,200	
Supplies	500	
Equipment	11,000	
Accounts Payable		$ 2,300
Capital		24,000
Drawing	8,000	
Service Income		22,200
Supplies Expense	200	
Salary Expense	8,200	
Rent Expense	7,400	
	$48,500	$48,500

Chapter 4

Recording Transactions

4.1 INTRODUCTION

In the preceding chapters we discussed the nature of business transactions and the manner in which they are analyzed and classified. The primary emphasis was the *why* rather than the *how* of accounting operations; we aimed at an understanding of the *reason* for making the entry in a particular way. We showed the effects of transactions by making entries in "T" accounts. However, these entries do not provide the necessary data for a particular transaction nor do they provide a chronological record of transactions. The missing information is furnished by the journal.

4.2 THE JOURNAL

The journal, or day book, is the book of original entry for accounting data. Subsequently the data is transferred or *posted* to the ledger, the book of subsequent or *secondary* entry. The various transactions are evidenced by sales tickets, purchase invoices, check stubs, etc. On the basis of this evidence the transactions are entered in chronological order in the journal. The process is called *journalizing*.

There are a number of different journals that may be used in a business. For our purposes they may be grouped into (1) general journals and (2) specialized journals. The latter type, which are used in businesses with a large number of repetitive transactions, are described in Chapter 5. To illustrate journalizing, we here use the general journal whose standard form is shown below.

GENERAL JOURNAL *Page*

Date (1)	Description (2)	P. R. (3)	Debit (4)	Credit (5)
197—				
Oct. 7	*Cash*	1	10,000	
	John Hennessy, Capital	50		10,000
	(6) *Invested cash in the business*			

4.3 JOURNALIZING

We describe the entries in the general journal according to the numbering above.

(1) ***Date.*** The year, month, and day of the first entry are written in the date column. The year and month do not have to be repeated for the additional entries until a new month occurs or a new page is needed.

(2) ***Description.*** The account title to be debited is entered on the first line, next to the date column. The name of the account to be credited is entered on the line below and indented.

(3) ***P.R. (Posting Reference).*** Nothing is entered in this column until the particular entry is posted; that is, until the amounts are transferred to the related ledger accounts. The posting process will be described in Sec. 4.4.

(4) **Debit.** The debit amount for each account is entered in this column. Generally there is only one item, but there could be two or more separate items.

(5) **Credit.** The credit amount for each account is entered in this column. Here again, there is generally only one account, but there could be two or more accounts involved with different amounts.

(6) **Explanation.** A brief description of the transaction is usually made on the line below the credit. Generally a blank line is left between the explanation and the next entry.

EXAMPLE 1.

To help in understanding the operation of the general journal, let us journalize the transactions previously described for Mr. Bagon's business (see page 35).

	P. R.	Debit	Credit
Transaction (1). Invested in business			
197—			
Jan. 4 Cash		*5,000*	
A. Bagon, Capital			*5,000*
Investment in law practice			
Transaction (2). Bought supplies			
4 Supplies on Hand		*300*	
Cash			*300*
Bought supplies for cash			
Transaction (3). Bought equpment on account			
4 Equipment		*2,500*	
Accounts Payable			*2,500*
Bought equipment from Altway			
Transaction (4). Fees earned			
15 Cash		*2,000*	
Fees Income			*2,000*
Received payment for services			
Transaction (5). Rent paid			
30 Rent Expense		*500*	
Cash			*500*
Paid rent for month			
Transaction (6). Paid salaries			
30 Salaries Expense		*200*	
Cash			*200*
Paid salaries of part-time help			
Transaction (7). Payment on account			
31 Accounts Payable		*1,000*	
Cash			*1,000*
Payment on account to Altway			
Transaction (8). Count of supplies			
31 Supplies Expense		*200*	
Supplies on Hand			*200*
Supplies used during the month			
Transaction (9). Withdrawal for personal use			
31 A. Bagon, Drawing		*300*	
Cash			*300*
Personal withdrawal			

4.4 POSTING

The process of transferring information from the journal to the ledger for the purpose of summarizing is called *posting*. Primarily a clerical task, posting is ordinarily carried out in the following steps:

(1) **Record the amount and date.** The date and the amounts of the debits and credits are entered in the appropriate accounts.

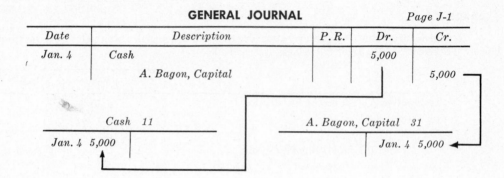

(2) **Record the posting reference in the account.** The number of the journal page is entered in the account (broken arrows below).

(3) **Record the posting in the journal.** For cross-referencing, the code number of the account is now entered in the P.R. column of the journal (solid arrows).

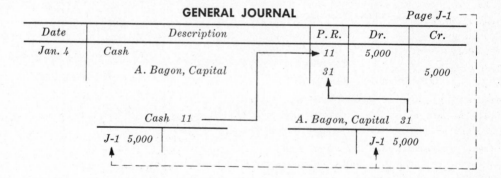

EXAMPLE 2.

The results of the posting from the journal of A. Bagon (see page 51) appear below.

ASSETS	=	LIABILITIES	+	CAPITAL

Cash 11		Accounts Payable 21		A. Bagon, Capital 31
(1) 5,000	300 (2)	(7) 1,000	2,500 (3)	5,000 (1)
(4) 2,000	500 (5)			
	200 (6)			A. Bagon, Drawing 32
	1,000 (7)			(2) 300
	300 (9)			

(continued next page)

	ASSETS	=	LIABILITIES +	CAPITAL

ASSETS = LIABILITIES + CAPITAL

Supplies on Hand 12	Fees Income 41
(2) 300	200 (8)		2,000 (4)
Equipment 13	Rent Expense 51
(3) 2,500	(5) 500
	Salaries Expense 52
	(6) 200
	Supplies Expense 53
	(8) 200

A. Bagon, Lawyer
Trial Balance
January 31, 197–

	Debit	Credit
Cash	$4,700	
Supplies on Hand	100	
Equipment	2,500	
Accounts Payable		$1,500
A. Bagon, Capital		5,000
A. Bagon, Drawing	300	
Fees Income		2,000
Rent Expense	500	
Salaries Expense	200	
Supplies Expense	200	
	$8,500	$8,500

A. Bagon, Lawyer
Income Statement
for the month ended January 31, 197–

Fees Income		$2,000
Expenses		
Rent Expense	$500	
Salaries Expense	200	
Supplies Expense	200	
Total Expenses		900
Net Income		$1,100

A. Bagon, Lawyer
Balance Sheet
January 31, 197–

ASSETS

Current Assets		
Cash	$4,700	
Supplies on Hand	100	
Total Current Assets		$4,800
Fixed Assets		
Equipment		2,500
Total Assets		$7,300

LIABILITIES

Accounts Payable	$1,500

CAPITAL

Capital, January 1	$5,000	
Add: Net Income	1,100	
	6,100	
Less: Drawing	300	
Capital, January 31		5,800
Total Liabilities and Capital		$7,300

Summary

(1) The initial book for recording all transactions is known as the _____.

(2) Another name and description of the journal is _____.

(3) The process of transferring information from the journal to the ledger is known as _____.

(4) The list of code numbers that identify the entries in the journal is called the _____ _____.

(5) Asset account numbers begin with the number _____, while liabilities begin with ____.

(6) All capital account numbers begin with the number ____.

(7) All income account numbers begin with ____, while expense account numbers begin with ____.

(8) The process of recording transactions in the journal is termed _____.

(9) The complete process of accounting is called the _____.

Answers:
(1)	journal	(4)	chart of accounts	(7)	4, 5
(2)	book of original entry	(5)	1, 2	(8)	journalizing
(3)	posting	(6)	3	(9)	accounting cycle

Solved Problems

4.1. What is a compound journal entry?

SOLUTION

An entry having more than one debit or more than one credit is called a compound entry. For example, land was bought (debit for $10,000, with a down payment of cash (credit) of $4,000 and a mortgage (credit) of $6,000.

4.2. How does the incorrect posting of a debit as a credit affect the trial balance?

SOLUTION

The trial balance will be out of balance by twice the amount incorrectly posted. For example, if a $200 debit to cash is posted as a credit, there will be $400 in credits and 0 in debits, making a net difference of $400.

4.3. In the shaded space below each entry, write a brief explanation of the transaction that might appear in the general journal.

(a)	Equipment	8,000	
	Cash		2,000
	Accounts Payable, William Smith		6,000
(b)	Accounts Payable, William Smith	4,000	
	Notes Payable		4,000
(c)	Accounts Payable, William Smith	2,000	
	Cash		2,000

SOLUTION

(a)	Equipment	8,000	
	Cash		2,000
	Accounts Payable, William Smith		6,000
	Purchase of equipment, 25% for cash, balance on account		
(b)	Accounts Payable, William Smith	4,000	
	Notes Payable		4,000
	Notes payable in settlement of account payable		
(c)	Accounts Payable, William Smith	2,000	
	Cash		2,000
	Settlement of the accounts payable		

4.4. Dr. Jon Voity, Dentist, began his practice, investing in the business the following assets:

Cash	$ 2,600
Supplies	1,400
Equipment	12,500
Furniture	3,000

Record the opening entry in the journal.

	Debit	Credit

SOLUTION

	Debit	Credit
Cash	2,600	
Supplies	1,400	
Equipment	12,500	
Furniture	3,000	
Jon Voity, Capital		19,500

4.5. If in Problem 4.4 Dr. Voity owed a balance on the equipment of $3,500, what would the opening entry then be?

	Debit	Credit

SOLUTION

	Debit	Credit
Cash	2,600	
Supplies	1,400	
Equipment	12,500	
Furniture	3,000	
Accounts Payable		3,500
Jon Voity, Capital		16,000

4.6. Record the following entries in the general journal for the Acom Cleaning Company.

(a) Invested $12,000 cash in the business.
(b) Paid $1,000 for office furniture.
(c) Bought equipment costing $8,000, on account.
(d) Received $2,200 in cleaning income.
(e) Paid 1/5 of the amount owed on the equipment.

	Debit	Credit
(a)		
(b)		
(c)		
(d)		
(e)		

SOLUTION

		Debit	Credit
(a)	Cash	12,000	
	Acom, Capital		12,000
(b)	Office Furniture	1,000	
	Cash		1,000
(c)	Equipment	8,000	
	Accounts Payable		8,000
(d)	Cash	2,200	
	Cleaning Income		2,200
(e)	Accounts Payable	1,600	
	Cash		1,600

4.7. Record the following entries in the general journal for the Tusten Medical Group.

(*a*) Invested $18,000 in cash, $4,800 in supplies, and $12,200 in equipment to begin the Tusten Medical Group.

(*b*) Received $2,400 from cash patients for the week.

(*c*) Invested additional cash of $5,000 in the firm.

		Debit	Credit
(*a*)			
(*b*)			
(*c*)			

SOLUTION

		Debit	Credit
(*a*)	Cash	18,000	
	Supplies Inventory	4,800	
	Equipment	12,200	
	Tusten, Capital		35,000
(*b*)	Cash	2,400	
	Fees Income		2,400
(*c*)	Cash	5,000	
	Tusten, Capital		5,000

4.8. If, in Problem 4.7, the Tusten Medical Group billed patients for the month for $1,600, present the necessary journal entry.

SOLUTION

Accounts Receivable	1,600	
Fees Income		1,600
To record services rendered on account		

4.9. If the Medical Group (see Problems 4.7 and 4.8) received $545 from patients who were billed last month, what entry would be necessary to record this information?

SOLUTION

Cash	545	
Accounts Receivable		545
Received cash on account		

4.10. Refer to Problems 4.8 and 4.9. When payment is received from billed patients (accounts receivable), why isn't the income account credited?

SOLUTION

Fees Income had been recorded in the previous month, when the service had been rendered. On the accrual basis, income, as well as expense, is recorded in the period of service or use, not in the period of payment.

4.11. Post the following journal entries for the Canny Taxi Company to the "T" accounts below. Disregard folio numbers at this time.

		P. R.	Debit	Credit
(a)	Cash		6,000	
	Canny, Capital			6,000
(b)	Equipment		4,000	
	Accounts Payable			3,000
	Cash			1,000
(c)	Accounts Payable		3,000	
	Cash			3,000
(d)	Cash		1,500	
	Fares Income			1,500
(e)	Salaries Expense		600	
	Cash			600

Cash	Equipment	Accounts Payable

Fares Income	Salaries Expense

Canny, Capital

SOLUTION

Cash		Equipment		Accounts Payable	
(a) 6,000	(b) 1,000	(b) 4,000		(c) 3,000	(b) 3,000
(d) 1,500	(c) 3,000				
	(e) 600	**Fares Income**		**Salaries Expense**	
			(d) 1,500	(e) 600	
Canny, Capital					
	(a) 6,000				

4.12. Use the balances of the "T" accounts in Problem 4.11 to prepare a trial balance.

Canny Taxi Company Trial Balance		
Cash		
Equipment		
Accounts Payable		
Capital		
Fares Income		
Salaries Expense		

SOLUTION

Canny Taxi Company		
Trial Balance		
Cash	$2,900	
Equipment	4,000	
Accounts Payable		0
Capital		$6,000
Fares Income		1,500
Salaries Expense	600	
	$7,500	$7,500

4.13. Journalize the following transactions: (a) Larry Adams opened a dry cleaning store on March 1, 197–, investing $12,000 cash, $6,000 in equipment, and $4,000 worth of supplies; (b) bought $2,600 worth of equipment on account from J. Laym, Inc., Invoice 101; (c) received $2,800 from cash sales for the month; (d) paid rent, $200; (e) paid salaries, $600; (f) paid $1,600 on account to J. Laym, Inc.; (g) withdrew $500 for personal use; (h) used $1,000 worth of supplies during the month.

	Debit	Credit
(a)		
(b)		
(c)		
(d)		
(e)		
(f)		
(g)		
(h)		

SOLUTION

		Debit	Credit
(a)	Cash	12,000	
	Supplies on Hand	4,000	
	Equipment	6,000	
	L. Adams, Capital		22,000
	Investment in business		
(b)	Equipment	2,600	
	Accounts Payable		2,600
	J. Laym, Inc. Invoice 101		
(c)	Cash	2,800	
	Cleaning Income		2,800
	Sales for month		
(d)	Rent Expense	200	
	Cash		200
	Rent for month		
(e)	Salaries Expense	600	
	Cash		600
	Salaries for month		
(f)	Accounts Payable	1,600	
	Cash		1,600
	Paid J. Laym, Inc. on account		
(g)	L. Adams, Drawing	500	
	Cash		500
	Personal withdrawal		
(h)	Supplies Expense	1,000	
	Supplies on Hand		1,000
	Supplies used during month		

4.14. Post from the journal in Problem 4.13 to the following accounts:

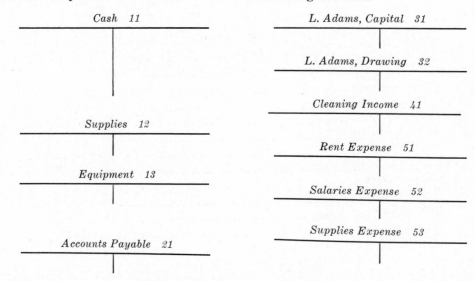

Cash   11   L. Adams, Capital   31

Supplies   12   L. Adams, Drawing   32

Equipment   13   Cleaning Income   41

Accounts Payable   21   Rent Expense   51

Salaries Expense   52

Supplies Expense   53

SOLUTION

Cash 11		L. Adams, Capital 31
(a) J-4 12,000	(d) J-4 200	(a) J-4 22,000
(c) J-4 2,800	(e) J-4 600	
	(f) J-4 1,600	
	(g) J-4 500	

L. Adams, Drawing 32

(g) J-4 500

Supplies 12

(a) J-4 4,000	(h) J-4 1,000

Cleaning Income 41

(c) J-4 2,800

Equipment 13

(a) J-4 6,000
(b) J-4 2,600

Rent Expense 51

(d) J-4 200

Salaries Expense 52

(e) J-4 600

Accounts Payable 21

(f) J-5 1,600	(b) J-4 2,600

Supplies Expense 53

(h) J-4 1,000

4.15. From the information obtained in Problem 4.14, prepare a trial balance for Adams Dry Cleaning Company.

Adams Dry Cleaning Company		
Trial Balance		
Cash		
Supplies on Hand		
Equipment		
Accounts Payable		
L. Adams, Capital		
L. Adams, Drawing		
Cleaning Income		
Rent Expense		
Salaries Expense		
Supplies Expense		

SOLUTION

Adams Dry Cleaning Company		
Trial Balance		
Cash	$11,900	
Supplies on Hand	3,000	
Equipment	8,600	
Accounts Payable		$ 1,000
L. Adams, Capital		22,000
L. Adams, Drawing	500	
Cleaning Income		2,800
Rent Expense	200	
Salaries Expense	600	
Supplies Expense	1,000	
	$25,800	$25,800

4.16. The trial balance for Vanguard Playhouse on October 31, 197–, was as follows.

Vanguard Playhouse
Trial Balance
October 31, 197–

Cash	$ 2,400	
Accounts Receivable	1,500	
Supplies Inventory	350	
Equipment	11,200	
Building	10,000	
Accounts Payable		$ 9,450
Notes Payable		12,000
Vanguard Playhouse, Capital		4,000
	$25,450	$25,450

Selected transactions for November were as follows:

(*a*)   Nov. 2:   Paid $1,000 due on the notes payable

(*b*)   Nov. 8:   Paid $3,000 on account

(*c*)   Nov. 15:   Receipts for the two-week period totaled $8,400

(*d*)   Nov. 22:   Bought an additional projector at a cost of $15,500 with a cash down payment of $5,000, the balance to be paid within one year

(*e*)   Nov. 30:   Paid salaries of $1,600

Using this data, transfer the October 31 balances to the ledger accounts below, prepare journal entries for the month of November, and post to the ledger accounts.

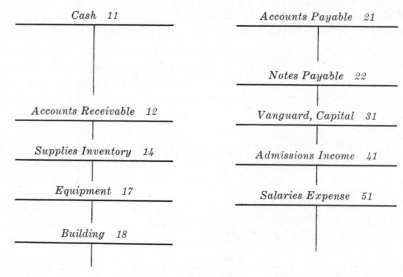

JOURNAL				*Page J-6*
Date	Description	P.R.	Debit	Credit

JOURNAL *Page J-6 (continued)*

SOLUTION

JOURNAL

Date	Description	P. R.	Debit	Credit
197–				
Nov. 2	Notes Payable	22	1,000	
	Cash	11		1,000
	Payment of installment note			
Nov. 8	Accounts Payable	21	3,000	
	Cash	11		3,000
	Payment on outstanding accounts			
Nov. 15	Cash	11	8,400	
	Admissions Income	41		8,400
	Receipts for the two-week period to date			
Nov. 22	Equipment	17	15,500	
	Cash	11		5,000
	Accounts Payable	21		10,500
	Purchase of a projector with cash payment,			
	balance due in one year			
Nov. 30	Salaries Expense	51	1,600	
	Cash	11		1,600
	Salaries paid to employees			

Cash 11

Bal. 2,400	(a) J-6 1,000
J-6 8,400	(b) J-6 3,000
	(d) J-6 5,000
	(e) J-6 1,600

Accounts Receivable 12

Bal. 1,500	

Supplies Inventory 14

Bal. 350	

Equipment 17

Bal. 11,200	
J-6 15,500	

Building 18

Bal. 10,000	

Accounts Payable 21

(b) J-6 3,000	Bal. 9,450
	(d) J-6 10,500

Notes Payable 22

(a) J-6 1,000	Bal. 12,000

Vanguard, Capital 31

	Bal. 4,000

Admissions Income 41

	(c) J-6 8,400

Salaries Expense 51

(e) J-6 1,600	

4.17. For Vanguard Playhouse (Problem 4.16), prepare (*a*) a trial balance and (*b*) a balance sheet as of November 30, 197–.

(a)

Vanguard Playhouse		
Trial Balance		
November 30, 197–		
Cash		
Accounts Receivable		
Supplies Inventory		
Equipment		
Building		
Accounts Payable		
Notes Payable		
Vanguard, Capital		
Admissions Income		
Salaries Expense		

(b)

Vanguard Playhouse		
Balance Sheet		
November 30, 197–		
ASSETS		
Current Assets		
Total Current Assets		
Fixed Assets		
Total Fixed Assets		
Total Assets		
LIABILITIES AND CAPITAL		
Current Liabilities		
Total Current Liabilities		
Vanguard, Capital, November 30, 197–		
Total Liabilities and Capital		
*(Additional space to compute Capital)		

SOLUTION

(a)

Vanguard Playhouse		
Trial Balance		
November 30, 197–		
Cash	$ 200	
Accounts Receivable	1,500	
Supplies Inventory	350	
Equipment	26,700	
Building	10,000	
Accounts Payable		$16,950
Notes Payable		11,000
Vanguard, Capital		4,000
Admissions Income		8,400
Salaries Expense	1,600	
	$40,350	$40,350

(b)

Vanguard Playhouse		
Balance Sheet		
November 30, 197–		
ASSETS		
Current Assets		
Cash	$ 200	
Accounts Receivable	1,500	
Supplies Inventory	350	
Total Current Assets		$ 2,050
Fixed Assets		
Equipment	26,700	
Building	10,000	
Total Fixed Assets		36,700
Total Assets		$38,750
LIABILITIES AND CAPITAL		
Current Liabilities		
Accounts Payable	16,950	
Notes Payable	11,000	
Total Current Liabili'es		27,950
*Vanguard, Capital, November 30, 197–		10,800
Total Liabilities and Capital		$38,750

*To obtain the capital balance as of November 30, first determine
the net income for the period (income statement).

Admissions Income	$ 8,400	
Less: Salaries Expense	1,600	
Net Income	$ 6,800	

Since there is no drawing involved, add the net income to the
beginning capital:

Capital, November 1	$ 4,000	
Add: Net Income	6,800	
Capital, November 30	$10,800	

Chapter 5

Repetitive Transactions

5.1 INTRODUCTION

In earlier sections, the accounting principles discussed were illustrated in terms of small businesses having relatively few transactions. Each transaction was recorded by means of an entry in the general journal, then posted to the related account in the general ledger.

Such a simple system becomes altogether too slow and cumbersome when transactions of various categories occur by the hundreds or thousands monthly. In that case, it is more practical to group the repetitive transactions according to type (sales, purchases, cash, etc.) and to provide a separate *special journal* for each type. Entries not of a repetitive nature, such as corrections, adjusting entries, and closing entries, will still be entered in the general journal.

5.2 ADVANTAGES OF SPECIAL JOURNALS

The advantages of using special journals where there are numerous repetitive transactions may be summarized as follows:

(1) *Reduces detailed recording.* In the special journal, each transaction is entered on a single line which is designed to provide all necessary information. For example, a sales transaction is recorded on a single line indicating a debit to the customer's account and giving the customer's name, the date, the amount, and any other desired data (such as the invoice number). Under the special-journal concept, individual posting is eliminated. Only one posting for the total amount is made to the appropriate ledger account at the end of the month. Thus, if a firm had 1,000 sales on account during the month, the sales account would be credited once, not 1,000 times.

(2) *Permits better division of labor.* Each special journal can be handled by a different person, who will become more familiar with the special work and therefore more efficient. Just as important: journalizing can now be done by a number of people working simultaneously, rather than consecutively.

(3) *Permits better internal control.* Having separate journals allows the work to be arranged in such a way that no one person has conflicting responsibilities; for example, the receipt and the recording of cash. Thus, no employee can steal received cash and then make a journal entry to conceal the theft.

5.3 SPECIAL LEDGERS (SUBSIDIARY LEDGERS)

Further simplification of the general ledger is brought about by the use of subsidiary ledgers. In particular, for those businesses which sell goods on credit and find it necessary to maintain a separate account with each customer and with each creditor, a special *accounts receivable ledger* and an *accounts payable ledger* eliminate multiple entries in the general ledger.

The advantages of special or subsidiary ledgers are similar to those of special journals. These are:

(1) **Reduces ledger detail.** Most of the information will be in the subsidiary ledger, and the general ledger will be reserved chiefly for summary or total figures. Therefore, it will be easier to prepare the financial statements.

(2) **Permits better division of labor.** Here again, each special or subsidiary ledger may be handled by a different person. Therefore, one person may work on the general ledger accounts while another person may simultaneously work on the subsidiary ledger.

(3) **Permits a different sequence of accounts.** In the general ledger, it is desirable to have the accounts in the same sequence as in the balance sheet and income statement. As a further aid, it is desirable to use numbers to locate and reference the accounts, as explained in Sec. 3.5. However, in connection with accounts receivable or accounts payable, which involve names of customers or companies, it is preferable to have the accounts in *alphabetical* sequence.

(4) **Permits better internal control.** Better control is maintained if a person other than the person responsible for the general ledger is responsible for the subsidiary ledger. For example, the accounts receivable or customers' ledger trial balance should agree with the balance of the accounts receivable account in the general ledger. The general ledger account acts as a *controlling account*, and the subsidiary ledger must agree with the control. No unauthorized entry could be made in the subsidiary ledger, as it would immediately put that record out of balance with the control account.

The idea of control accounts introduced above is an important one in accounting. Any group of similar accounts may be removed from the general ledger and a controlling account substituted for it. Not only is another level of error-protection thereby provided, but the time needed to prepare the general ledger trial balance and the financial statements becomes further reduced.

5.4   USE OF SPECIAL JOURNALS

The principal special journals are the sales journal, purchases journal, cash receipts journal, and cash disbursements journal.

We shall describe each and illustrate the relationship between the special journal and the general ledger, on the one hand, and, on the other hand, the relationship between the special journal and the subsidiary ledger. Also, it is desirable to point out in each case the relationship of the controlling account to the subsidiary ledger.

SALES JOURNAL

The entry for the individual sale on account is a debit to Accounts Receivable (and to the customer's account) and a credit to Sales. Only sales on account are recorded in the sales journal. Cash sales ordinarily do not require the customer's name and are recorded in the cash receipts journal, usually in daily total.

Referring to Example 1 below, we have the following procedure for recording and posting the sales journal:

1. Record the sale on account in the sales journal.

2. Post from the sales journal to the individual accounts in the subsidiary ledger.

3. Record the posting of the individual accounts in the post reference (P.R.) column. A check mark indicates that the posting has been made.

4. At the end of the month, total the amount of sales made on account. This total is posted in the general ledger to the accounts receivable account (12) as a debit and to the sales account (41) as a credit. In the general ledger the source of the entry (S-1) is entered in each account.

EXAMPLE 1.

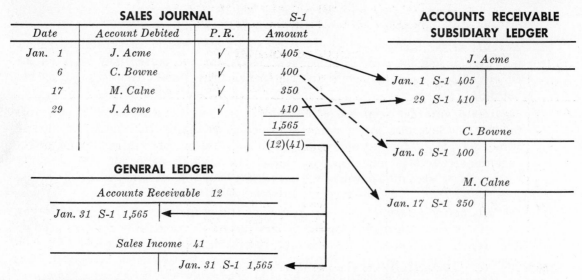

The balances in the accounts receivable ledger may be summarized by listing each customer and the amount he owes. The accounts receivable trial balance should agree with the controlling account.

EXAMPLE 2.

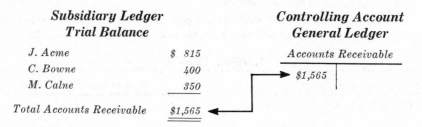

PURCHASES JOURNAL

In most businesses, purchases are made regularly and are evidenced by purchase invoices issued to creditors. In previous chapters the entry to record the purchase of goods on account had the following form:

Purchases	(Debit)
Accounts Payable	(Credit)

Where there are many transactions for purchases of merchandise for resale, for supplies to be used in the business, for equipment, etc., the labor-saving features of a special purchases journal may be utilized. The basic principles that apply to the sales journal also apply to the purchases journal. However, because of the variety of items that are purchased, more columns are needed in the purchases journal.

For the sales journal (see Example 2) the subsidiary ledger trial balance total (accounts receivable) equaled the controlling account in the general ledger. In the purchases journal the individual transactions with creditors (accounts payable) are posted to the creditor's account in the subsidiary ledger, while the total is posted to the controlling account, Accounts Payable.

EXAMPLE 3.

January 2:   Purchased merchandise from Altman Company, $2,000
January 8:   Purchased supplies on account from Bay Company, $600
January 15:   Purchased equipment on account from Calloway Company, $5,000

January 15:   Purchased land from J. Smith on account, $1,000
January 21:   Purchased additional supplies from Bay Company, $200
January 28:   Purchased additional merchandise from Altman Company, $1,000

PURCHASES JOURNAL
P-1 (1)

Date	Account Credited	P. R.	Acct. Pay. Cr.	Purch. Dr.	Supp. Dr.	Sundry		
						Accounts Debited	P. R.	Amt.
Jan. 2	(2) Altman Company	√	2,000	2,000				
8	Bay Company	√	600		600			
15	Calloway Company	√	5,000			Equipment	18	5,000
15	J. Smith	√	1,000			Land	17	1,000
21	Bay Company	√	200		200	(4)		
28	Altman Company	√	1,000	1,000				
		(3)	9,800	3,000	800			6,000
			(21)	(51)	(14)			(√)

NOTES: (1) P-1 denotes the page number (1) of the purchases journal.

(2) The individual amounts will be posted as credits to their respective accounts in the accounts payable subsidiary ledger. The check marks in the purchases journal indicate such postings.

(3) Accounts Payable, Purchases, and Supplies are posted to the respective accounts in the general ledger as totals only.

(4) The sundry amount of $6,000 is not posted as a total; instead, the individual amounts are posted, as many different accounts may be affected each month.

GENERAL LEDGER

Supplies Inventory 14		Accounts Payable 21	
Jan. 31 P-1 800			Jan. 31 P-1 9,800

Land 17	
Jan. 15 P-1 1,000	

Equipment 18		Purchases 51	
Jan. 15 P-1 5,000		Jan. 31 P-1 3,000	

ACCOUNTS PAYABLE SUBSIDIARY LEDGER

Altman Company		Bay Company	
	Jan. 2 P-1 2,000		Jan. 8 P-1 600
	28 P-1 1,000		21 P-1 200

Calloway Company		J. Smith	
	Jan. 15 P-1 5,000		Jan. 15 P-1 1,000

To prove that the accounts payable ledger is in balance, the total owed to the three companies must agree with the balance in the accounts payable control account.

		Accounts Payable	
Altman Company	$3,000		
Bay Company	800	P-1 $9,800	
Calloway Company	5,000		
J. Smith	1,000		
Total	$9,800		

CASH RECEIPTS JOURNAL

Transactions involving cash are recorded in either the cash receipts or the cash disbursements journal. Items that increase cash position are recorded in the cash receipts journal. Increases in cash may come from such sources as collections from customers, receipts from cash sales, investments, and collection of interest and principal on notes held by the firm (notes receivable).

The procedure for recording and posting the cash receipts journal is described below and illustrated in Example 4.

1. The total of the cash column is posted as a debit to the cash account.
2. Each amount is posted to the individual customer's account. The total is posted as a credit to the accounts receivable account in the general ledger.
3. The total of the sales credit column is posted as a credit to the sales account.
4. Each item in the sundry account is posted individually to the general ledger. The total of the sundry account is not posted.
5. The accuracy of the journal (that is, the equality of debits and credits) is verified by adding the three credit columns and comparing the total with the debit column.

EXAMPLE 4.

The month of July saw the following cash-increasing transactions.

July 2:   Received $600 from J. Acme in partial settlement of his bill
July 5:   Returned defective merchandise bought for cash and received $80 in settlement
July 14:   Cash sales for the first half of the month, $800
July 24:   Received a check from C. Bowne in full settlement of his account, $400
July 30:   Cash sales for the second half of the month, $720

As shown in Example 2, there are balances in Mr. Acme's and Mr. Bowne's accounts of $815 and $400, respectively.

CASH RECEIPTS JOURNAL   CR-1

Date	Account Credited	P. R.	Cash Dr.	Acct. Rec. Cr.	Sales Cr.	Sundry Acct. Cr.	Amt.
July 2	J. Acme	√	600	600			
5	Purchase Returns	52	80				80
14	Sales	√	800		800		
24	C. Bowne	√	400	400			
30	Sales	√	720		720		
			2,600	1,000	1,520		80
			(11)	(12)	(41)		(√)

GENERAL LEDGER

Cash 11	
July 31 CR-1 2,600	

Sales 41	
	July 31 CR-1 1,520

Accounts Receivable 12	
Bal. 1,215	July 31 CR-1 1,000

Purchase Returns 52	
	July 5 CR-1 80

ACCOUNTS RECEIVABLE SUBSIDIARY LEDGER

J. Acme	
Bal. 815	July 1 CR-1 600

C. Bowne	
Bal. 400	July 28 CR-1 400

CASH DISBURSEMENTS JOURNAL

The cash disbursements journal is used to record all transactions that *reduce* cash. These transactions may arise from payments to creditors, cash purchases (of supplies, equipment, or merchandise), the payment of expenses, (salary, rent, insurance, etc.), as well as from personal withdrawals.

The procedure for recording and posting the cash disbursements journal parallels that for the cash receipts journal:

1. A check is written each time a payment is made; the check numbers provide a convenient reference, and they help in controlling cash and in reconciling the bank account.

2. The cash credit column is posted in total to the general ledger at the end of the month.

3. Debits to Accounts Payable represent cash paid to creditors. These individual amounts will be posted to the creditors' accounts in the accounts payable subsidiary ledger. At the end of the month the total of the accounts payable column is posted to the general ledger.

4. The sundry column is used to record debits for any account that cannot be entered in the other special columns. These would include purchases of equipment, inventory, payment of expenses, and cash withdrawals. Each item is posted separately to the general ledger. The total of the sundry column is not posted.

EXAMPLE 5.

CASH DISBURSEMENTS JOURNAL   CD-1

Date	Description	P.R.	Check No.	Cash Cr.	Accounts Payable Dr.	Sundry Debits Account	Amount
Feb. 2	Bay Company	√	1	600	600		
8	Rent Expense	52	2	220			220
15	Salary Expense	53	3	1,900			1,900
21	Purchases	51	4	1,600			1,600
24	Salaries Expense	53	5	1,900			1,900
				6,220	600		5,620
				(11)	(21)		(√)

GENERAL LEDGER

Cash 11

Feb. 28 CD-1 6,220

Rent Expense 52

Feb. 8 CD-1 220

Accounts Payable 21

Feb. 28 CD-1 600 | Bal. 600

Salaries Expense 53

Feb. 15 CD-1 1,900
24 CD-1 1,900

Purchases 51

Feb. 21 CD-1 1,600

ACCOUNTS PAYABLE SUBSIDIARY LEDGER

Bay Company

Feb. 2 CD-1 600 | Bal. 800*

*From the purchases journal, Example 3.

5.5 DISCOUNTS

To induce a buyer to make payment before the amount is due, the seller may allow the buyer to deduct a certain percent of the bill. If payment is due within a stated number of days after the date of invoice, the number of days will usually be preceded by the letter "n", signifying net. For example, bills due in 30 days would be indicated by n/30.

A two-percent discount offered if payment is made within ten days would be indicated by 2/10. If the buyer has a choice of either paying the amount less 2% within the ten-day period or paying the entire bill within 30 days, the terms would be written as 2/10, n/30.

EXAMPLE 6.

A sales invoice totaling $800 and dated January 2 has discount terms of 2/10, n/30. If the purchaser pays on or before January 12 (10 days after the date of purchase), he may deduct $16 ($800 × 2%) from the bill and pay only $784. If he chooses not to pay within the discount period, he is obligated to pay the entire amount of $800 by February 1.

From the point of view of the seller, the discount is a sales discount; the purchaser would consider it a purchase discount. If a business experiences a great number of sales and purchase discounts, then special columns would be added in the cash receipts and cash disbursements journals.

Sales Discount appears as a reduction of Sales in the income statement. Purchase Discount appears as a reduction of Purchases in the Cost of Goods Sold section of the income statement.

5.6 RETURN OF MERCHANDISE

Many factors in business will cause a return of merchandise: damaged goods, incorrect size or style, or a price not agreed upon. Returns associated with purchases are recorded as purchase returns and allowances, and those associated with sales are recorded as sales returns and allowances.

PURCHASE RETURNS AND ALLOWANCES

If a firm has many purchase returns, a purchase returns and allowances journal should be used. However, for illustrative purposes, entries for the return of purchases (bought on account) are here made in the general journal:

	P. R.	Debit	Credit
Accounts Payable, Smith and Company	√ 21	420	
Purchase Returns and Allowances	52		420

The debit portion of the accounts payable is posted to the accounts payable account in the general ledger, and also to the accounts payable subsidiary ledger. Because the controlling account and the customer's account are both debited, a diagonal line is needed in the post reference column to show both postings. For items involving a return for cash, the cash receipts journal is used.

ACCOUNTS PAYABLE LEDGER	GENERAL LEDGER	
Smith and Company	*Accounts Payable 21*	*Purchase Returns 52*
J-1 420	Bal. 800	J-1 420	Bal. 800		J-1 420

Purchase Returns and Allowances appears in the income statement as a reduction of Purchases.

SALES RETURNS AND ALLOWANCES

If many transactions occur during the year, in which customers return goods bought on account, a special journal known as the sales returns and allowances journal would be used. However, where sales returns are infrequent the general journal is sufficient.

The entry to record returns of sales on account in the general journal would be:

	P. R.	Debit	Credit
Sales Returns and Allowances	42	600	
Accounts Receivable, Murphey Company	√ 12		600

The accounts receivable account, which is credited, is posted both in the accounts receivable controlling account and in the accounts receivable ledger.

ACCOUNTS RECEIVABLE LEDGER   **GENERAL LEDGER**

Murphey Company	
Bal. 900	J-1 600

Accounts Receivable 12	
Bal. 900	J-1 600

Sales Returns 42	
J-1 600	

If the sales returns involve the payment of cash, it would appear in the cash disbursements journal.

Sales Returns and Allowances appears in the income statement as a reduction of Sales Income.

5.7 TYPES OF LEDGER ACCOUNT FORMS

The "T" account has been used for most illustrations of accounts thus far. The disadvantage of the "T" account is that it requires totaling the debit and the credit columns in order to find the balance. As it is necessary to have the balance of a customer's or creditor's account available at any given moment, an alternate form of the ledger, the three-column account, may be used. The advantage of the form is that an extra column, "Balance," is provided, so that the amount the customer owes is always shown. As each transaction is recorded, the balance is updated. Below is an illustration of an accounts receivable ledger account using this form.

A. Lapinsky

Date	P. R.	Debit	Credit	Balance
Jan. 2	S-1	650		650
4	S-1	409		1,059
8	CD-1		500	559

Summary

(1) The journal used to record sales of merchandise on account is known as the _____ journal.

(2) The sale of merchandise for cash would appear in the _____ journal.

(3) It is common practice to divide the ledger in a large business into three separate ledgers, known as the _____, _____, and _____ ledgers.

(4) The total of the sales journal is posted at the end of the month as a debit to Accounts Receivable and a credit to _____.

(5) The only column in the purchases journal that will not be posted in total at the end of the month is the _____ column.

(6) Sales Discount and Purchase Discount appear in the _____ statement as reductions of Sales and of Purchases, respectively.

(7) Terms of 2/10, n/30 on a $750 purchase of January 4, paid within the discount period, would provide a discount of $____.

(8) Accounts Receivable and Accounts Payable in the general ledger may be classified as _____.

Answers: (1) sales;   (2) cash receipts;   (3) general, accounts receivable, accounts payable;   (4) Sales; (5) sundry;   (6) income;   (7) 15;   (8) controlling accounts

Solved Problems

5.1.   For each of the following transactions, indicate with a check mark the journal in which it should be recorded.

(a) Purchase of merchandise on account

(b) Purchase of merchandise for cash

(c) Receipt of cash from a customer in settlement of an account

(d) Cash sales for the month

(e) Payment of salaries

(f) Sales of merchandise for cash

(g) Sales of merchandise on account

(h) Cash refunded to customer

(i) Sale of a fixed asset for cash

(j) Notes payable sent to creditor in settlement of an account

	Cash Receipts Journal	Cash Disburs. Journal	Sales Journal	Purchases Journal	General Journal
(a)					
(b)					
(c)					
(d)					
(e)					
(f)					
(g)					
(h)					
(i)					
(j)					

SOLUTION

	Cash Receipts Journal	Cash Disburs. Journal	Sales Journal	Purchases Journal	General Journal
(a)				√	
(b)		√			
(c)	√				
(d)	√				
(e)		√			
(f)	√				
(g)			√		
(h)		√			
(i)	√				
(j)					√

5.2. Record the following transactions in the sales journal.

January 1:   Sold merchandise on account to Fleischer Company, $550

January 4:   Sold merchandise on account to Gerard Company, $650

January 18:   Sold merchandise on account to Harke Company, $300

January 29:   Sold additional merchandise to Harke Company, $100

SALES JOURNAL   S-1

Date	Account Debited	P.R.	Amount

SOLUTION

SALES JOURNAL   S-1

Date	Account Debited	P.R.	Amount
Jan. 1	Fleischer Company	√	550
4	Gerard Company	√	650
18	Harke Company	√	300
29	Harke Company	√	100
			1,600

5.3. Post the customers' accounts in Problem 5.2 to the accounts receivable subsidiary ledger and prepare a schedule of accounts receivable.

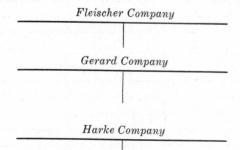

SCHEDULE OF ACCOUNTS RECEIVABLE

Fleischer Company	
Gerard Company	
Harke Company	

SOLUTION

Fleischer Company

Jan. 1 S-1 550	

Gerard Company

Jan. 4 S-1 650	

Harke Company

Jan. 18 S-1 300	
29 S-1 100	

SCHEDULE OF ACCOUNTS RECEIVABLE

Fleischer Company	550
Gerard Company	650
Harke Company	400
	1,600

5.4.   For Problem 5.2, make the entries needed to record the sales for the month.

Accounts Receivable   12

Sales Income   41

SOLUTION

Accounts Receivable   12

Jan. 31 S-1 1,600	

Sales Income   41

	Jan. 31 S-1 1,600

5.5.   What is the net proceeds of goods sold on March 10 for $750, terms 2/10, n/30, if payment is made (*a*) on March 18? (*b*) on March 22?

SOLUTION

(*a*) $750 \times 2\% = \$15$ (*b*) $750 (the discount period ended March 20)
$750 - \$15 = \$735$

5.6.   Record the following transactions in the purchases journal.

   April. 2:   Purchased merchandise on account from Kane Company, $450

   April 5:   Purchased supplies on account from Lane Supply House, $180

   April 20:   Purchased merchandise on account from Hanson Company, $400

   April 24:   Purchased additional supplies on account from Lane Supply House, $50

   April 29:   Purchased equipment on account from Olin Equipment, $1,600

PURCHASES JOURNAL   *P-1*

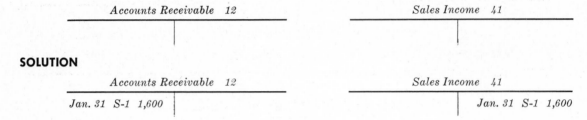

Date	Account Credited	P. R.	Acct. Pay. Cr.	Purch. Dr.	Supp. Dr.	Sundry		
						Acct. Dr.	P. R.	Amt.

SOLUTION

PURCHASES JOURNAL   P-1

Date	Account Debited	P.R.	Acct. Pay. Cr.	Purch. Dr.	Supp. Dr.	Sundry		
						Acct. Dr.	P.R.	Amt.
Apr. 2	Kane Company	√	450	450				
5	Lane Supply House	√	180		180			
20	Hanson Company	√	400	400				
24	Lane Supply House	√	50		50			
29	Olin Equipment	√	1,600			Equipment		1,600
			2,680	850	230			1,600

5.7. Post the information from Problem 5.6 into the accounts payable subsidiary ledger and prepare a schedule of accounts payable.

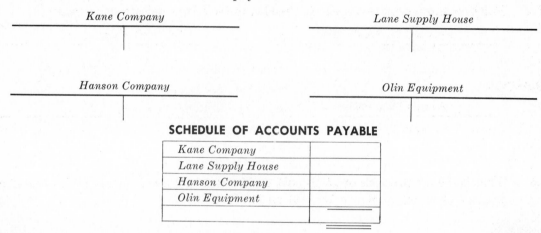

Kane Company

Lane Supply House

Hanson Company

Olin Equipment

SCHEDULE OF ACCOUNTS PAYABLE

Kane Company	
Lane Supply House	
Hanson Company	
Olin Equipment	

SOLUTION

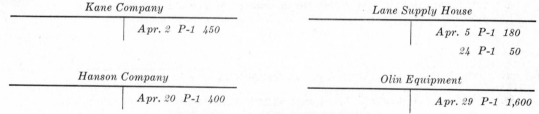

Kane Company

Apr. 2 P-1 450

Lane Supply House

Apr. 5 P-1 180
24 P-1   50

Hanson Company

Apr. 20 P-1 400

Olin Equipment

Apr. 29 P-1 1,600

SCHEDULE OF ACCOUNTS PAYABLE

Kane Company	450
Lane Supply House	230
Hanson Company	400
Olin Equipment	1,600
	2,680

5.8. Post the purchases journal totals from Problem 5.6 to the accounts in the general ledger.

GENERAL LEDGER

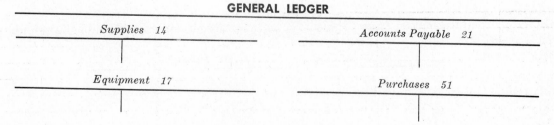

Supplies   14

Accounts Payable   21

Equipment   17

Purchases   51

SOLUTION

GENERAL LEDGER

Supplies 14		Accounts Payable 21	
Apr. 30 P-1 230			Apr. 30 P-1 2,680

Equipment 17		Purchases 51	
Apr. 29 P-1 1,600		Apr. 30 P-1 850	

5.9. Record the following transactions in the cash receipts journal.

> January 2: Received $510 from L. Harmon in full settlement of his account
>
> January 10: Received $615 from B. Elder in settlement of his account
>
> January 14: Cash sales for a two-week period, $3,400
>
> January 20: Sold $200 of office supplies [not a merchandise item] to Smith Company as a service
>
> January 24: The owner made an additional investment of $1,500
>
> January 30: Cash sales for the last two weeks, $2,620

CASH RECEIPTS JOURNAL   CR-1

Date	Account Cr.	P. R.	Cash Dr.	Acct. Rec. Cr.	Sales Cr.	Sundry Cr.

SOLUTION

CASH RECEIPTS JOURNAL   CR-1

Date	Account Cr.	P. R.	Cash Dr.	Acct. Rec. Cr.	Sales Cr.	Sundry Cr.
Jan. 2	L. Harmon	✓	510	510		
10	B. Elder	✓	615	615		
14	Sales	✓	3,400		3,400	
20	Office Supplies	15	200			200
24	Capital	31	1,500			1,500
30	Sales	✓	2,620		2,620	
			8,845	1,125	6,020	1,700

5.10. Post the information from Problem 5.9 into the accounts receivable subsidiary ledger.

ACCOUNTS RECEIVABLE LEDGER

L. Harmon		B. Elder	
Bal. 510		Bal. 615	

SOLUTION

ACCOUNTS RECEIVABLE LEDGER

L. Harmon		B. Elder	
Bal. 510	Jan. 2 CR-1 510	Bal. 615	Jan. 10 CR-1 615

5.11. Post the cash receipts journal totals from Problem 5.9 to the accounts in the general ledger.

GENERAL LEDGER

Cash 11		Capital 31	
			Bal. 6,500

Accounts Receivable 12	
Bal. 3,000	

Office Supplies 15		Sales 41	
Bal. 3,500			

SOLUTION

GENERAL LEDGER

Cash 11		Capital 31	
Jan. 31 CR-1 8,845			Bal. 6,500
			Jan. 24 CR-1 1,500

Accounts Receivable 12			
Bal. 3,000	Jan. 31 CR-1 1,125	Sales 41	
			Jan. 31 CR-1 6,020

Office Supplies 15	
Bal. 3,500	Jan. 20 CR-1 200

5.12. Record the following transactions in the cash disbursements journal.

March 1:	Paid rent for the month, $320 (Check #16)
March 7:	Paid J. Becker $615 for his February invoice (Check #17)
March 10:	Bought store supplies for cash, $110 (Check #18)
March 15:	Paid salaries for the two-week period, $685 (Check #19)
March 23:	Paid B. Cone for February invoice, $600 (Check #20)
March 30:	Paid salaries for the second half of the month, $714 (Check #21)

CASH DISBURSEMENTS JOURNAL
CD-1

Date	Check No.	Account Dr.	P. R.	Cash Cr.	Acct. Pay. Dr.	Sundry Dr.

SOLUTION

CASH DISBURSEMENTS JOURNAL   CD-1

Date	Check No.	Account Dr.	P. R.	Cash Cr.	Acct. Pay. Dr.	Sundry Dr.
Mar. 1	16	Rent Expense		320		320
7	17	J. Becker	√	615	615	
10	18	Store Supplies		110		110
15	19	Salaries Expense		685		685
23	20	B. Cone	√	600	600	
30	21	Salaries Expense		714		714
				3,044	1,215	1,829

5.13. Post the information from Problem 5.12 into the accounts payable subsidiary ledger.

ACCOUNTS PAYABLE LEDGER

J. Becker	B. Cone
Bal. 615	Bal. 600

SOLUTION

ACCOUNTS PAYABLE LEDGER

J. Becker		B. Cone	
Mar. 7 CD-1 615	Bal. 615	Mar. 23 CD-1 600	Bal. 600

5.14. Post the cash disbursements journal from Problem 5.12 to the accounts in the general ledger.

GENERAL LEDGER

Cash   11

Bal. 4,200

Store Supplies   15

Accounts Payable   21

Bal. 1,840

Rent Expense   51

Salaries Expense   52

SOLUTION

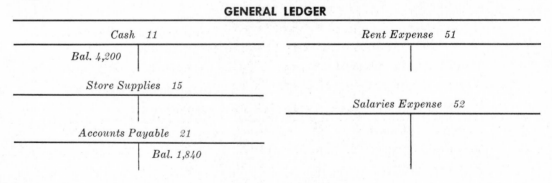

GENERAL LEDGER

Cash   11

Bal. 4,200 | Mar. 30 CD-1 3,044

Store Supplies   15

Mar. 10 CD-1 110

Accounts Payable   21

Mar. 30 CD-1 1,215 | Bal. 1,840

Rent Expense   51

Mar. 1 CD-1 320

Salaries Expense   52

Mar. 15 CD-1 685
30 CD-1 714

5.15. The cash receipts journal below utilizes a special column for sales discount. Record the following cash transactions in the journal.

May 2: Received a check for $588 from A. Banks in settlement of his $600 April invoice

May 12: Received $686 in settlement of the April invoice of $700 from J. Johnson

May 26: Received a check for $495 in settlement of B. Simpson's April account of $500

CASH RECEIPTS JOURNAL   CR-1

Date	Account Cr.	P.R.	Cash Dr.	Sales Disc. Dr.	Acct. Rec. Cr.	Sundry Dr.

SOLUTION

CASH RECEIPTS JOURNAL   CR-1

Date	Account Cr.	P.R.	Cash Dr.	Sales Disc. Dr.	Acct. Rec. Cr.	Sundry Dr.
May 2	A. Banks		588	12	600	
12	J. Johnson		686	14	700	
26	B. Simpson		495	5	500	
			1,769	31	1,800	

5.16. The cash disbursements journal below utilizes the special column Purchases Discount. Record the cash transactions into the cash disbursements journal.

June 2: Paid J. Thompson $490 in settlement of our April invoice for $500, Check #24

June 10: Sent a check to B. Rang, $297, in settlement of the May invoice of $300, Check #25

June 21: Paid A. Johnson $588 in settlement of the $600 invoice of last month, Check #26

CASH DISBURSEMENTS JOURNAL   CD-1

Date	Check No.	Account Dr.	P.R.	Cash Cr.	Pur. Disc. Cr.	Acct. Pay. Dr.	Sundry Dr.

SOLUTION

CASH DISBURSEMENTS JOURNAL   CD-1

Date	Check No.	Account Dr.	P.R.	Cash Cr.	Pur. Disc. Cr.	Acct. Pay. Dr.	Sundry Dr.
June 2	24	J. Thompson		490	10	500	
10	25	B. Rang		297	3	300	
21	26	A. Johnson		588	12	600	
				1,375	25	1,400	

5.17. All transactions affecting the cash account of Park Company for the month of January, 1973, are presented below.

January 1: Received cash from Alden Company for the balance due on their account, $1,600, less 2% discount

January 5: Received payment from Walk Company on account, $1,550

January 8: Paid rent for the month, $650, Check #165

January 10: Purchased supplies for cash, $614, Check #166

January 14: Cash sales for the first half of the month, $5,280

January 15: Paid bi-weekly salaries, $1,600, Check #167

January 19: Received $406 in settlement of a $400 note receivable plus interest

January 19: Received payment from J. Cork of $500, less 1% discount

January 20: Paid B. Simmons $686 in settlement of our $700 invoice, Check #168

January 24: Paid $450 on account to L. Hann, Check #169

January 27: Paid H. Hiram $800, less 2%, on account, Check #170

January 30: Paid bi-weekly salaries, $1,680, Check #171

Record the above transactions in both the cash receipts and cash disbursements journals.

CASH RECEIPTS JOURNAL   CR-1

Date	Account Cr.	P. R.	Cash Dr.	Sales Disc. Dr.	Sales Cr.	Acct. Rec. Cr.	Sundry Cr.

CASH DISBURSEMENTS JOURNAL   CD-1

Date	Check No.	Account Dr.	P. R.	Cash Cr.	Pur. Disc. Cr.	Acct. Pay. Dr.	Sundry Dr.

SOLUTION

CASH RECEIPTS JOURNAL   CR-1

Date	Account Cr.	P. R.	Cash Dr.	Sales Disc. Dr.	Sales Cr.	Acct. Rec. Cr.	Sundry Cr.
Jan. 1	Alden Co.	√	1,568	32		1,600	
5	Walk Co.	√	1,550			1,550	
14	Sales	√	5,280		5,280		
19	Notes Rec.						400
19	Interest Inc.		406				6
19	J. Cork	√	495	5		500	
			9,299	37	5,280	3,650	406

CASH DISBURSEMENTS JOURNAL   CD-1

Date	Check No.	Account Dr.	P. R.	Cash Cr.	Pur. Disc. Cr.	Acct. Pay. Dr.	Sundry Dr.
Jan. 8	165	Rent Exp.		650			650
10	166	Supplies		614			614
15	167	Salaries Exp.		1,600			1,600
20	168	B. Simmons	√	686	14	700	
24	169	L. Hann	√	450		450	
27	170	H. Hiram	√	784	16	800	
30	171	Salaries Exp.		1,680			1,680
				6,464	30	1,950	4,544

5.18. The Johnston Company transactions involving purchases and sales for the month of January are presented below. All purchases and sales are made on account.

> January 3: Sold merchandise to Acme Supply Company, $440
>
> January 5: Purchased merchandise from Balfour Corporation, $7,200
>
> January 10: Sold merchandise to Mennon Company, $345
>
> January 10: Sold merchandise to Blant Company, $2,400
>
> January 14: Purchased from Wyde Equipment $750 worth of equipment
>
> January 17: Purchased office supplies from Gold Supply, $850
>
> January 21: Purchased merchandise from Caldon Company, $6,240
>
> January 28: Returned damaged merchandise purchased from Balfour Corporation, receiving credit of $300
>
> January 30: Issued credit of $60 to Acme Supply Company for defective goods returned to us

Record the transactions in the sales, purchases, and general journals.

SALES JOURNAL   S-1

January

Date	Account Debited	P. R.	Amount

PURCHASES JOURNAL   P-1

Date	Account Cr.	P. R.	Acct. Pay Cr.	Pur. Dr.	Supp. Dr.	Sundry Acct. Dr.	P. R.	Amount

GENERAL JOURNAL   J-1

Date	Description	P. R.	Debit	Credit

SOLUTION

SALES JOURNAL   S-1

Date	Account Debited	P. R.	Amount
Jan. 3	Acme Supply Company	√	440
10	Mennon Company	√	345
10	Blant Company	√	2,400
			3,185

PURCHASES JOURNAL   P-1

Date	Account Cr.	P. R.	Acct. Pay. Cr.	Pur. Dr.	Supp. Dr.	Sundry Account Dr.	P. R.	Amount
Jan. 5	Balfour Corp.	√	7,200	7,200				
14	Wyde Equip.		750			Equipment		750
17	Gold Supply		850		850			
21	Caldon Co.	√	6,240	6,240				
			15,040	13,440	850			750

GENERAL JOURNAL   J-1

Date	Description	P. R.	Debit	Credit
Jan. 28	Accounts Payable, Balfour Corp.		300	
	Purchase Returns			300
Jan. 30	Sales Returns		60	
	Accounts Receivable, Acme Supply			60

5.19. William Drew began business on March 1. The transactions completed by the Drew Company for the month of March are listed below. Record these transactions, using the various journals provided.

March 1: Deposited $14,000 in a bank account for the operation of Drew Company

March 2: Paid rent for the month, $600, Check #1

March 4: Purchased equipment on account from Andon Equipment, $10,000

March 7: Purchased merchandise on account from Baily Company, $1,200

March 7: Cash sales for the week, $1,650

March 10: Issued Check #2 for $150, for store supplies

March 11: Sold merchandise on account to Manny Company, $600

March 12: Sold merchandise on account to Nant Company, $350

March 14: Paid bi-weekly salaries of $740, Check #3

March 14: Cash sales for the week, $1,800

March 16: Purchased merchandise on account from Cotin Company, $1,100

March 17: Issued Check #4 to Baily Company for March 7 purchase, less 2%

March 18: Bought $250 worth of store supplies from Salio Supply House on account

March 19: Returned defective merchandise of $200 to Cotin Company and received credit

March 19: Sold merchandise on account to Olin Company, $645

March 21: Issued Check #5 to Andon Equipment for $500, in part payment of equipment purchase

March 22:   Received check from Nant Company in settlement of their March 12 purchase, less 2% discount

March 22:   Purchased merchandise from Canny Corporation for cash, $750, Check #6

March 23:   Cash sales for the week, $1,845

March 24:   Purchased merchandise on account from Daily Corporation, $850

March 25:   Sold merchandise on account to Pallit Corporation $740

March 26:   Purchased additional supplies, $325, from Salio Supply House

March 27:   Received check from Manny Company in settlement of their account, less 1% discount

March 30:   Cash sales for the week, $1,920

March 30:   Received $300 on account from Olin Company

March 31:   Paid bi-weekly salaries, $810, Check #7

GENERAL JOURNAL   J-1

Date	Description	P. R.	Debit	Credit

CASH RECEIPTS JOURNAL   CR-1

Date	Account Cr.	P. R.	Cash Dr.	Sales Disc. Dr.	Acct. Rec. Cr.	Sales Cr.	Sundry Acct. Cr.

CASH DISBURSEMENTS JOURNAL   CD-1

Date	Check No.	Account Dr.	P. R.	Cash Cr.	Pur. Disc. Cr.	Acct. Pay. Dr.	Sundry Acct. Dr.

PURCHASES JOURNAL   P-1

Date	Account Cr.	P.R.	Acct. Pay. Cr.	Pur. Dr.	Store Supp. Dr.	Office Supp. Dr.	Sundry Acct. Dr.		
							Acct.	P.R.	Amount

SALES JOURNAL   S-1

Date	Account Debited	P.R.	Accounts Receivable Dr. Sales Cr.

SOLUTION

GENERAL JOURNAL   J-1

Date	Description	P.R.	Debit	Credit
Mar. 19	Accounts Payable, Cotin Co.	√ / 21	200	
	Purchase Returns and Allowances	52		200
	Defective goods			

CASH RECEIPTS JOURNAL   CR-1

Date	Account Credited	P.R.	Cash Dr.	Sales Disc. Dr.	Acct. Rec. Cr.	Sales Cr.	Sundry Acct. Cr.
Mar. 1	Drew Company, Capital	31	14,000				14,000
7	Sales	√	1,650			1,650	
14	Sales	√	1,800			1,800	
22	Nant Company	√	343	7	350		
23	Sales	√	1,845			1,845	
30	Manny Company	√	594	6	600		
30	Sales	√	1,920			1,920	
30	Olin Company	√	300		300		
			22,452	13	1,250	7,215	14,000
			(11)	(42)	(12)	(41)	(√)

CASH DISBURSEMENTS JOURNAL   CD-1

Date	Check No.	Account Debited	P.R.	Cash Cr.	Pur. Disc. Cr.	Acct. Pay. Dr.	Sundry Acct. Dr.
Mar. 2	1	Rent Expense	54	600			600
10	2	Store Supplies	14	150			150
14	3	Salaries Expense	55	740			740
17	4	Baily Company	√	1,176	24	1,200	
21	5	Andon Equipment	√	500		500	
22	6	Purchases	51	750			750
31	7	Salaries Expense	55	810			810
				4,726	24	1,700	3,050
				(11)	(51)	(21)	(√)

PURCHASES JOURNAL

P-1

Date	Account Cr.	P.R.	Acct. Pay. Cr.	Pur. Dr.	Store Supp. Dr.	Office Supp. Dr.	Sundry Acct. Dr.		
							Acct.	P.R.	Amount
Mar. 4	Andon Equipment	√	10,000				Equip.	19	10,000
7	Baily Company	√	1,200	1,200					
16	Cotin Company	√	1,100	1,100					
18	Salio Supply House	√	250		250				
24	Daily Corporation	√	850	850					
26	Salio Supply House	√	325		325				
			13,725	3,150	575				10,000
			(21)	(51)	(14)				(√)

SALES JOURNAL

S-1

Date	Account Debited	P.R.	Accounts Receivable Dr. Sales Cr.
Mar. 11	Manny Company	√	600
12	Nant Company	√	350
19	Olin Company	√	645
25	Pallit Corporation	√	740
			2,335
			(12)(41)

5.20. Based upon the work in Problem 5.19, post all transactions to the appropriate accounts in the general ledger, the accounts receivable ledger, and the accounts payable ledger.

GENERAL LEDGER

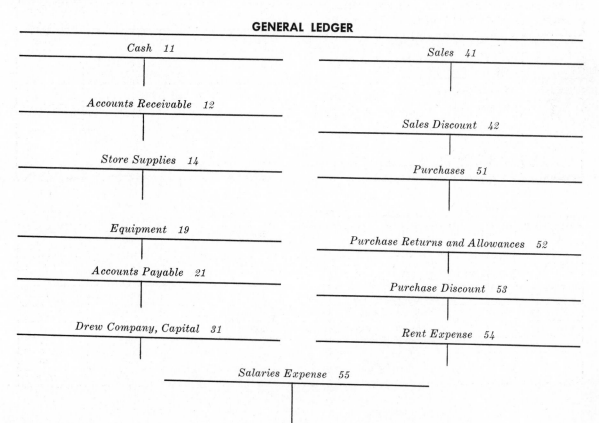

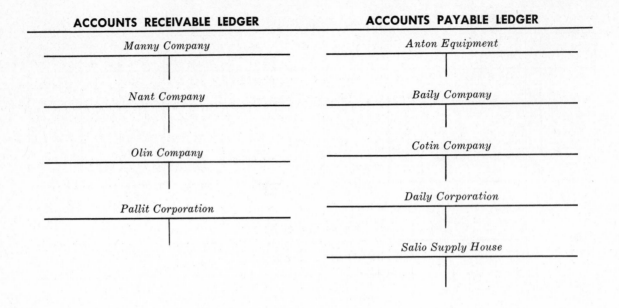

ACCOUNTS RECEIVABLE LEDGER	**ACCOUNTS PAYABLE LEDGER**
Manny Company	Anton Equipment
Nant Company	Baily Company
Olin Company	Cotin Company
Pallit Corporation	Daily Corporation
	Salio Supply House

SOLUTION

GENERAL LEDGER

Cash   11

Mar. 31 CR-1	22,452	Mar. 31 CD-1	4,726
	17,726		

Sales   41

	Mar. 31 S-1	2,335
	31 CR-1	7,215
		9,550

Accounts Receivable   12

Mar. 31 S-1	2,335	Mar. 31 CR-1	1,250
	1,085		

Sales Discount   42

Mar. 31 CR-1	13

Store Supplies   14

Mar. 10 CD-1	150
31 P-1	575
	725

Purchases   51

Mar. 22 CD-1	750
31 P-1	3,150
	3,900

Equipment   19

Mar. 4 P-1	10,000

Purchase Returns and Allowances   52

	Mar. 19 P-1	200

Accounts Payable   21

Mar. 19 J-1	200	Mar. 31 P-1	13,725
31 CD-1	1,700		11,825

Purchase Discount   53

	Mar. 31 CD-1	24

Drew Company, Capital   31

	Mar. 1 CR-1	14,000

Rent Expense   54

Mar. 2 CD-1	600

Salaries Expense   55

Mar. 14 CD-1	740
31 CD-1	810
	1,550

ACCOUNTS RECEIVABLE LEDGER	ACCOUNTS PAYABLE LEDGER

Manny Company

Mar. 11 S-1 600	Mar. 30 CR-1 600

Nant Company

Mar. 12 S-1 350	Mar. 22 CR-1 350

Olin Company

Mar. 19 S-1 645	Mar. 30 CR-1 300

Pallit Corporation

Mar. 25 S-1 740	

Andon Equipment

Mar. 21 CD-1 500	Mar. 4 P-1 10,000

Baily Company

Mar. 17 CD-1 1,200	Mar. 7 P-1 1,200

Cotin Company

Mar. 19 J-1 200	Mar. 16 P-1 1,100

Daily Corporation

	Mar. 24 P-1 850

Salio Supply House

	Mar. 18 P-1 250
	26 P-1 325

5.21. Based upon the information in Problems 5.19 and 5.20, prepare (a) a schedule of accounts receivable, (b) a schedule of accounts payable, (c) a trial balance.

(a)

Drew Company
Schedule of Accounts Receivable
March 31, 1973

Olin Company	
Pallit Corporation	

(b)

Drew Company
Schedule of Accounts Payable
March 31, 1973

Andon Equipment	
Cotin Equipment	
Daily Corporation	
Salio Supply House	

(c)

Drew Company
Trial Balance
March 31, 1973

Cash		
Accounts Receivable		
Store Supplies		
Equipment		
Accounts Payable		
Drew Company, Capital		
Sales		
Sales Discount		
Purchases		
Purchase Returns and Allowances		
Purchase Discount		
Rent Expense		
Salaries Expense		

SOLUTION

(a)

Drew Company	
Schedule of Accounts Receivable	
March 31, 1973	
Olin Company	$ 345
Pallit Corporation	740
	$1,085

(b)

Drew Company	
Schedule of Accounts Payable	
March 31, 1973	
Andon Equipment	$ 9,500
Cotin Company	900
Daily Corporation	850
Salio Supply House	575
	$11,825

(c)

Drew Company		
Trial Balance		
March 31, 1973		
Cash	$17,726	
Accounts Receivable	1,085	
Store Supplies	725	
Equipment	10,000	
Accounts Payable		$11,825
Drew Company, Capital		14,000
Sales		9,550
Sales Discount	13	
Purchases	3,900	
Purchase Returns and Allowances		200
Purchase Discount		24
Rent Expense	600	
Salaries Expense	1,550	
	$35,599	$35,599

Chapter 6

Adjusting and Closing Procedures

6.1 INTRODUCTION: THE ACCRUAL BASIS OF ACCOUNTING

As mentioned in Chapter 2, accounting records are kept on the *accrual basis,* except in the case of very small businesses. This means that *revenue is recognized when earned, regardless of when cash is actually collected, and expense is matched to the revenue, regardless of when cash is paid out.* Most revenue is earned when goods or services are delivered. At this time title to the goods or services is transferred and there is created a legal obligation to pay for such goods or services. Some revenue is recognized on a time basis, such as rental income, and is earned when the specified period of time has passed. The accrual concept demands that expenses be kept in step with revenue, so that each month sees only that month's expenses applied against the revenue for that month. The necessary matching is brought about through a type of journal entry. In this chapter we shall discuss these *adjusting entries,* and also the *closing entries* through which the adjusted balances are ultimately transferred to balance sheet accounts at the end of the fiscal year.

6.2 ADJUSTING ENTRIES COVERING RECORDED DATA

To adjust expense or income items that have already been recorded only a reclassification is required; that is, amounts have only to be transferred from one account (e.g., Prepaid Insurance) to another (Insurance Expense). The following seven examples will show how adjusting entries are made for the principal types of *recorded expenses.*

EXAMPLE 1. Prepaid Insurance.

Assume that a business paid a $1,200 premium on April 1 for one year's insurance in advance. This represents an increase in one asset (prepaid expense) and a decrease in another asset (cash). Thus, the entry would be:

Prepaid Insurance	*1,200*	
Cash		*1,200*

At the end of April, 1/12 of the $1,200, or $100, had expired or been used up. Therefore, an adjustment has to be made, decreasing or crediting Prepaid Insurance and increasing or debiting Insurance Expense. The entry would be:

Insurance Expense	*100*	
Prepaid Insurance		*100*

Thus, $100 would be shown as Insurance Expense in the income statement for April and the balance of $1,100 would be shown as Prepaid Expense in the balance sheet.

EXAMPLE 2. Prepaid Taxes.

Assume that on April 1 a business made the quarterly property tax payment of $600. At that time the transaction would be recorded with a debit to Prepaid Taxes, and a credit to Cash, for $600. Since the payment covers 3 months, the tax expense will be $200 per month. The entries would be as follows:

April 1	*Prepaid Property Taxes*	*600*	
	Cash		*600*
April 30	*Property Tax Expense*	*200*	
	Prepaid Property Taxes		*200*

The balance to be shown on the balance sheet of April 30 for Prepaid Property Taxes would be $400.

EXAMPLE 3. Prepaid Rent.

Assume that on March 1 a business paid $1,500 to cover rent for the balance of the year. The full amount would have been recorded as a prepaid expense in March. Since there is a 10-month period involved, the rent expense each month is $150. The balance of Prepaid Rent would be $1,350 at the beginning of April. The adjusting entry for April would be:

Rent Expense	*150*	
Prepaid Rent		*150*

At the end of April, the balance in the prepaid rent account would be $1,200.

EXAMPLE 4. Prepaid Interest.

Assume that the business found it necessary to take a loan of $5,000 from the local bank on April 1. The period of the loan was 2 months, with interest of 6% a year. When interest is deducted in advance, or discounted, there is prepaid interest involved. On April 1 the entry would be:

Cash	*4,950*	
Prepaid Interest	*50*	
Loan Payable		*5,000*

The prepaid interest, an asset, was computed as follows:

$$\$5,000 \times 6\% \text{ per year} \times 1/6 \text{ year} = \$50$$

At the end of April the adjusting entry would be:

Interest Expense	*25*	
Prepaid Interest		*25*

EXAMPLE 5. Supplies on Hand.

A type of prepayment which is somewhat different from those previously described is the payment for office or factory supplies. Assume that on April 1, $400 worth of supplies were purchased on credit. This would increase assets and also increase liabilities. At the end of April, when expense and revenue are to be matched and statements prepared, a count of the amount on hand will be made. Assume that the inventory count shows that $250 of supplies are still on hand. Then the amount consumed during April was $150 ($400 − $250). The two entries would be as follows:

April 1	*Supplies on Hand*	*400*	
	Accounts Payable		*400*
April 30	*Supplies Expense*	*150*	
	Supplies on Hand		*150*

Supplies Expense of $150 will be included in the April income statement; Supplies on Hand of $250 will be included as an asset on the balance sheet of April 30.

In each of the above examples the net effect of the adjusting entry is to credit the same account as was originally debited. Examples 6 and 7 illustrate what are called *valuation* or *offset accounts*.

EXAMPLE 6. Allowance for Uncollectible Accounts.

A business with many accounts receivable will reasonably expect to have some losses from uncollectible accounts. It will not be known which specific accounts will not be collected, but past experience furnishes an estimate of the total uncollectible amount.

Assume that a company estimates that 1% of sales on account will be uncollectible. Then, if such sales are $10,000 for April, it is estimated that $100 will be uncollectible. The actual loss may not definitely be determined for a year or more, but the loss attributed to April sales would call for an adjusting entry.

Uncollectible Accounts Expense	*100*	
Allowance for Uncollectible Accounts		*100*

If the balance in Accounts Receivable at April 30 was $9,500 and the previous month's balance in Allowance for Uncollectible Accounts was $300, the balance sheet at April 30 would show the following:

Accounts Receivable	*9,500*	
Less: Allowance for Uncollectible Accounts	*400*	*9,100*

EXAMPLE 7.   Accumulated Depreciation.

This also is a valuation or offset account, which means that the balance is offset against the related asset account.   In the case of property, plant, and equipment it is desirable to know the original cost as well as the value after depreciation.   Assume that machinery costing $15,000 was purchased on February 1 of the current year and was expected to last 10 years.   With the straight-line method of accounting (i.e., equal charges each period), the depreciation would be $1,500 a year, or $125 a month.   The adjusting entry would be as follows:

Depreciation Expense	*125*	
Accumulated Depreciation		*125*

At the end of April, Accumulated Depreciation would have a balance of $375, representing three months' accumulated depreciation.   The account would be shown in the balance sheet as follows:

Machinery	*15,000*	
Less: Accumulated Depreciation	*375*	*14,625*

Adjustment of *recorded revenue* (unearned income) takes place as in the following two examples.   Note that unearned income represents a liability, since something remains to be done before the revenue is actually earned.

EXAMPLE 8.   Unearned Rent.

Assume that rent of $400 was received on March 15, for April rent.   The following entries would be made:

March 15 *Cash*	*400*	
Unearned Rent		*400*

At the end of April, when the rent had been earned, Unearned Rent would be debited.

April 30 *Unearned Rent*	*400*	
Rent Income		*400*

EXAMPLE 9.   Unearned Commissions.

Assume that $300 was received on April 1, for commissions for 3 months.   At the end of April, Unearned Commissions would be debited, and Earned Commissions Income would be credited, for $100. The entries would be as follows:

April 1 *Cash*	*300*	
Unearned Commissions		*300*
April 30 *Unearned Commissions*	*100*	
Earned Commissions Income		*100*

6.3   ADJUSTING ENTRIES COVERING UNRECORDED DATA

In the previous section we discussed various kinds of adjustments to accounts to which entries had already been made. Now we consider those instances in which an expense has been incurred or an income earned but the applicable amount has not been recorded during the month. For example, if salaries are paid on a weekly basis, the last week of the month may apply to two months. If April ends on a Tuesday, then the first two days of the week will apply to April and be an April expense, while the last three days will be a May expense.

To arrive at the proper total for salaries for the month of April, we must include along with the April payrolls that were paid in April, the two days' salary that was not paid until May. Thus, we make an entry to *accrue* the two days' salary. To accrue means to collect or accumulate.

The following two examples show adjusting entries for the most important types of *unrecorded expenses* (accrued expenses).

EXAMPLE 10. Accrued Salaries.

Assume that April 30 falls on Tuesday for the last weekly payroll period. Then, two days of that week will apply to April, three days to May. The payroll for the week amounted to $2,500, of which $1,000 applied to April and $1,500 to May. The entries would be as follows:

April 30	Salaries Expense	1,000	
	Accrued Salaries		1,000

When the payment of the payroll is made — say, on May 8 — the entry would be as follows:

May 8	Salaries Expense	1,500	
	Accrued Salaries	1,000	
	Cash		2,500

As can be seen above, $1,000 was charged to expense in April and $1,500 in May. The debit to Accrued Salaries of $1,000 in May merely canceled the credit entry made in April, when the liability was set up for the April salaries expense.

EXAMPLE 11. Accrued Interest.

At the end of the accounting period the interest accrued on any business liabilities should be recognized in the accounts. Assume that instead of interest being prepaid on the $5,000 loan described in Example 4, the interest is due when the loan is due. In that case, there would be accrued interest for April of $25, and the following adjusting entry would be required for April:

April 30	Interest Expense	25	
	Accrued Interest Payable		25

Most businesses would have some *unrecorded revenue* (accrued income); that is, income earned but not yet received. Generally, this would be interest earned on notes from customers, rent earned on premises rented to a tenant, or various other items for which income had been earned but had not yet been collected.

EXAMPLE 12. Accrued Interest Income.

A business holds a note receivable from a customer for $10,000. The note, due in 3 months, bears interest at 6% and was issued on March 1. The total interest would be $150 ($10,000 × 6% per year × 1/4 year). By the end of April, interest for two months had been earned. The following adjusting entry would be required for April:

April 30	Accrued Interest Receivable	50	
	Interest Income		50

When the note is settled by the customer in May, he would pay the principal plus the interest, as shown below:

May 31	Cash	10,150	
	Note Receivable		10,000
	Accrued Interest Receivable		100
	Interest Income		50

As can be seen, the interest earned was $50 a month. Therefore, Accrued Interest Receivable was debited $50 for March and $50 for April. The same entry was not necessary for May, since the note was settled at the end of May.

6.4 CLOSING ENTRIES

The information for the month-to-month adjusting entries and the related financial statements can be obtained from the worksheet, whose use will be fully described in Chapter 7. After the income statement and balance sheet have been prepared from the worksheet for the last month in the fiscal year, a summary account — variously known as Expense and Income Summary, Profit and Loss Summary, etc. — is set up. Then, by means of *closing entries*, each expense account is credited so as to produce a zero balance, and the total amount for the closed-out accounts is debited to Expense and Income Summary. Similarly, the individual revenue accounts are closed out by debiting, and the total amount is credited to the summary account. Thus, the new fiscal year starts with zero balances in the income and expense accounts, while the Expense and Income Summary balance gives the net income or the net loss for the old year.

EXAMPLE 13.

To illustrate closing procedure, we refer to the accounts of Alan Bagon.

Alan Bagon
Trial Balance
April 30, 197–

Cash	$4,700	
Supplies on Hand	100	
Equipment	2,500	
Accounts Payable		$1,500
Alan Bagon, Capital		5,000
Alan Bagon, Drawing	300	
Income from Fees		2,000
Rent Expense	500	
Salaries Expense	200	
Supplies Expense	200	
	$8,500	$8,500

The closing entries are as follows.

(1) **Close out revenue accounts.** Debit the individual revenue accounts and credit the total to Expense and Income Summary. Here, there is only one income account.

April 30	Income from Fees	2,000	
	Expense and Income Summary		2,000

(2) **Close out expense accounts.** Credit the individual expense accounts and debit the total to Expense and Income Summary.

April 30	Expense and Income Summary	900	
	Rent Expense		500
	Salaries Expense		200
	Supplies Expense		200

(3)   **Close out the Expense and Income Summary account.** If there is a profit, the credit made for total income in (1) above will exceed the debit made for total expense in (2) above. Therefore, to close out the balance to zero, a debit entry will be made to Expense and Income Summary. A credit will be made to the capital account to transfer the net income for the period. If expenses exceed income, then a loss has been sustained and a credit would be made to Expense and Income Summary and a debit to the capital account. Based on the information given, the entry is:

April 30   Expense and Income Summary   1,100

Alan Bagon, Capital   1,100

(4)   **Close out the drawing account.** The drawing account would be credited for the total amount of the drawings for the period and the capital account debited for that amount. The difference between net income and drawing for the period represents the net change in the capital account for the period. The net income of $1,100, less drawings of $300, results in a net increase of $800 in the capital account. The closing entry for the drawing account is:

April 30   Alan Bagon, Capital   300

Alan Bagon, Drawing   300

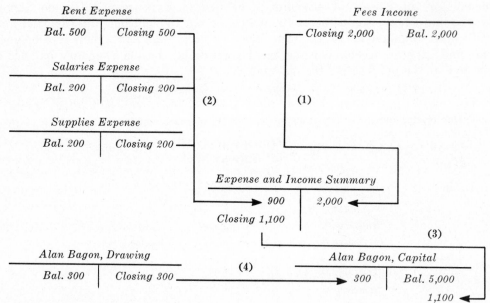

After the closing entries (1) through (4) are made, the various accounts will appear as below. The income and expense accounts and the drawing account are ruled off or closed out, thus showing no balance. The net profit for the period and the drawing account balance were transferred to Alan Bagon, Capital, a balance sheet account.

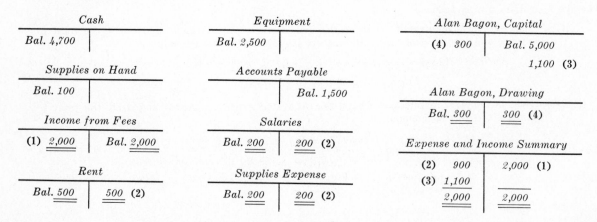

6.5 POST-CLOSING TRIAL BALANCE

After the closing entries are made, only balance sheet accounts — assets, liabilities, and capital — remain open.   A trial balance of these accounts is thus a *post-closing trial balance.*

EXAMPLE 14.

Alan Bagon
Post-Closing Trial Balance
April 30, 197–

Cash	$4,700	
Supplies on Hand	100	
Equipment	2,500	
Accounts Payable		$1,500
Alan Bagon, Capital		5,800
	$7,300	$7,300

Summary

(1)   The basis of accounting that recognizes revenue when earned, regardless of when cash is received, and matches the expenses to the revenue, regardless of when cash is paid out, is known as the _____.

(2)   An adjusting entry that records the expired amount of prepaid insurance would create the _____ account.

(3)   Supplies on hand is classified as an _____ and appears in the _____, while supplies expense is an _____ and appears in the _____.

(4)   Both Allowance for Uncollectible Accounts and Accumulated Depreciation appear in the balance sheet as _____ from their related assets.

(5)   Accrued Salaries is treated in the balance sheet as a _____, while Salaries Expense appears in the income statement as an _____.

(6)   Income that has been earned but not yet received is known as _____ _____.

(7)   Expenses that have been incurred but not yet paid for are known as _____ _____.

(8)   The revenue and expense accounts are closed out to the summary account known as _____.

(9)   Eventually, all income, expense, and drawing accounts, including summaries, will be closed into the _____ account.

(10)   The post-closing trial balance will involve only _____ , _____, and _____ accounts.

Answers: (1) accrual basis;   (2) insurance expense;   (3) asset, balance sheet, expense, income statement; (4) deductions;   (5) liability account, expense account;   (6) unrecorded revenue or accrued income;   (7) unrecorded expenses or accrued expenses;   (8) Expense and Income Summary; (9) capital;   (10) asset, liability, capital.

Solved Problems

6.1. A business pays weekly salaries of $10,000 on Friday for the five-day week. Show the adjusting entry when the fiscal period ends on (*a*) Tuesday; (*b*) Thursday.

(*a*)

(*b*)

SOLUTION

(*a*)	Salaries Expense	4,000	
	Salaries Payable		4,000
(*b*)	Salaries Expense	8,000	
	Salaries Payable		8,000

6.2. An insurance policy covering a two-year period was purchased on November 1 for $600. The amount was debited to Prepaid Insurance. Show the adjusting entry for the two-month period ending December 31.

SOLUTION

Insurance Expense	50*	
Prepaid Insurance		50

$$*\frac{600}{2}\frac{\text{dol}}{\text{yr}} \times \frac{2}{12}\ \text{yr}\ =\ \$50$$

6.3. Office supplies purchases of $900 were debited to Office Supplies on Hand. A count of the supplies at the end of the period showed $500 still on hand. Make the adjusting entry at the end of the period.

SOLUTION

Office Supplies Expense	400	
Office Supplies on Hand		400

6.4. Machinery costing $12,000, purchased November 30, is being depreciated at the rate of 10% per year. Show the adjusting entry for December 31.

SOLUTION

Depreciation Expense, Machinery	100*	
Accumulated Depreciation, Machinery		100

* $12,000 \times 10\%$ per year $\times \frac{1}{12}$ year $= \$100$

6.5. The business received $6,000 as an advance payment for work to be done for a customer. At the end of the year, $4,000 of the services had been performed. Prepare the adjusting entry if the original amount had been credited to Unearned Income.

SOLUTION

Unearned Income (Unrealized Income)	4,000	
Service Income (Realized Income)		4,000

6.6. The Willet Wilkinson Company's before-closing trial balance shows service revenue of $10,000 and interest income of $2,000. The expenses are: salaries, $6,000; rent, $2,000; depreciation, $1,500; and interest, $500. Give the closing entries to be made to Expense and Income Summary for (a) income and (b) expense.

(a)

(b)

SOLUTION

(a)
Service Income	10,000	
Interest Income	2,000	
Expense and Income Summary		12,000

(b)
Expense and Income Summary	10,000	
Salaries Expense		6,000
Rent Expense		2,000
Depreciation Expense		1,500
Interest Expense		500

6.7. Using Problem 6.6(a) and (b), prepare the closing entry for net income, and (c) post the transactions to the Expense and Income Summary and to the capital account, which had a prior balance of $20,000. Finally, close out the applicable account.

(Turn page for "T" account forms.)

Expense and Income Summary	Willet Wilkinson, Capital
(b) 10,000 (a) 12,000	Bal. 20,000
(c) ?	

SOLUTION

Expense and Income Summary	2,000	
Willet Wilkinson, Capital		2,000

Expense and Income Summary	Willet Wilkinson, Capital
(b) 10,000 (a) 12,000	Bal. 20,000
(c) 2,000	(c) 2,000
12,000 12,000	

6.8. After all revenue and expense accounts were closed at the end of the fiscal year, the Expense and Income Summary had a debit total of $100,000 and a credit total of $150,000. The capital account for William Whyte had a credit balance of $50,000 and William Whyte, Drawing had a debit balance of $35,000. Journalize the closing entries.

SOLUTION

Expense and Income Summary	50,000	
William Whyte, Capital		50,000
William Whyte, Capital	35,000	
William Whyte, Drawing		35,000

6.9. Based upon the balances below, prepare entries to close out (a) revenue accounts, (b) expense accounts, (c) Expense and Income Summary, (d) drawing account.

P. Silver, Capital		22,000
P. Silver, Drawing	6,000	
Service Revenue		12,000
Interest Income		1,500
Wages and Salaries Expense	8,000	
Rent Expense	4,000	
Depreciation Expense	3,000	
Interest Expense	2,000	

(a)

(b)

(c)

(d)

SOLUTION

(a)	Service Income	12,000	
	Interest Income	1,500	
	Expense and Income Summary		13,500
(b)	Expense and Income Summary	17,000	
	Wages and Salaries Expense		8,000
	Rent Expense		4,000
	Depreciation Expense		3,000
	Interest Expense		2,000
(c)	P. Silver, Capital	3,500*	
	Expense and Income Summary		3,500
(d)	P. Silver, Capital	6,000	
	P. Silver, Drawing		6,000

* 3,500 represents a net loss and is debited to the capital account

Chapter 7

Summarizing and Reporting
via the Worksheet

7.1 INTRODUCTION

The recording of transactions and the adjusting and closing procedures have been discussed in previous chapters. It is reasonable to expect that among the hundreds of computations and clerical tasks involved some errors will occur, such as posting a debit as a credit. Today many financial records are maintained on the computer or on mechanical bookkeeping systems. The use of machine time to correct errors can be very costly and can bring painful questions from high financial executives.

One of the best ways yet developed of avoiding errors in the permanent accounting records, and also of simplifying the work at the end of the period, is to make use of an informal record called the *worksheet*.

7.2 WORKSHEET PROCEDURES FOR A SERVICE BUSINESS

We are already familiar with the types of accounts found in a service business — i.e. a business in which revenue comes from services rendered — so we shall first discuss the worksheet for such a business.

The worksheet is usually prepared in pencil on a large sheet of accounting stationery called analysis paper. On the worksheet the ledger accounts are adjusted, balanced, and arranged in proper form for preparing the financial statements. All procedures can be reviewed quickly and the adjusting and closing entries can be made in the formal records with less chance of error. Moreover, with the data for the income statement and balance sheet already proved out on the worksheet, these statements can be prepared more quickly.

For a typical service business we may suppose the worksheet to have 10 money columns; namely, a debit and a credit column for five groups of figures: (1) Trial Balance, (2) Adjustments, (3) Adjusted Trial Balance, (4) Income Statement, and (5) Balance Sheet. (Later on, with practice, the adjusted trial balance columns may be eliminated.) The steps in completing the worksheet are then:

1. Enter the trial balance figures from the ledger.
2. Enter the adjustments.
3. Compute the adjusted trial balances.
4. Extend the adjusted trial balance figures to either the income statement or balance sheet columns.
5. Total the income statement columns and the balance sheet columns.
6. Enter the net income or net loss.

EXAMPLE 1.

Prepare the worksheet for the Wilderotter Company, whose ledger balances appear below.

Wilderotter Company
Trial Balance
May 31, 197–

Cash	$ 3,510	
Accounts Receivable	3,010	
Allowance for Uncollectible Accounts		$ 205
Supplies on Hand	1,050	
Prepaid Rent	400	
Equipment	18,000	
Accumulated Depreciation		3,000
Notes Payable		4,000
Accounts Payable		2,175
Salaries Payable		400
R. G. Wilderotter, Capital		13,690
R. G. Wilderotter, Drawing	3,000	
Service Fees		10,500
Salaries Expense	4,600	
Misc. Expense	400	
	$33,970	$33,970

1. **Enter the trial balance figures.** The balance of each general ledger account is entered in the appropriate trial balance column of the worksheet (see Fig. 7-1, page 104). The balances summarize all the transactions for May before any adjusting entries have been applied.

2. **Enter the adjustments.** After the trial balance figures have been entered and the totals are in agreement, the adjusting entries should be entered in the second pair of columns. The related debits and credits are keyed by letters so that they may be rechecked quickly for any errors. The letters should be in proper sequence, beginning with the accounts at the top of the page.

(a) *Uncollectible accounts.* Experience has shown that losses from uncollectible accounts have averaged approximately 1% of sales. Therefore, the business expects to collect 99% of the sales of any given month. The loss is really an expense of the month in which the sales are made. Since there is no account listed for uncollectible accounts expense, the account title should be written in at the bottom of the sheet. The entry is as follows:

Uncollectible Accounts Expense	125	
Allowance for Uncollectible Accounts		125

(b) *Supplies.* In order to determine the amount of supplies used, it is necessary to make a count of the amount on hand on May 31. The amount was found to be $550 worth. The balance at the beginning of the month plus purchases during May amounted to $1,050. Therefore, $1,050 − $550 = $500 worth of supplies must have been used in May. There is no account for supplies expense, so the account name must be written in at the bottom of the worksheet. The adjusting entry is:

Supplies Expense	500	
Supplies on Hand		500

(c) *Rent.* Rent of $600 for 6 months was paid in advance on March 1. Therefore, the original amount charged to Prepaid Rent has been reduced by $100 charged to expense in March and $100 in April. The account name, Rent Expense, should be written in at the bottom of the worksheet. The adjusting entry for May is as follows:

Rent Expense	100	
Prepaid Rent		100

(d) *Depreciation.* The equipment is being written off over a 10-year period using the straight-line method. Thus, $1,800 a year, or $150 a month, is being charged to expense. The title Depreciation Expense will also have to be written in at the bottom of the worksheet. The entry will be:

Depreciation Expense	150	
Accumulated Depreciation		150

WILDEROTTER COMPANY Worksheet May 31, 197__

ACCOUNT TITLE	ACCT. NO.	TRIAL BALANCE Debit	TRIAL BALANCE Credit	ADJUSTMENTS Debit	ADJUSTMENTS Credit	ADJUSTED TRIAL BALANCE Debit	ADJUSTED TRIAL BALANCE Credit	INCOME STATEMENT Debit	INCOME STATEMENT Credit	BALANCE SHEET Debit	BALANCE SHEET Credit
Cash		3510				3510				3510	
Accounts Receivable		3010				3010				3010	
Allowance for Uncollectible Accounts			205		(a) 125		330				330
Supplies on Hand		1050			(b) 500	550				550	
Prepaid Rent		400			(c) 100	300				300	
Equipment		18000				18000				18000	
Accumulated Depreciation			3000		(d) 150		3150				3150
Notes Payable			4000				4000				4000
Accounts Payable			2175				2175				2175
Taxes Payable			400				400				400
R.B. Wilderotter, Capital			13690				13690				13690
R.B. Wilderotter, Drawing		3000				3000				3000	
Sales			10500				10500		10500		
Salaries Expense		4600		(e) 200		4800		4800			
Misc. Expense		400				400		400			
		33970	33970								
Rent Expense				(c) 100		100		100			
Uncollectible Accounts Expense				(a) 125		125		125			
Supplies Expense				(b) 500		500		500			
Depreciation Expense				(d) 150		150		150			
Salaries Payable					(e) 200		200				200
Interest Expense				(f) 20		20		20			
Interest Payable					(f) 20		20				20
				1095	1095	34465	34465	6095		28370	23965
Net Income								4405			4405
								10500	10500	28370	28370

Fig. 7-1

(e) *Salaries.* The salaries amount in the trial balance column would include only the payments which have been recorded and paid during the month. The portion which was earned in May but paid in June, because the weekly pay period ended in June, would not be included. If the amount is $200, the accrued entry would be:

Salaries Expense   200

  Salaries Payable   200

The account title Salaries Payable will also have to be written in on the worksheet.

(f) *Interest.* On the note payable there is accrued interest for one month. Assuming that the note bears 6% interest, the accrued interest would be $20 ($4,000 $\times$ 6% $\times$ 1/12). The entry will be:

Interest Expense   20

  Interest Payable   20

3. **Compute the adjusted trial balances.** The individual balances in the trial balance and adjustments columns are added across (*cross-footed*) to compute the amounts to be entered in the adjusted trial balance columns. Accounts such as Cash, Accounts Receivable, and Equipment are not affected by the adjustments, and the trial balance figures are carried directly to the adjusted trial balance columns. After the footings (the totals of the trial balance column and the adjustments column) have been proven, the total debits should equal the total credits in the adjusted trial balance columns.

4. **Extend the adjusted trial balance figures to either the income statement or balance sheet columns.** The process of extending the balances horizontally should begin with the account at the top of the sheet. The revenue and expense accounts should be extended to the income statement columns; the assets, liabilities, and capital to the balance sheet columns. Each figure is extended to only one of the columns. After the adjusted trial balance column totals have been proved out, then the income statement columns and the balance sheet columns should also prove out.

5. **Total the income statement columns and the balance sheet columns.** The difference between the debit and credit totals in both sets of columns should be the same amount, which represents net income or net loss for the period.

6. **Enter the net income or net loss.** In Fig. 7-1 the credit column total in the income statement is $10,500, the debit column total is $6,095. The credit column, or income side, is the larger, representing a net income of $4,405 for the month. Since net income increases capital, the net income figure should go on the credit side of the balance sheet. The balance sheet credit column total of $23,965 plus net income of $4,405 totals $28,370, which equals the debit column total. Since both the income statement columns and balance sheet columns are in agreement, it is a simple matter to prepare the formal income statement and balance sheet.

If there had been a loss, the debit or expense column in the income statement would have been the larger and the loss amount would have been entered in the credit column in order to balance the two columns. As a loss would decrease the capital, it would be entered in the balance sheet debit column.

7.3 WORKSHEET PROCEDURES FOR A MERCHANDISING BUSINESS

Merchandising (trading) businesses are those whose income derives largely from buying or selling goods rather than from rendering services. In addition to the accounts discussed in Sec. 7.2, the worksheet for a merchandising business will carry: Inventory, Cost of Goods Sold, Purchases, Transportation-In, and Purchase Returns and Allowances.

Let us discuss these new accounts separately, and then illustrate their handling on the worksheet.

INVENTORY AND COST OF GOODS SOLD

Inventory represents the value of goods on hand either at the beginning or the end of the accounting period. The beginning balance would be the same amount as the ending balance of the previous period. Generally, not all purchases of merchandise are sold in the same period; so unsold merchandise must be counted and priced, and the total recorded in the ledger as Ending Inventory. The amount of this inventory will be shown as an asset in the balance sheet. The amount of goods sold during the period will be shown as Cost of Goods Sold in the income summary. The relevant data might look like:

Beginning Inventory	*$ 5,000*
Add: Purchases	*8,000*
Goods Available for Sale	*$13,000*
Less: Ending Inventory	*7,000*
Cost of Goods Sold	*$ 6,000*

We have not said anything about how the inventory balance is actually computed. This important question forms the subject of Chapter 11.

PURCHASES

It is preferable for managerial purposes to maintain a separate account for purchases rather than including them in the inventory account. The account includes only merchandise purchased for retail; purchases of machinery, trucks, etc., to be used in the business are debited to the particular asset account.

The journal entry to record a merchandise purchase is as follows:

Purchases	*500*	
Accounts Payable (or Cash)		*500*

At the end of the period the total in the purchases account is closed to the expense and income summary account.

TRANSPORTATION-IN

The cost of transportation, such as freight or trucking, is part of the cost of merchandise. Where the purchaser pays the transportation-in, a separate account should be maintained. The entry to record the payment of transportation-in is as follows:

Transportation-In	*112.67*	
Accounts Payable (or Cash)		*112.67*

Transportation-In is combined with Purchases in the income statement as follows:

Partial Income Statement
for the year ended December 31, 197—

Sales			*$45,000*
Cost of Goods Sold			
Inventory, January 1		*$10,000*	
Purchases	*$25,000*		
Transportation-In	*1,000*	*26,000*	
Goods Available for Sale		*$36,000*	
Inventory, December 31		*12,000*	
Cost of Goods Sold			*24,000*
Gross Profit on Sales			*$21,000*

PURCHASE RETURNS AND ALLOWANCES

Sometimes goods purchased may be found to be unsatisfactory for use. The entire shipment may be returned to the vendor or the vendor may allow a reduction in price. A return of $600 of goods to the vendor is shown as follows:

Accounts Payable	*600*	
Purchase Returns and Allowances		*600*

Where it was decided to keep the goods if an allowance of $150 is made on the price, the entry would be:

FLANNERY ROOFING SUPPLY COMPANY   Worksheet   Month ended November 30, 197_

ACCOUNT TITLE	ACCT. NO.	TRIAL BALANCE DEBIT	TRIAL BALANCE CREDIT	ADJUSTMENTS DEBIT	ADJUSTMENTS CREDIT	ADJUSTED TRIAL BALANCE DEBIT	ADJUSTED TRIAL BALANCE CREDIT	INCOME STATEMENT DEBIT	INCOME STATEMENT CREDIT	BALANCE SHEET DEBIT	BALANCE SHEET CREDIT
Cash		9100								8900	
Accounts Receivable		5500			(a)500					5500	
Inventory Oct. 31		9700		(b)12000	(b)9700					12000	
Prepaid Insurance		3200			(c)150					3050	
Building		25000								25000	
Accumulated Depreciation			8500		(e)100						8600
Accounts Payable			4000								4000
Salaries Payable			1000								1000
William Flannery, Capital			30000								30000
William Flannery, Drawing		3000								3000	
Expense and Income Summary				(a)9700	(b)12000			9700	12000		
Service Fee			56000						56000		
Sales Returns and Allowances		3300						3300			
Purchases		35000						35000			
Purchases Returns and Allowances			1500						1500		
Transportation-In		1000						1000			
Salaries Expense		5000						5000			
Insurance Expense		800		(c)150				950			
Rent Expense		400		(d)200				600			
		101000	101000								
Depreciation Expense				(e)100				100			
				22150	22150			55650	69500	57450	13850
Net Income								13850			57450
								69500	69500	57450	57450

Fig. 7-2

Accounts Payable	*150*	
Purchase Returns and Allowances		*150*

In the income statement, Purchase Returns and Allowances would be shown as follows:

Cost of Goods Sold		
Inventory, January 1		*$10,000*
Purchases	*$25,000*	
Less: Purchase Returns and Allowances	*600*	
Net Purchases	*$24,400*	
Transportation-In	*1,000*	*25,400*
Goods Available for Sale		*$35,400*
Inventory, December 31		*12,000*
Cost of Goods Sold		*$23,400*

EXAMPLE 2.

Figure 7-2, page 107, shows the worksheet for the Flannery Roofing Supply Company. Trial balances from the ledgers are entered in the first two money columns, and the remainder of the worksheet is prepared very much as in Example 1.

Observe that the adjusted trial balance columns, present in Fig. 7-1, have been dropped. Aside from this, the only significant difference from Fig. 7-1 arises from the presence of the account Inventory. The inventory appearing in the trial balance is the inventory at the end of the previous month. The inventory at the end of November amounted to $12,000, and this is debited to Inventory and credited to Expense and Income Summary in the adjustments columns:

Inventory	*12,000*	
Expense and Income Summary		*12,000*

The Beginning Inventory of $9,700 must now be closed out to Expense and Income Summary as follows:

Expense and Income Summary	*9,700*	
Inventory		*9,700*

The net effect of these entries is indicated below.

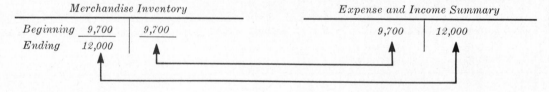

Merchandise Inventory		*Expense and Income Summary*	
Beginning *9,700*	*9,700*	*9,700*	*12,000*
Ending *12,000*			

Summary

(1)   The balances of the accounts appearing in the worksheet in the first two columns are obtained from the _____.

(2)   The title of the account that shows losses from sales for which payment had not been collected in a given period is _____.

(3)   The ten-column worksheet can be reduced to eight columns by the elimination of the

_____.

(4)   If the total of the debit column of the income statement in the worksheet is larger than the total of the credit column of the income statement, the balance is said to be a _____ for the period.

(5)   The merchandise inventory that is on hand at the end of the period will appear in the

_____.

(6) Beginning inventory plus net purchases will equal _____.

(7) The transportation-in account is combined with the _____ account in the income statement.

(8) In recording both beginning inventory and ending inventory as an adjusting entry, the _____ account is used.

(9) When goods purchased are found to be unsatisfactory, the account _____ _____ is created to arrive at net purchases.

Answers: (1) ledger; (2) Uncollectible Accounts Expense; (3) adjusted trial balance columns; (4) net loss; (5) balance sheet; (6) goods available for sale; (7) purchases; (8) Expense and Income Summary; (9) Purchase Returns and Allowances.

Solved Problems

7.1. The Folk Company purchased merchandise costing $150,000. What is the cost of goods sold under each assumption below?

	Beginning Inventory	Ending Inventory
(a)	100,000	60,000
(b)	75,000	50,000
(c)	50,000	30,000
(d)	0	10,000

SOLUTION

	Beginning Inventory	+ Purchases	− Ending Inventory	= Cost of Goods Sold
(a)	100,000	150,000	60,000	190,000
(b)	75,000	150,000	50,000	175,000
(c)	50,000	150,000	30,000	170,000
(d)	0	150,000	10,000	140,000

7.2. Compute the cost of goods sold from the following information: Beginning Inventory, $20,000; Purchases, $70,000; Purchase Returns and Allowances, $3,000; Transportation-In, $1,000; Ending Inventory, $34,000.

SOLUTION

Beginning Inventory		$20,000
Purchases	$70,000	
Purchase Returns and Allowances	3,000	
Net Purchases	$67,000	
Transportation-In	1,000	68,000
Total Available		$88,000
Ending Inventory		34,000
Cost of Goods Sold		$54,000

7.3. Journalize the following data:

(a) Merchandise inventory, January 1, $31,800; December 31, $38,500.

(b) Prepaid insurance before adjustment $1,540. It was found that $460 had expired during the year.

(c) Office supplies physically counted on December 31 were worth $120. The original balance of Supplies on Hand was $750.

(d) Office salaries for a five-day week ending on Friday average $2,500. The last payday was on Friday, December 27.

		Dr.	Cr.
(a)			
(b)			
(c)			
(d)			

SOLUTION

		Dr.	Cr.
(a)	*Expense and Income Summary*	31,800	
	Merchandise Inventory		31,800
	Merchandise Inventory	38,500	
	Expense and Income Summary		38,500
(b)	*Insurance Expense*	460	
	Prepaid Insurance		460
(c)	*Office Supplies Expense*	630	
	Office Supplies on Hand		630
(d)	*Office Salaries Expense*	1,000	
	Salaries Payable (December 30 and 31)		1,000

7.4. For each situation below, determine the missing figures.

	Beginning Inventory	Purchases During Period	Ending Inventory	Cost of Goods Sold
(a)	$18,000	$40,000	_____	$35,000
(b)	_____	41,000	$15,000	42,000
(c)	21,000	37,000	20,000	_____
(d)	27,000	_____	25,000	38,000

SOLUTION

(a) $23,000; (b) $16,000; (c) $38,000; (d) $36,000

7.5. Prepare an income statement based upon the data below.

Merchandise Inventory	Jan. 1, 197–	$ 21,000
Merchandise Inventory	Dec. 31, 197–	24,000
Purchases		66,000
Sales		103,000
Purchase Returns		2,000
Total Selling Expenses		15,500
Total General Expenses		22,400
Sales Returns		3,000

Income Statement		

SOLUTION

Income Statement		
Sales Income		$103,000
Less: Sales Returns		3,000
Net Sales		$100,000
Cost of Goods Sold		
Merchandise Inventory, Jan. 1	$21,000	
Purchases	$66,000	
Less: Purchase Returns	2,000	64,000
Goods Available for Sale		$85,000
Less: Merchandise Inventory, Dec. 31		24,000
Cost of Goods Sold		61,000
Gross Profit		$ 39,000
Expenses		
Total Selling Expenses	15,500	
Total General Expenses	22,400	
Total Expenses		37,900
Net Profit		$ 1,100

7.6. From the partial view of the worksheet below, determine the net income or loss.

Income Statement		Balance Sheet	
Dr.	Cr.	Dr.	Cr.
29,500	36,200	52,400	45,700

SOLUTION

$$36,200 \text{ (total credits of income statement)}$$
$$-29,500 \text{ (total debits of income statement)}$$
$$6,700 \text{ (net income)}$$

	Income Statement		Balance Sheet	
	Dr.	Cr.	Dr.	Cr.
	29,500	36,200	52,400	45,700
Net Income 6,700				6,700
	36,200	36,200	52,400	52,400

7.7. A section of the worksheet is presented below. Enter the adjustment required for Inventory, if it is assumed that Ending Inventory was $38,000.

Title	Trial Balance		Adjustments	
	Dr.	Cr.	Dr.	Cr.
Merchandise Inventory	32,400			
Expense and Income Summary				

SOLUTION

Title	Trial Balance		Adjustments	
	Dr.	Cr.	Dr.	Cr.
Merchandise Inventory	32,400		38,000	32,400
Expense and Income Summary			32,400	38,000

7.8. Using the information in Problem 7.7, extend the accounts in the worksheet.

Title	Income Statement		Balance Sheet	
	Dr.	Cr.	Dr.	Cr.
Merchandise Inventory				
Expense and Income Summary				

SOLUTION

Title	Income Statement		Balance Sheet	
	Dr.	Cr.	Dr.	Cr.
Merchandise Inventory			38,000	
Expense and Income Summary	32,400	38,000		

7.9. The following selected accounts are taken from the ledger of C. Gold Co. Place check marks in the appropriate columns to which the accounts will be extended in the worksheet.

	Title	Income Statement		Balance Sheet	
		Dr.	Cr.	Dr.	Cr.
1.	Cash				
2.	Accounts Receivable				
3.	Merchandise Inventory				
4.	Accounts Payable				
5.	C. Gold, Drawing				
6.	C. Gold, Capital				
7.	Expense and Income Summary				
8.	Depreciation Expense				
9.	Sales Income				
10.	Salaries Payable				

SOLUTION

	Income Statement		Balance Sheet	
	Dr.	Cr.	Dr.	Cr.
1.			√	
2.			√	
3.			√	
4.				√
5.			√	
6.				√
7.	√	√		
8.	√			
9.		√		
10.				√

7.10. Based on the worksheet's income statement columns below, prepare an income statement.

Expense and Income Summary	26,400	28,200
Sales Income		62,500
Purchases	31,400	
Rent Expense	6,000	
Salaries Expense	18,300	
Depreciation Expense	500	

SOLUTION

Sales Income		$62,500
Cost of Goods Sold		
Merchandise Inventory (beginning)	$26,400	
Purchases	31,400	
Goods Available for Sale	57,800	
Merchandise Inventory (ending)	28,200	
Cost of Goods Sold		29,600
Gross Profit		$32,900
Operating Expenses		
Rent Expense	$ 6,000	
Salaries Expense	18,300	
Depreciation Expense	500	
Total Expenses		24,800
Net Income		$ 8,100

7.11. From the following trial balances and adjustments information, prepare an 8-column worksheet.

P. C. Silver Company
Trial Balance
December 31, 197–

Account Title	Trial Balance		Adjustments		Income Statement		Balance Sheet	
	Dr.	Cr.	Dr.	Cr.	Dr.	Cr.	Dr.	Cr.
Cash	7,000							
Accounts Receivable	3,500							
Prepaid Rent	3,000							
Supplies	800							
Equipment	6,200							
Accounts Payable		4,500						
P. C. Silver, Capital		12,000						
Fees Income		10,000						
Salaries Expense	4,600							
General Expense	1,400							
	26,500	26,500						

Adjustments information is:

   (a) Rent expired for year, $1,200

   (b) Supplies on hand, $200

   (c) Salaries accrued, $400

SOLUTION

P. C. Silver Company
Worksheet
December 31, 197–

Account Title	Trial Balance Dr.	Cr.	Adjustments Dr.	Cr.	Income Statement Dr.	Cr.	Balance Sheet Dr.	Cr.
Cash	7,000						7,000	
Accounts Receivable	3,500						3,500	
Prepaid Rent	3,000			(a) 1,200			1,800	
Supplies	800			(b) 600			200	
Equipment	6,200						6,200	
Accounts Payable		4,500						4,500
P. C. Silver, Capital		12,000						12,000
Fees Income		10,000				10,000		
Salaries Expense	4,600		(c) 400		5,000			
General Expense	1,400				1,400			
	26,500	26,500						
Rent Expense			(a) 1,200		1,200			
Supplies Expense			(b) 600		600			
Salaries Payable				(c) 400				400
			2,200	2,200	8,200	10,000	18,700	16,900
Net Income					1,800			1,800
					10,000	10,000	18,700	18,700

7.12. From the information in Problem 7.11, prepare all adjusting and closing entries.

ADJUSTING ENTRIES

(a)

(b)

(c)

CLOSING ENTRIES

(a)

(b)

(c)

SOLUTION

ADJUSTING ENTRIES

(a)	Rent Expense	1,200	
	Prepaid Rent		1,200
(b)	Supplies Expense	600	
	Supplies		600
(c)	Salaries Expense	400	
	Salaries Payable		400

CLOSING ENTRIES

(a)	Fees Income	10,000	
	Expense and Income Summary		10,000
(b)	Expense and Income Summary	8,200	
	Salaries Expense		5,000
	General Expense		1,400
	Rent Expense		1,200
	Supplies Expense		600
(c)	Expense and Income Summary	1,800	
	P. C. Silver, Capital		1,800

7.13. From the data of Problem 7.11, prepare the income statement and balance sheet.

P. C. Silver Company		
Income Statement		
for the period ending December 31, 197—		
Fees Income		
Expenses		
Salaries Expense		
General Expense		
Rent Expense		
Supplies Expense		
Total Expenses		
Net Income		

P. C. Silver Company			
Balance Sheet			
December 31, 197—			

ASSETS		LIABILITIES AND CAPITAL	
Current Assets		Liabilities	
Cash		Accounts Payable	
Accounts Receivable		Salaries Payable	
Prepaid Rent		Total Liabilities	
Supplies		Capital	
Total Current Assets		Capital, January 1, 197–	
Fixed Assets		Add: Net Income	
Equipment		Capital, December 31, 197–	
Total Assets		Total Liabilities and Capital	

SOLUTION

P. C. Silver Company		
Income Statement		
for the period ending December 31, 197—		
Fees Income		$10,000
Expenses		
Salaries Expense	$5,000	
General Expense	1,400	
Rent Expense	1,200	
Supplies Expense	600	
Total Expenses		8,200
Net Income		$ 1,800

P. C. Silver Company
Balance Sheet
December 31, 197—

ASSETS		LIABILITIES AND CAPITAL		
Current Assets		Liabilities		
Cash	$ 7,000	Accounts Payable		$ 4,500
Accounts Receivable	3,500	Salaries Payable		400
Prepaid Rent	1,800	Total Liabilities		$ 4,900
Supplies	200	Capital		
Total Current Assets	$12,500	Capital, January 1, 197—	$12,000	
Fixed Assets		Add: Net Income	1,800	
Equipment	6,200	Capital, December 31, 197—		13,800
Total Assets	$18,700	Total Liabilities and Capital		$18,700

7.14. Trial balances of the Altman Sales Company, as of December 31, are as follows:

Cash	$14,200	
Accounts Receivable	6,500	
Merchandise Inventory	38,100	
Supplies	4,200	
Prepaid Insurance	8,000	
Equipment	15,100	
Accumulated Deprec.		$ 3,400
Accounts Payable		11,200
J. Altman, Capital		37,200
J. Altman, Drawing	2,400	
Sales Income		98,200
Purchases	42,100	
Purchase Returns		300
Salaries Expense	11,200	
Rent Expense	4,500	
Misc. Gen. Expense	4,000	

Prepare an eight-column worksheet, using the following additional information for year-end adjustments: (*a*) merchandise inventory on December 31, $42,500; (*b*) supplies inventory, December 31, $4,000; (*c*) insurance expired during this year, $2,000; (*d*) depreciation for the current year, $800; (*e*) salaries accrued on December 31, $400.

Account Title	Trial Balance Dr.	Trial Balance Cr.	Adjustments Dr.	Adjustments Cr.	Income Statement Dr.	Income Statement Cr.	Balance Sheet Dr.	Balance Sheet Cr.

SOLUTION

Account Title	Trial Balance Dr.	Trial Balance Cr.	Adjustments Dr.	Adjustments Cr.	Income Statement Dr.	Income Statement Cr.	Balance Sheet Dr.	Balance Sheet Cr.
Cash	14,200						14,200	
Accounts Receivable	6,500						6,500	
Merchandise Inven.	38,100		(a) 42,500	(a) 38,100			42,500	
Supplies	4,200			(b) 200			4,000	
Prepaid Insurance	8,000			(c) 2,000			6,000	
Equipment	15,100						15,100	
Accumulated Deprec.		3,400		(d) 800				4,200
Accounts Payable		11,200						11,200
J. Altman, Capital		37,200						37,200
J. Altman, Drawing	2,400						2,400	
Sales Income		98,200				98,200		
Purchases	42,100				42,100			
Purchase Returns		300				300		
Salaries Expense	11,200		(e) 400		11,600			
Rent Expense	4,500				4,500			
Misc. Gen. Expense	4,000				4,000			
	150,300	150,300						
Exp. and Inc. Sum.			(a) 38,100	(a) 42,500	38,100	42,500		
Supplies Expense			(b) 200		200			
Insurance Expense			(c) 2,000		2,000			
Depreciation Exp.			(d) 800		800			
Salaries Payable				(e) 400				400
			84,000	84,000	103,300	141,000	90,700	53,000
Net Income					37,700			37,700
					141,000	141,000	90,700	90,700

7.15. From the information in Problem 7.14, prepare all necessary adjusting and closing entries.

ADJUSTING ENTRIES

(a)

(b)

(c)

(d)

(e)

CLOSING ENTRIES

(a)

(b)

(c)

(d)

SOLUTION

ADJUSTING ENTRIES

(a)	Merchandise Inventory	42,500	
	Expense and Income Summary		42,500
	Expense and Income Summary	38,100	
	Merchandise Inventory		38,100
(b)	Supplies Expense	200	
	Supplies		200
(c)	Insurance Expense	2,000	
	Prepaid Insurance		2,000
(d)	Depreciation Expense	800	
	Accumulated Depreciation		800
(e)	Salaries Expense	400	
	Salaries Payable		400

CLOSING ENTRIES

(a)	Sales Income	98,200	
	Purchase Returns	300	
	Expense and Income Summary		98,500
(b)	Expense and Income Summary	65,200	
	Purchases		42,100
	Salaries Expense		11,600
	Rent Expense		4,500
	Misc. General Expense		4,000
	Supplies Expense		200
	Insurance Expense		2,000
	Depreciation Expense		800
(c)	Expense and Income Summary	37,700	
	J. Altman, Capital		37,700
(d)	J. Altman, Capital	2,400	
	J. Altman, Drawing		2,400

7.16. From the information in Problem 7.14 prepare all financial statements.

Altman Sales Company		
Income Statement		
December 31, 197—		

Altman Sales Company		
Capital Statement		
December 31, 197—		

Altman Sales Company		
Balance Sheet		
December 31, 197—		

SOLUTION

Altman Sales Company		
Income Statement		
December 31, 197—		
Sales Income		$98,200
Cost of Goods Sold		
Merchandise Inventory, Jan. 1	$38,100	
Purchases	$42,100	
Less: Purchase Returns	300	41,800
Goods Available for Sale		79,900
Less: Merchandise Inventory, Dec. 31		42,500
Cost of Goods Sold		37,400
		$60,800
Operating Expenses		
Salaries Expense	$11,600	
Rent Expense	4,500	
Insurance Expense	2,000	
Supplies Expense	200	
Depreciation Expense	800	
Misc. General Expense	4,000	
Total Expenses		$23,100
Net Income		$37,700

Altman Sales Company		
Capital Statement		
December 31, 197—		
Capital, January 1, 197—		$37,200
Net Income	$37,700	
Less: Drawing	2,400	
Increase in Capital		35,300
Capital, December 31, 197—		$72,500

Altman Sales Company		
Balance Sheet		
December 31, 197—		
ASSETS		
Current Assets		
Cash	$14,200	
Accounts Receivable	6,500	
Merchandise Inventory	42,500	
Supplies	4,000	
Prepaid Insurance	6,000	
Total Current Assets		$73,200
Fixed Assets		
Equipment	$15,100	
Less: Accumulated Depreciation	4,200	10,900
Total Assets		$84,100
LIABILITIES AND CAPITAL		
Current Liabilities		
Accounts Payable	$11,200	
Salaries Payable	400	
Total Current Liabilities		$11,600
Capital, December 31, 197—		72,500
Total Liabilities and Capital		$84,100

Examination II

Chapters 4-7

1. Contrast the journal and the ledger.

2. What effect does the incorrect posting of a debit as a credit have on the trial balance?

3. Distinguish between prepaid expenses and accrued expenses.

4. What are adjusting entries? Closing entries?

5. Interpret the balance in the supplies on hand account at the end of the accounting period (a) before adjustment; (b) after adjustment.

6. In the table below, indicate in which of the five journals each transaction is to be recorded.

	Cash Payments	Cash Receipts	Sales	Purchases	General
(1) Sale of merchandise for cash		(√)			
(2) Sale of merchandise on account					
(3) Cash refunded to a customer					
(4) Receipt of cash from a customer in settlement of an account					
(5) Purchase of merchandise for cash					
(6) Purchase of merchandise on account					
(7) Payment of salaries					
(8) Note payable sent to a creditor in settlement of an account					
(9) Payment of interest on the mortgage					
(10) Received a note in settlement of a customer's account					

7. The balances of the accounts of the Judith Playhouse, as of November 30, were as follows:

Judith Playhouse
Trial Balance
November 30

Cash	$10,000	
Accounts Receivable	2,100	
Supplies	600	
Equipment	12,000	
Building	9,000	
Accounts Payable		$ 6,500
Notes Payable		12,000
Judith Playhouse, Capital		15,200
	$33,700	$33,700

Selected transactions for the month of December were:

(*a*)   Dec. 1:   Bought new theatrical equipment for $3,000, paying half in cash and giving our note for the balance

(*b*)   Dec. 10:   Paid $1,000 due on the notes payable

(*c*)   Dec. 14:   Receipts for the two-week period (admissions income) totaled $9,600

(*d*)   Dec. 20:   Paid utilities, $150

(*e*)   Dec. 24:   Paid $1,000 for five-year insurance policy on the theatre

(*f*)   Dec. 28:   Paid monthly salaries, $1,250

Journalize the transactions.

8.   (*a*) Weekly salaries of $8,000 are payable on Friday, for a five-day week. What is the adjusting entry if the fiscal period ends on Wednesday?

(*b*) An insurance policy covering a four-year period was purchased on February 1, for $1,200. What is the adjusting entry on December 31?

(*c*) Office supplies of $700 were debited to Office Supplies on Hand. At the end of the month, the account shows $300 worth still on hand. Prepare the adjusting entry.

9.   In the following assume a fiscal year extending from January 1 through December 31.

(*a*) A machine costing $8,000 was purchased on October 31 and is being depreciated at the rate of 10% per year. What amount will appear as the adjusting entry on December 31?

(*b*) An insurance policy covering a six-year period was purchased on March 1 for $1,800. What amount will appear as an expense on the income statement at the end of the year? What amount will appear on the balance sheet as an asset?

10.   After all revenue and expense accounts of the Gold Silver Company were closed at the end of the year, the expense and income summary had a debit balance of $125,000 and a credit balance of $190,000. The capital account had a credit balance of $72,000, while the drawing account had a debit balance of $12,000. Journalize the closing entries.

11.   Prepare an 8-column worksheet for the Honest Taxi Company for the month of September. Balances in the ledger as of August 31 appear below.

Cash	$ 2,230
Supplies	5,100
Prepaid Insurance	600
Equipment	15,000
Accumulated Depreciation	3,000
Honest Taxi Company, Capital	19,600
Honest Taxi Company, Drawing	700
Fares Income	3,950
Salaries Expense	1,400
Maintenance Expense	620
Miscellaneous Expense	900

Adjustment data for September 30, are as follows:

Supplies on hand	$1,800
Expired insurance	200
Depreciation on equipment	350
Salaries payable	190

Honest Taxi Company
Worksheet
September 30, 197–

Account Title	Trial Balance		Adjustments		Income Statement		Balance Sheet	
	Dr.	Cr.	Dr.	Cr.	Dr.	Cr.	Dr.	Cr.
Cash	2,230							
Supplies	5,100							
Prepaid Ins.	600							
Equipment	15,000							
Accum. Deprec.		3,000						
Capital		19,600						
Drawing	700							
Fares Income		3,950						
Salaries Exp.	1,400							
Maint. Exp.	620							
Misc. Exp.	900							
	26,550	26,550						

12. On the basis of Question 11, journalize the closing entries needed.

13. The trial balance of the Harmin Company, before adjustments of December 31, 197–, includes the following selected accounts:

Merchandise Inventory	$160,000
Sales	840,000
Sales Returns	40,000
Purchases	620,000
Transportation	2,000

Merchandise Inventory on December 31 totals $135,000.

(a) Present the income statement, through Gross Profit on Sales, for the Harmin Company. (b) Present the journal entries necessary to adjust the merchandise inventory at December 31.

14. The accounts and the balances appearing in the ledger of the Capo Company, as of December 31, 197–, are listed below.

Cash	$73,200	J. Capo, Drawing	$ 3,000
Accounts Receivable	11,000	Sales	244,000
Merchandise Inventory	33,000	Sales Returns	1,200
Supplies	3,600	Purchases	115,000
Prepaid Insurance	1,400	Transportation	2,000
Equipment	10,000	Salaries Expense	18,000
Accumulated Depreciation	2,000	Rent Expense	4,000
Accounts Payable	8,200	Advertising Expense	2,600
Notes Payable	6,000	Maintenance and Repairs	3,000
J. Capo, Capital	22,500	Miscellaneous Expense	1,700

The data for the year-end adjustments are as follows:

Merchandise inventory on December 31	$28,600
Supplies inventory on December 31	1,100
Insurance expired during the year	950
Depreciation for the current year	750
Salaries accrued at December 31	350

Prepare an eight-column worksheet.

Account Title	Trial Balance Dr.	Trial Balance Cr.	Adjustments Dr.	Adjustments Cr.	Income Statement Dr.	Income Statement Cr.	Balance Sheet Dr.	Balance Sheet Cr.
Cash	73,200							
Acct. Rec.	11,000							
Merch. Inv.	33,000							
Supplies	3,600							
Prepaid Ins.	1,400							
Equipment	10,000							
Accum. Deprec.		2,000						
Acct. Pay.		8,200						
Notes Pay.		6,000						
Capo, Capital		22,500						
Capo, Drawing	3,000							
Sales		244,000						
Sales Returns	1,200							
Purchases	115,000							
Transportation	2,000							
Salaries Exp.	18,000							
Rent Exp.	4,000							
Adv. Exp.	2,600							
Maint. Exp.	3,000							
Misc. Exp.	1,700							
	282,700	282,700						

Answers to Examination II

1. The journal is a book of original entry which contains a *chronological* record of transactions. Each transaction is recorded first in the journal, which specifies the accounts to be debited and credited, along with a brief explanation of the transaction. The ledger is the complete set of accounts. It takes various physical forms, depending on whether the accounting is manual or machine.

2. The trial balance will be out of balance by twice the amount of incorrect posting.

3. Prepaid expenses are those paid in advance of consumption; accrued expenses are those for which the consumption precedes the payment.

4. *Adjusting entries* are those required at the end of the accounting period to make the accounts properly reflect the results of operations for the period and the financial position at the end of the period. *Closing entries* are those which summarize the activities of the period, matching the inflow of income with the outflow of expenses to arrive at the net increase or decrease in owners' equity for the period. They separate the operations of one period from those of another. The accounts that are closed are the nominal or temporary accounts, which are really only extensions of the capital accounts.

5. (*a*) The balance before adjustment is the balance at the beginning of the period plus the amount purchased during the period. It includes both the amount on hand and the amount used.

   (*b*) The balance after adjustment includes only the inventory of supplies on hand at the end of the period. The amount used has been transferred to the supplies expense account.

6.

	Cash Payments	Cash Receipts	Sales	Purchases	General
(1)		√			
(2)			√		
(3)	√				
(4)		√			
(5)	√				
(6)				√	
(7)	√				
(8)					√
(9)	√				
(10)					√

7. (*a*) Equipment   3,000
              Cash   1,500
              Notes Payable   1,500

   (*b*) Notes Payable   1,000
              Cash   1,000

   (*c*) Cash   9,600
              Admissions Income   9,600

   (*d*) Utilities Expense   150
              Cash   150

   (*e*) Prepaid Insurance   1,000
              Cash   1,000

   (*f*) Salaries Expense   1,250
              Cash   1,250

8. (*a*) Salaries Expense   4,800
              Salaries Payable   4,800
           [3 × (8,000/5) = 4,800]

   (*b*) Insurance Expense   275
              Prepaid Insurance   275
           [1,200 ÷ 4 = 300; 11/12 × 300 = 275]

   (*c*) Supplies Expense   400
              Supplies   400

9. (a) $133.33   [$8,000 × 10% = $800; 1/6 × $800 = $133.33]

    (b)   Expense: $ 250   [$1,800 ÷ 6 = $300; 5/6 × $300 = $250]

          Asset: $1,550   [$1,800 − $250 = $1,550]

10.   *Expense and Income Summary*   65,000

            Capital   65,000

      Capital   12,000

            Drawing   12,000

11.

Honest Taxi Company
Worksheet
September 30, 197–

Account Title	Trial Balance		Adjustments		Income Statement		Balance Sheet	
	Dr.	Cr.	Dr.	Cr.	Dr.	Cr.	Dr.	Cr.
Cash	2,230						2,230	
Supplies	5,100			(a) 3,300			1,800	
Prepaid Ins.	600			(b) 200			400	
Equipment	15,000						15,000	
Accum. Deprec.		3,000		(c) 350				3,350
Capital		19,000						19,600
Drawing	700						700	
Fares Income		3,950				3,950		
Salaries Exp.	1,400		(d) 190		1,590			
Maint. Exp.	620				620			
Misc. Exp.	900				900			
	26,550	26,550						
Supp. Exp.			(a) 3,300		3,300			
Ins. Exp.			(b) 200		200			
Deprec. Exp.			(c) 350		350			
Salaries Pay.				(d) 190				190
			4,040	4,040	6,960	3,950	20,130	23,140
Net Loss						3,010	3,010	
					6,960	6,960	23,140	23,140

12.   *Fares Income*   3,950

            Expense and Income Summary   3,950

      Expense and Income Summary   6,960

            Salaries Expense   1,590

            Maintenance Expense   620

            Miscellaneous Expense   900

            Supplies Expense   3,300

            Insurance Expense   200

            Depreciation Expense   350

      Capital   3,010

            Expense and Income Summary   3,010

      Capital   700

            Drawing   700

13. (a)

Harmin Company
Income Statement
for the period ending December 31, 197–

Sales		$840,000
Less: Sales Returns		40,000	$800,000
Cost of Goods Sold		
Merchandise Inv. (beg.)		160,000
Purchases	$620,000	
Transportation	2,000	622,000
Goods Available for Sale		782,000
Less: Merchandise Inv. (end)		135,000
Cost of Goods Sold			647,000
Gross Profit on Sales			$153,000

(b)

Expense and Income Summary	160,000	
Merchandise Inventory		160,000
Merchandise Inventory	135,000	
Expense and Income Summary		135,000

14.

Account Title	Trial Balance Dr.	Trial Balance Cr.	Adjustments Dr.	Adjustments Cr.	Income Statement Dr.	Income Statement Cr.	Balance Sheet Dr.	Balance Sheet Cr.
Cash	73,200						73,200	
Acct. Rec.	11,000						11,000	
Merch. Inv.	33,000		(a) 28,600	(a) 33,000			28,600	
Supplies	3,600			(b) 2,500			1,100	
Prepaid Ins.	1,400			(c) 950			450	
Equipment	10,000						10,000	
Accum. Deprec.		2,000		(d) 750				2,750
Acct. Pay.		8,200						8,200
Notes Pay.		6,000						6,000
Capo, Capital		22,500						22,500
Capo, Drawing	3,000						3,000	
Sales		244,000				244,000		
Sales Returns	1,200				1,200			
Purchases	115,000				115,000			
Transportation	2,000				2,000			
Salaries Exp.	18,000		(e) 350		18,350			
Rent Exp.	4,000				4,000			
Adv. Exp.	2,600				2,600			
Maint. Exp.	3,000				3,000			
Misc. Exp.	1,700				1,700			
	282,700	282,700						
Exp. & Inc. Sum.			(a) 33,000	(a) 28,600	33,000	28,600		
Supp. Exp.			(b) 2,500		2,500			
Ins. Exp.			(c) 950		950			
Deprec. Exp.			(d) 750		750			
Salaries Pay.				(e) 350				350
			66,150	66,150	185,050	272,600	127,350	39,800
Net Income					87,550			87,550
					272,600	272,600	127,350	127,350

Chapter 8

Revenue, Expenses, and Net Income

8.1 WHAT IS REVENUE?

Revenue is the inflow of resources resulting from the delivery of goods or services in the effort to produce a profit. The revenue which derives from the principal business of the firm is called *operating revenue*, the term *other revenue* is used for any incidental gains, such as sales of noncurrent assets or retirement of noncurrent liabilities.

8.2 RECOGNITION OF REVENUE

Revenue should be recognized at the earliest point at which it is secured, measurable, and earned. There are three general bases for deciding when that point has been reached.

Sales basis. Recognition occurs at the time the company's products or services are *delivered* to the customer. This is the most frequently used basis.

Production basis. Revenue may be recognized at the completion of production and before a sale is made if there is a guaranteed market. For example, gold and certain other products have assured sales prices and thus revenue can be recognized when the product is ready. Revenue is sometimes recognized *before* production is complete or an exchange has taken place. For example, in the case of long-term construction projects, which may extend two or three years or more, revenue is recognized according to the percentage of completion. If the job is 50% complete, then 50% of the expected earnings is recognized in the current period.

Collection basis. Revenue is recognized only when cash is actually collected from customers. Also called the *cash basis,* it is used by doctors, lawyers, etc., and by small businesses with little or no amount of inventory. Retail stores that sell goods on the installment plan and recognize revenue as collections call this basis the *installment basis.*

8.3 REVENUE REDUCTIONS

Closely related to the earning of revenue are the reductions and adjustments which must be made in order to arrive at the proper revenue amount. There are three principal types.

Sales returns and allowances. If the customer returns goods or if the goods or services are faulty, an allowance is made to the customer. The result is a decrease in sales. The debit is made to a separate account in order that records can be maintained and control exerted over such returns and allowances.

EXAMPLE 1.

If cash is returned, the entry is as follows:

Sales Returns and Allowances	*100*	
Cash		*100*

If the customer's account is credited, the entry is:

Sales Returns and Allowances	*100*
Accounts Receivable	*100*

Cash discounts. Often a discount is offered to customers to encourage payment before the normal credit date. Generally it is 2 percent for payment within 10 days, or the full amount is due in 30 days. These terms are abbreviated to "2/10, n/30." A discount is an expense of the business and is now generally shown as a reduction of sales. Less desirably, the discount may be considered a payment of interest for receiving cash early, and shown as sales expense.

EXAMPLE 2.

The entry to record the cash discount when a customer pays his bill of $400 within the discount period is:

Cash	*392*	
Cash Discount	*8*	
Accounts Receivable		*400*

Credit losses. Experience shows that a small percentage of credit sales will never be collected. This amount can be closely estimated and provided for in the accounts.

EXAMPLE 3.

Assume that 1% of the sales on account during the period will be uncollectible. Then, if the sales on account were $100,000 and the accounts receivable balance at the year end was $25,000, the transaction will be as follows:

Uncollectible Accounts Expense	*1,000*	
Allowance for Uncollectible Accounts		*1,000*

The debit is an expense to be deducted from Sales, the allowance is a valuation account (see Sec. 6.2) to be deducted from Accounts Receivable.

Income Statement

Sales	*$100,000*	
Less: Uncollectible Accounts Expense	*1,000*	
Net Sales		*$99,000*

Balance Sheet

Accounts Receivable	*$25,000*	
Less: Allowance for Uncollectible Accounts	*1,000*	*$24,000*

8.4　SALES TAXES

Sales taxes are not revenue and should be separately recorded and paid. Thus if a sale of $100 is made and the state, city, or other retail tax is 6%, then the entry is as follows:

Cash	*106*	
Sales		*100*
Sales Taxes Payable		*6*

8.5   WHAT IS AN EXPENSE?

The consumption of resources in the effort to produce revenue is expense. It is important that an expense be matched with the revenue to which it relates. There are two forms of expenses: *consumption of goods* (cost of goods sold, supplies, depreciation of property, etc.) and *consumption of services* (salaries, wages, rent, interest, taxes, etc.).

It is useful to distinguish an expense, as just defined, from a cost and from an expenditure. A *cost* — say, the cost of merchandise — does not expire in the usual sense. The merchandise is sold rather than consumed, and one speaks of "cost of goods sold," not of an expense. An *expenditure* is merely the payment for an item, which may be either an expense item, such as salaries, or a capital item, such as equipment.

8.6   PREPAID, DEFERRED, AND ACCRUED ITEMS

There are a number of revenue and expense items which have all or a part of their balance recognized as income or expense in succeeding periods. In fact, the accrual method of accounting rests on recognizing income or expense only in the specific period in which income is *earned* or expense *incurred* (see Sec. 6.1).

Prepaid items. These are commodities or services purchased but unconsumed at the end of the accounting period (prepaid expenses) or revenue received but not earned (prepaid revenue). The portion used or earned during the period is expense or income, the remainder will be an expense or income normally in the next period. Prepaid expenses are ordinarily included as current assets. Unearned revenue will be included as a current liability unless the income will apply to more than one year.

EXAMPLE 4.

Prepaid rent of $600 is entered as:

Cash	*600*	
Unearned Rent Collected		*600*

If the advance is only for a month or a quarter and will be earned before the year end, it may be recorded as earned upon receipt:

Cash	*600*	
Earned Revenue		*600*

Deferred items. These result from the postponement of the recognition of an expense already paid or of a revenue already received, if the deferment will extend more than one year. They would ordinarily be shown on the balance sheet as noncurrent assets, under a caption such as Deferred Charges or Other Assets or Deferred Credits.

EXAMPLE 5.

The company has a substantial investment in patterns and molds used in producing machine parts. The patterns and molds are amortized over a four-year period. On January 1, $5,000 worth of patterns and molds were purchased for cash.

Deferred Charges	*5,000*	
Cash		*5,000*

By December 31 of the same year, one-fourth ($1,250) of the asset had been used up.

Patterns and Molds Expense	*1,250*	
Deferred Charges		*1,250*

Accrued items.   *Expenses or revenues that have gradually accumulated but have not yet been recognized in the accounts.*   An accrued expense may be shown on the balance sheet without the word "accrued" occurring; for instance, "salaries payable." Similarly, accrued revenue may appear as "interest receivable," etc. Since these items relate to a short period, they are classified respectively as current liabilities and current assets.

EXAMPLE 6.

The payroll for salaries is $1,250 weekly, or $250 per day, and is paid the week after it is earned. The month of March ended on Tuesday and thus two days' pay, or $500, had accrued and was unpaid on March 31.   The entry on March 31 is:

Salaries Expense	500	
Salaries Payable		500

8.7   WHAT IS NET INCOME?

Net income is the excess of the earned inflow of resources over the consumption of resources used in earning that inflow.   Thus, it is gross sales, less sales reductions and all costs and expenses incurred in earning the sales.

8.8   FORMS OF THE INCOME STATEMENT

The definition of net income given in Sec. 8.7, together with the division of revenue into operating and other revenue (Sec. 8.1), implies the following general scheme for the income statement.

   REVENUE (SALES)   *(Inflow of resources)*
– COSTS AND EXPENSES *(Consumption of resources, such as merchandise, wages, salaries, rent)*
   NET INCOME FROM OPERATIONS   *(Excess of revenue over operating expenses)*
+ OTHER INCOME   *(Incidental, nonoperating income, such as interest income)*
– OTHER EXPENSES   *(Incidental, nonoperating expense, such as loss on sale of assets)*
   NET INCOME   *(Excess of revenue over all expenses; an increase in capital)*

This basic plan can be adapted to the needs of a particular concern through the inclusion of various intermediary captions and subtotals.   Differing treatments of extraordinary items are also possible.   Examples 7 through 10 display the forms of income statement most commonly found.

EXAMPLE 7.   Classified Multiple-Step Form.

(a)	*Sales Revenue*			
	Gross Sales			$700,000
	Less: Sales Returns and Allowances		$ 15,300	
	Cash Discounts on Sales		12,400	27,700
	Net Sales			$672,300
(b)	*Cost of Goods Sold (66.1%)*			
	Beginning Inventory		$ 58,700	
	Purchases	$400,000		
	Less: Purchase Returns and Allowances	12,100		
	Net Purchases	$387,900		
	Transportation-In	43,200	431,100	
	Goods Available for Sale		489,800	
	Less: Ending Inventory		45,600	
	Cost of Goods Sold			444,200

(continued next page)

(c) Gross Profit on Sales (33.9%)			$228,100
(d) Operating Expenses			
Selling Expenses			
Sales Salaries and Commissions	$ 30,000		
Sales Travel	15,000		
Advertising and Promotion	28,000		
Delivery Expense	7,000		
Other Selling Expenses	5,000	85,000	
General and Administrative Expenses			
Administrative Salaries	$ 32,000		
Insurance	8,000		
Depreciation of Office Equipment	3,000		
Other Administrative Expenses	12,000	55,000	
Total Operating Expenses			140,000
(e) Operating Income			$ 88,100
(f) Other Revenues			
Interest	$ 7,000		
Dividends	3,000	$ 10,000	
(g) Other Expenses			
Interest Expense		2,100	7,900
Net Income Before Taxes			$ 96,000
Federal and State Income Taxes			50,000
(h) Net Income			$ 46,000

In this form of income statement a number of subcategories of cost and expense are used. The key items are labeled with letters and we will describe them briefly.

(a)   This is the total of all charges to customers.

(b)   This is one of the most important sections of the income statement. It shows the cost of the goods sold to customers during the period and the relationship to sales. This relationship (66.1%) can be conveniently compared with the figures for other periods.

(c)   The amount of gross profit (gross margin) must be sufficient to pay all expenses (other than those in Cost of Goods Sold) and to yield a reasonable return or profit. The percentage (33.9%), or gross profit ratio, is a key control figure in managing a business. The selling price must be kept in such relationship to cost as to yield a desired gross profit. To improve the gross profit ratio, sales prices may be increased or costs decreased. Favorable or unfavorable trends can be easily seen by comparing the gross profit ratio with the ratios for other periods.

(d)   These are the expenses necessary in carrying on the operations of the business. They do not include unusual expenses or financial expenses not of an operating nature, which are classed separately.

(e)   This is the amount by which the gross profit exceeds the total operating expense. It measures the degree of profitability from operations, before nonoperating items are considered.

(f)   Another example is Gain on Disposal of Plant Assets.

(g)   Another example is Loss on Disposal of Plant Assets. Like Other Revenues, this nonoperating item is offset and the net amount is shown in the summary column of the income statement.

(h)   This represents the net increase in capital for the period. (Had capital decreased, the figure would have been called *net loss*.)

EXAMPLE 8.   Classified, Single-Step Form.

Revenues		
Net Sales		$672,300
Interest		7,000
Dividends		3,000
Total Revenues		$682,300
Expenses		
Wages, Salaries, and Employee Benefits	$ 90,200	
Merchandise and Supplies	424,600	
Payments for Services	42,400	
Depreciation	6,500	
Rent	8,000	
Property Taxes	12,500	
Interest	2,100	
Federal and State Income Taxes	50,000	
Total Expenses		636,300
Net Income		$ 46,000

Proponents of the single-step form maintain that only the final figure, net income, is significant. Often the expenses are grouped according to type of expense (e.g., selling) rather than by their nature. Notice that in this form all revenue — operating and other — appears at the top of the statement.

EXAMPLE 9.   All-Inclusive Form.

Sales Revenue		$672,300
Cost of Goods Sold		444,200
Gross Margin		$228,100
Operating Expenses		140,000
Operating Income		$ 88,100
Other Income (net)		7,900
Net Income Before Taxes		$ 96,000
Income Taxes		50,000
Income Before Extraordinary Loss		$ 46,000
Flood Loss	$40,000	
Less: Applicable Taxes	16,000	24,000
Net Income		$ 22,000

This form, unlike those of Examples 7 and 8, reflects all *extraordinary gains and losses*; that is, those arising from such unusual events as earthquakes, riots, embezzlements, etc. Only prior-period adjustments (Sec. 8.10) are excluded. Note that the income tax relating to the extraordinary item is shown separately and the net amount after tax is deducted.

EXAMPLE 10.   Current Operating Performance Form.

Sales Revenues	$672,300
Cost of Goods Sold	444,200
Gross Margin	$228,100
Operating Expenses	140,000
Operating Income	$ 88,100
Other Income (net)	7,900
Net Income Before Taxes	$ 96,000
Income Taxes	50,000
Net Income	$ 46,000

8.9   RETAINED EARNINGS

Even though the reported net income for the current year differs between the all-inclusive form and the current operating performance form, the ultimate effect on retained earnings is the same. Under the current operation performance concept, the $24,000 flood loss of Example 9 would be charged directly to retained earnings, but also the net income credited would be greater. Thus, if we assume a beginning balance of $50,000, the ending balance will be $72,000 under both concepts:

	All-Inclusive Form	Current Operating Performance Form
Beginning Balance	$50,000	$50,000
Add: Net Income	22,000	46,000
Less: Flood Loss (net)		(24,000)
Ending Balance	$72,000	$72,000

8.10   PRIOR-PERIOD ADJUSTMENTS

Unlike the extraordinary items described above, prior-period adjustments are typical of the customary activities of the company. The AICPA defines them as:

material adjustments which (*a*) can be specifically identified with and directly related to the business activities of particular prior periods, and (*b*) are not attributable to economic events occurring subsequent to the date of the financial statements for the prior period, and (*c*) depend primarily on determinations by persons other than management and (*d*) were not susceptible of reasonable estimation prior to such determination.

Examples of prior-period adjustments are (1) significant litigation settlements and (2) material, nonrecurring adjustments or settlement of income taxes.

Normal adjustments and corrections resulting from the use of estimates are not considered prior-period adjustments. For example, a change in the estimated useful life of an asset — even a material asset — is not a prior-period adjustment. Adjustments of estimated liabilities that are not material should be considered as normal recurring items and should be included among the operations of the current period.

Prior-period adjustments should be reflected as adjustments (separate from related income taxes) of the opening balance of Retained Earnings.

EXAMPLE 11.

Retained Earnings (beginning of year)		
As previously reported		$50,000
Prior-Period Adjustments		
Additional Income Taxes	$12,000	
Loss of Compensation Suit	10,000	22,000
As restated		$28,000
Net Income		21,000
		$49,000
Dividends		
Preferred	$ 3,000	
Common	6,000	
Retained Earnings (end of year)		$40,000

Summary

(1) At the time goods are produced, in most firms it is not known exactly how much will be received for them or even if they will be sold. Therefore, revenue is recognized only when goods are _____.

(2) Where there is a guaranteed market for the product, revenue is recognized when the _____ is completed.

(3) For long-term construction projects, revenue is recognized on the basis of the _____ of completion.

(4) On the collection basis of accounting, revenue is recognized only when _____ is collected.

(5) The principal types of revenue reductions and adjustments are _____ _____, _____, and _____.

(6) Resources consumed in the effort to produce revenue are termed _____.

(7) Commodities or services purchased but unconsumed at the end of the period represent _____ expenses.

(8) An expense that has gradually accumulated but has not yet been recognized in the accounts is called an _____ expense.

(9) Gross sales, less sales reductions, costs, and expenses, is called _____.

(10) The _____ form of income statement shows various categories of cost and expense.

Answers: (1) delivered; (2) production; (3) percentage; (4) cash; (5) sales returns and allowances, cash discounts, credit losses; (6) expenses; (7) prepaid; (8) accrued; (9) net income; (10) multiple-step

Solved Problems

8.1. The C-L Company produces parts which are sold to auto manufacturers. During 197– the company collected $200,000 in cash. Of this amount $35,000 represented collections of accounts receivable balances at the end of the previous year. Accounts receivable balances at the end of the current year are $45,000. How much revenue should be recognized for the current year (*a*) on the accrual basis? (*b*) on the cash basis?

SOLUTION

(*a*) The revenue or sales for the period would be $210,000.

Total Collections	*$200,000*
Less: Sales for Previous Year	*35,000*
Sales Made and Collected	*165,000*
Sales Made but Not Yet Collected	*45,000*
Sales for Current Year	*$210,000*

(*b*) Sales for the year would be $200,000, representing the amount of cash collected during the year.

8.2. The Jack McLaurin Company leased a store to a tenant in December 1971 for $6,000 for the following calendar year, receivable upon signing of the lease. How much revenue should be reported for 1971 and for 1972 (*a*) on the accrual basis? (*b*) on the cash basis?

SOLUTION

	1971	1972
Accrual basis	0	$6,000
Cash basis	$6,000	0

8.3. The Gary Charles Mining Company produces lead, silver, and gold. The price of lead fluctuates widely, but the prices for silver and gold are fixed by the government. In 197– the costs of production for the year were: lead, $600,000; silver, $500,000; and gold, $400,000. The following percentages of production were sold: lead, 75% for $550,000; silver, 80% for $600,000; and gold, 50% for $300,000. The sales prices of the production unsold were: lead, $200,000; silver, $150,000; and gold, $160,000. What is the revenue for 197–?

	Sales	On Hand	Total Revenue
Lead			
Silver			
Gold			

SOLUTION

	Sales	On Hand	Total Revenue
Lead	$ 550,000	– –	$ 550,000
Silver	600,000	$150,000	750,000
Gold	300,000	160,000	460,000
	$1,450,000	$310,000	$1,760,000

8.4. The Henry Hogg Company has a $1,000,000 construction contract which was 25% complete at the end of the first year (with $250,000 revenue recognized) and 75% complete at the end of the second year. How much revenue should be reported for the second year?

SOLUTION

The total revenue to be reported on the contract to date is $750,000. This amount, less that previously reported, or $500,000, is the amount to be reported for the second year.

8.5. The Harold Dalton Company had sales of $150,000 for 197–. The sales returns and allowances were $5,000 for the year, including the December 15 allowance of $500 to Kenneth Connolly. Prepare (a) the journal entry to record the Connolly transaction and (b) the revenue section of the income statement for the year.

(a)

(b)

SOLUTION

(a)	Sales Returns and Allowances	500	
	Accounts Receivable		500
(b)	Revenue		
	Sales	$150,000	
	Less: Sales Returns and Allowances	5,000	
	Net Sales		$145,000

8.6. The Harold Dalton Company also had sales discounts of $2,000 for the year. Prepare the revenue section of the income statement based on the data in Problem 8.5.

SOLUTION

Revenue			
Sales		$150,000	
Less: Sales Returns			
and Allowances	$5,000		
Sales Discounts	2,000	7,000	
Net Sales			$143,000

8.7. The Alan Friedman Company paid $300 rent on November 30 for the following three months. Prepare the journal entry for Friedman's books at the end of the year, if the rent had been recorded as (a) Rent Expense and (b) Prepaid Rent.

(a)

(b)

SOLUTION

(a)	*Prepaid Rent*	200	
	Rent Expense		200
(b)	*Rent Expense*	100	
	Prepaid Rent		100

8.8. The Ross Dixon Company offers premiums to its customers upon receipt of coupons from its product Happybird. A bird food tray which costs the company 30¢ is given for every 10 coupons redeemed. During the current year there were 150,000 packages of Happybird sold, for which it is estimated that 10% of the coupons will be redeemed. What is the additional amount to be accrued for this year, if 10,000 coupons from this year's sales have already been redeemed?

SOLUTION

Estimated annual cost (150,000 × 10% × 3¢):	$450
Redeemed this year to date (10,000 × 3¢):	300
Amount to accrue at year end:	$150

8.9. From the information given below, compute the gross purchases for the year.

Cost of Goods Sold	$115,000
Beginning Inventory	38,500
Transportation-In	1,600
Ending Inventory	32,600
Purchase Returns	1,850

SOLUTION

The gross purchases are $109,350, computed as follows:

Total Goods Available		
Cost of Goods Sold	$115,000	
Add: Ending Inventory	32,600	
	$147,600	
Gross Purchases		
Total Goods Available	$147,600	
Less: Beginning Inventory	38,500	
	$109,100	
Add: Purchase Returns	1,850	
	$100,950	
Less: Transportation-In	1,600	
	$109,350	

8.10. Prepare journal entries for the following transactions for the Wilson Company.

June 1: Purchased merchandise on account from H. Brown, $500, at terms of 2/10, n/30

1: Sold merchandise to A. Pesnow, $1,000, receiving a 30-day, 6% note in exchange

1: Purchased delivery equipment from W. Green, $3,500, paying $500 and issuing a series of five 6% notes of $600 each, maturing at 30-day intervals

5: Paid invoice of H. Brown

15: Sold merchandise, $400, to S. Meyer, at terms of 2/10, n/30

17: Mr. Meyer returned $100 worth of goods purchased

24: Received check from S. Meyer settling his account

30: The electric bill for June is estimated to be $200

30: Interest accrual for the Pesnow note

30: Interest accrual for the Green notes

SOLUTION

1.		
1.		
1.		
5.		
15.		
17.		
24.		
30.		
30.		
30.		

SOLUTION

1.	Purchases	500	
	Accounts Payable, H. Brown		500
1.	Notes Receivable, A. Pesnow	1,000	
	Sales		1,000
1.	Delivery Equipment	3,500	
	Notes Payable		3,000
	Cash		500
5.	Accounts Payable, H. Brown	500	
	Cash		490
	Purchase Discount		10
15.	Accounts Receivable, S. Meyer	400	
	Sales		400
17.	Sales Returns and Allowances	100	
	Accounts Receivable, S. Meyer		100
24.	Cash	294	
	Sales Discount	6	
	Accounts Receivable, S. Meyer		300
30.	Electricity Expense	200	
	Accrued Expense, Electricity		200
30.	Interest Receivable	5	
	Accrued Interest Income		5
30.	Interest Expense	15	
	Accrued Interest Payable		15

Chapter 9

Cash and Its Control

9.1 INTRODUCTION

In most firms transactions involving the receipt and disbursement of cash far outnumber any other kinds of transactions. Cash is, moreover, the most liquid asset and most subject to theft and fraud. It then becomes essential to have a system of accounting procedures and records that will maintain adequate control over cash.

9.2 CLASSIFICATION OF CASH

Roughly speaking, cash is anything that a bank will accept for deposit and will credit to the depositor's account. More precisely:

(1) *Cash is a medium of exchange.* Thus, such items as

> currency
> coin
> demand deposits
> savings deposits
> petty cash funds
> bank drafts
> cashier's checks
> personal checks
> money orders

qualify as cash. There are other items which are usually under the control of the company cashier, which are not cash, such as postage stamps, postdated checks, and IOU's. Postage is prepaid expense; postdated checks are receivables; and IOU's are receivables or prepaid expenses, depending on whether they are to be collected or applied against employee expenses.

(2) *Cash is immediately available for payment of current debts.* Certificates of deposit are temporary investments rather than cash, since they cannot be immediately withdrawn. (Technically, savings accounts may not be withdrawn without notice to the bank, but generally this requirement is not enforced; hence, savings deposits were listed above as cash.) Likewise, a sinking fund specifically established to pay bond requirements or a deposit with a manufacturer for purchase of equipment is not available to pay other current obligations and, therefore, is not cash. Such items are generally shown on the balance sheet as noncurrent assets, while cash is listed as a current asset.

9.3 CONTROLLING CASH RECEIPTS

In a very small business the owner-manager can maintain control through personal contact and supervision. This kind of direct intervention must, in a firm of any size, be replaced by a system of internal control, exercised through accounting reports and records. We have already encountered the guiding principle of internal control in Sec. 5.3; namely, the separation of duties. No person assigned to handle cash should, at the same time, be in a position to make entries in the records affecting his own activities.

The specific controls applied to cash receipts may be summarized as:

1. All receipts should be banked promptly.
2. Receipts from cash sales should be supported by sales tickets, cash register tapes, etc.
3. Accountability should be established each time cash is transferred.
4. Persons receiving cash should not make disbursements of cash, record cash transactions, or reconcile bank accounts.

9.4 CONTROLLING CASH DISBURSEMENTS

The main ideas here are that payments be made only by properly authorized persons, that equivalent value be received, and that documents adequately support the payment. Following are specific internal controls relating to cash disbursements.

1. All disbursements, except petty cash payments, should be made by prenumbered check.
2. Vouchers and supporting documents should be submitted for review when checks are signed.
3. Persons who sign checks should not have access to cash receipts, should not have custody of funds or record cash entries, and should not reconcile bank accounts.

It is seen that special procedures will be needed for petty cash; these will be treated in Sec. 9.7.

9.5 CONTROLLING CASH BALANCES

The basic principle of separation of duties is evident in the specific controls for cash balances:

1. Bank reconciliations should be prepared by persons who do not receive cash or sign checks.
2. Bank statements and paid checks should be received unopened by the person reconciling the account.
3. All cash funds on hand should be closely watched and surprise counts made at intervals.

If the rule of Sec. 9.3, requiring the banking of all cash receipts, is followed, then it is clear that the monthly bank statement can be made a powerful control over cash balances. Hence the importance of reconciling bank balances.

9.6 RECONCILING THE BANK BALANCE

Each month, generally, the bank forwards to the depositor a statement of his account showing:

1. Beginning balance
2. Deposits made and other credits
3. Checks paid and other charges (debits)
4. Ending balance

Included in the envelope with the statement are the paid, or "canceled," checks and any other deductions or additions (debit or credit memoranda) to the account. A deduction may be a debit memorandum for bank service charges; an addition may be a credit memorandum for the proceeds of a note collected by the bank for the depositor.

Usually the balance of the bank statement and the balance of the depositor's account will not agree. To prove the accuracy of both records the reconciling differences have to be found and any necessary entries made. The reconciling items will fall into two broad groups: (1) those on the depositor's books but not recorded by the bank, and (2) those on the bank statement but not on the books.

ITEMS ON BOOKS BUT NOT ON BANK STATEMENT

Outstanding checks. These are checks issued by the depositor but not yet presented to the bank for payment. The total of these checks is to be *deducted* from the bank balance.

Deposits in transit. Cash receipts recorded by the company but too late to be deposited. The total of such deposits is to be *added* to the bank balance.

Bookkeeping errors. Errors in recording amounts of checks; for example, a transposition of figures. The item should be added to the bank balance if it was previously overstated on the books. If the item was previously understated on the books, the amount should be deducted.

ITEMS ON BANK STATEMENT BUT NOT ON BOOKS

Service charges. The bank generally deducts amounts for bank services. The exact amount is usually not known by the depositor until he receives the statement. The amount should be deducted from the book balance.

NSF (nonsufficient funds) checks. Checks which have been deposited but cannot be collected because of insufficient funds in the account of the drawer of the check. The bank then issues a debit memorandum charging the depositor's account. The amount should be deducted from the book balance.

Collections. The bank collects notes and other items for a small fee. The bank then adds the proceeds to the account and issues a credit memorandum to the depositor. Often there are unrecorded amounts at the end of the month. The amounts should be added to the book balance.

Bank errors. Bank errors should not be entered on the books. They should be brought to the attention of the bank and corrected by the bank. Journal entries should be made for any adjustments to the book accounts. The statement used in accounting for the differences between the bank balance and the depositor's balance is known as a *bank reconciliation.*

EXAMPLE 1.

The following information was available when the John Hennessey Company began to reconcile its bank balance on May 31, 197–: Balance per depositor's books, $1,640; Balance per bank statement, $2,420; Deposit in transit, $150; Checks outstanding – #650, $300 and #654, $240; Collection of $400 note plus interest of $8, $408; Collection fee for note, $10; Bank service charge, $8.

John Hennessey Company
Bank Reconciliation
May 31, 197–

Balance per bank	$2,420		Balance per books		$1,640
Add: Deposit in transit	150		Add: Proceeds of note		408
	$2,570				$2,048
Less:			Less:		
Outstanding checks			Collection fee	$10	
#650	$300		Service charge	8	
#654	240	540			18
Adjusted balance	$2,030		Adjusted balance		$2,030

Only reconciling items in the depositor's section (right side above) are to be recorded on the books. The reconciling items in the bank section (left side above) have already been recorded on the books and merely have not yet reached the bank. They will normally be included in the next bank statement.

To complete the reconcilement, the following two journal entries will be needed.

Cash	408	
Notes Receivable		400
Interest Income		8
Service Charge Expense	18	
Cash		18

9.7 PETTY CASH

Funds spent through the cash disbursements journal take the form of checks issued in payment of various liabilities. In addition, a business will have many expenditures of small amounts for which it is not practical to issue checks. Examples are postage, parcel post, delivery expense, and miscellaneous small items, which are paid for in cash through a petty cash fund.

Under the so-called *imprest system* a fund is established for a fixed petty cash amount, and this fund is periodically reimbursed by a single check for amounts expended. The steps in setting up and maintaining the petty cash fund are as follows:

(1) An estimate is made of the total of the small amounts likely to be disbursed over a short period, usually a month. A check is drawn for the estimated total and put into the fund. The only time an entry is made in the petty cash account is for the initial establishment of the fund, unless at some later time it is determined that this fund must be increased or decreased.

EXAMPLE 2.

Petty Cash	40	
Cash		40

(2) The individual in charge of petty cash usually keeps the money in a locked box along with petty cash vouchers, such as illustrated following Example 3. The petty cash voucher, when signed by the recipient, acts as a receipt and provides information concerning the transaction. As each payment is made, the voucher is entered in the petty cash record and placed with the balance of money in the petty cash box.

EXAMPLE 3.

PETTY CASH RECORD

Date	Explanation	Voucher	Receipts	Payments	Postage	Del.	Sundry
Jan. 1	Established		$40.00				
2	Postage on Sales	1		$ 4.50	$ 4.50		
4	Telegram	2		4.00	4.00		
8	Taxi Fare	3		5.00		$5.00	
10	Coffee for Overtime	4		2.00			$ 2.00
15	Stamps	5		8.00	8.00		
26	Cleaning Windows	6		8.00			8.00
			$40.00	$31.50	$16.50	$5.00	$10.00
	Bal.			8.50			
			$40.00	$40.00			
Feb . 1	Bal.		$ 8.50				
	Replenished Fund		$31.50				

PETTY CASH VOUCHER

No. _____   Date _____

Paid To _____   Amount _____

Reason _____

Received By _____

(3)   Proof of petty cash is obtained by counting the currency and adding the amount of all the vouchers in the cash box. The total should agree with the amount in the ledger for the petty cash fund. If it does not, the entry in the cash disbursements journal that records the reimbursement of the petty cash fund will have to include an account known as Cash Short and Over. A cash shortage is debited, a cash overage is credited, to this account. Cash Short and Over is closed out at the end of the year into the expense and income account and is treated as a general expense (if a debit balance) or miscellaneous income (if a credit balance).

EXAMPLE 4.

The petty cash fund established in Example 2 might yield the following entries for the first month:

Postage Expense	12.50	
Delivery Expense	5.00	
Miscellaneous General Expense	10.00	
Cash Short and Over	2.00	
Cash		29.50

9.8   PAYROLL TAXES AND DEDUCTIONS

An important part of accounting for cash is the proper computation of the taxes and deductions that accompany payroll disbursements.

The taxes required by law are indicated in Table 1. The FICA (Federal Insurance Contributions Act) tax helps pay for Federal programs for old age and disability benefits, Medicare, and insurance benefits to survivors. During the working years of an employee, funds will be set aside from his earnings (Social Security taxes). When the employee's earnings cease because of disability, retirement, or death, the funds are made available to his dependents or survivors. Under the act, *both* employees and employers are required to contribute based on the earnings of the employee.

Table 1.   Payroll Taxes

Tax	Paid by		Rate
	Employee	Employer	
FICA	Yes	Yes	5% on first $9,000 of employee's wages each year*
Fed. Income	Yes	No	Varies with exemptions; based upon table
Fed. Unemp.	No	Yes	0.4% of first $3,000
State Unemp.	No	Yes	Up to 2.75% of first $3,000

*Subject to statutory change.

EXAMPLE 5.

If, in a given payroll period, a total of $85 was withheld from employees' wages for Social Security taxes, the employer must remit $170 to the Government, representing the $85 contribution by his employees plus the employer's matching share.

Wages in excess of $9,000 paid to a worker in one calendar year are not subject to FICA taxes.

EXAMPLE 6.

B's earnings prior to this week were $8,600.   This week his salary is $200. His FICA deduction is $10.00 ($200 ×5%). If, however, B had earned $8,850 prior to this pay period, the amount of the FICA tax would be $7.50 ($150 × 5%).

If an individual works for more than one employer during a year, each employer must withhold and pay taxes on the first $9,000.   The employee would be granted a refund from the Government if he exceeds the $9,000 base.

Under the Federal Withholding Tax System (commonly known as "pay as you go"), federal income tax is collected in the year in which the income is received, rather than in the following year.   Thus, employers must withhold funds for the payment of federal income taxes of their employees.   The amount to be withheld depends upon the number of exemptions the employee is allowed (Form W-4), the amount of the employee's earnings, and his marital status.   Notice that the withholding of any wages represents, from the employer's viewpoint, a liability, because the employer must pay to the Government that amount which he withheld from the employee.

In addition to taxes, or involuntary deductions, there are a number of *voluntary deductions* made for the convenience of the employee.   They may include group insurance premiums, hospitalization programs, savings plans, retirement payments, union dues, and charitable contributions.   The two examples that follow reflect both tax and voluntary deductions.

EXAMPLE 7.

The payroll for the Moss Company as of January 31 is as follows:

SALARIES		DEDUCTIONS		NET PAY
		FICA Tax	$ 290	
Regular	$4,200	Fed. Inc. Tax	820	
Overtime	1,600	Union Dues	600	
Total	$5,800	Total Ded.	$1,710	$4,090

The entry to record the payroll information would be:

Salaries Expense	5,800	
FICA Taxes Payable		290
Federal Income Taxes Payable		820
Union Dues Payable		600
Salaries Payable		4,090

Upon payment of the payroll:

Salaries Payable	4,090	
Cash		4,090

Here the entire amount of the salaries earned during the week ($5,800) was subject to FICA because no individual employee had earned in excess of $9,000 at that time.

EXAMPLE 8.

In Example 7 assume that only $4,000 of the total salaries was subject to FICA. The entry to record the above information would be:

Salaries Expense	5,800	
FICA Taxes Payable		200*
Federal Income Taxes Payable		820
Union Dues Payable		600
Salaries Payable		4,180

*4,000 × 5%

Summary

(1) The system used to control the disbursement of cash for small expenditures is known as an _____ fund.

(2) Except for the initial entry to record the establishment of the petty cash fund, the petty cash account is not used except when the fund is to be _____ or _____.

(3) A debit balance in Cash Short and Over represents an _____, whereas a credit balance is _____.

(4) On the depositor's monthly bank statement, Other Deductions are listed as _____ memorandums, while Other Additions to his account are shown as _____ memorandums.

(5) The term "NSF check" means _____ and the amount is _____ from the depositor's balance.

(6) FICA taxes are paid by both the _____ and the _____ for the benefit of the _____.

(7) Federal Unemployment Tax is borne solely by the _____.

(8) The employer's portion of FICA taxes, Federal Unemployment taxes, and State Unemployment taxes is charged to the _____ account.

(9) A signed receipt acknowledging advances from petty cash is known as a _____ _____.

(10) Deposits recorded in the books of a depositor and not presented to the bank in time for inclusion in the bank statement are known as _____, while checks made by the depositor and deducted from his books, but not recorded in the bank statement, are known as _____.

Answers:	(1)	imprest (petty cash)	(6)	employer, employee, employee
	(2)	increased, decreased	(7)	employer
	(3)	expense, income	(8)	payroll tax expense
	(4)	debit, credit	(9)	petty cash voucher
	(5)	nonsufficient funds, deducted	(10)	deposits in transit, outstanding checks

Solved Problems

9.1.   Name five sources of cash receipts.

SOLUTION

> The following list contains the principal sources:
>
> 1. Sales of goods and services for cash.
> 2. Collections of accounts and notes from customers.
> 3. Renting of property.
> 4. Loans from individuals.
> 5. Loans from banks.
> 6. Customers' notes discounted.
> 7. New bonds issued.
> 8. New capital stock issued.
> 9. Sale of scrap, waste, and by-products.
> 10. Disposal of equipment.
> 11. Sale of other assets.

9.2.   Name five types of cash disbursements.

SOLUTION

> 1. Purchase of goods.
> 2. Purchase of supplies.
> 3. Payment of wages and salaries.
> 4. Purchase of equipment.
> 5. Payment of other operating expenses.
> 6. Purchase of securities.
> 7. Retirement of bank loans.
> 8. Retirement of stocks and bonds.
> 9. Miscellaneous payments (dividend payments, etc.).

9.3.   William James worked 46 hours during the first week in January of the current year. His pay rate is $2.50 per hour. Withheld from his wages were: FICA tax, 5%; federal income tax, $16.00; hospitalization, $4.50. Determine the necessary adjusting entry to record the payment to the employee.

SOLUTION

Salary Expense	*122.50**	
FICA Taxes Payable		*6.13*
Federal Income Taxes Payable		*16.00*
Hospitalization Payable		*4.50*
Salaries Payable		*95.87*
*40 hours × $2.50 per hour = $100.00 (regular)		
6 hours × $3.75 per hour = 22.50 (overtime)		
$122.50		

9.4. The total payroll for the Keane Company for the week ending May 31 was $24,000. Of the total amount, $18,000 was subject to FICA tax, $3,000 held for federal income tax, $1,500 held for bond savings plan, and the balance paid to their employees in cash. Present the journal entry necessary to record the payroll for this week, assuming that the FICA tax rate is 5%.

SOLUTION

Salaries Expense	24,000	
FICA Taxes Payable		900
Federal Income Taxes Payable		3,000
Bond Savings Payable		1,500
Cash		18,600

9.5. For the week ending April 30 the total amount of earnings was $18,000. Of that amount, earnings subject to FICA was $14,000 and the amount subject to unemployment compensation tax was $9,000. Present the general journal entry to record the employer's payroll tax for the week, assuming the following rates: FICA, 5%; State Unemployment, 2%; Federal Unemployment, 0.4%.

SOLUTION

Payroll Tax Expense	916	
FICA Taxes Payable		700
State Unemployment Insurance Payable		180
Federal Unemployment Insurance Payable		36

9.6. Below is the payroll data for three of the employees of the Ernst Company.

Employee	Amount Earned to Date	Gross Pay for Week
A	$2,400	$100
B	$2,900	$250
C	$4,000	$150

The company is located in a state that imposes an unemployment insurance tax of 2.4% on the first $3,000. Federal unemployment tax is 0.4%; FICA tax, 5%. Present the journal entry necessary to record the employer's payroll tax expense.

SOLUTION

The taxes are computed as follows:

	FICA	State	Federal
A	5.00 (5% × 100)	2.40 (2.4% × 100)	0.40 (0.004 × 100)
B	12.50 (5% × 250)	2.40 (2.4% × 100)	0.40 (0.004 × 100)
C	7.50 (5% × 150)		
Total	25.00	4.80	0.80

The journal entry is therefore:

Payroll Tax Expense	30.60	
FICA Taxes Payable		25.00
State Unemployment Insurance Payable		4.80
Federal Unemployment Insurance Payable		0.80

9.7. Transactions for the Eagan Company for the month of January, pertaining to the establishment of a petty cash fund, were as follows:

January 1: Established an imprest petty cash fund of $50

January 31: Box contained $6 cash and paid vouchers for transportation, $14; freight, $16; charity, $4; office supplies, $6; miscellaneous expense, $4

What are the journal entries necessary to record the petty cash information?

SOLUTION

Petty Cash	50	
Cash		50
Transportation Expense	14	
Freight Expense	16	
Charity Expense	4	
Office Supplies Expense	6	
Miscellaneous Expense	4	
Cash		44

9.8. If in Problem 9.7 the cash on hand was $9, record the January 31 reimbursement.

SOLUTION

Transportation Expense	14	
Freight Expense	16	
Charity Expense	4	
Office Supplies Expense	6	
Miscellaneous Expense	4	
Cash		41
Cash Short and Over		3

9.9. At the close of the day, the total cash sales as determined by the sales registers was $1,480. However, the total cash receipts was only $1,472. The error cannot be located at the present time. What entry should be made to record the cash sales for the day?

SOLUTION

Cash	1,472	
Cash Short and Over	8	
Sales Income		1,480

9.10. Indicate for Items 1-8 below, in order to produce equal adjusted balances for Blake Company, whether they should be:

(a) added to the bank statement balance
(b) deducted from the bank statement balance
(c) added to the depositor's balance
(d) deducted from the depositor's balance
(e) exempted from the bank reconciliation statement.

1. Statement includes a credit memorandum, $402, representing the collection of the proceeds of a note left at the bank.
2. A credit memorandum representing the proceeds of a loan, $4,200, made to Blake Company by the bank.
3. Deposits in transit totaled $3,000.
4. Seven outstanding checks totaling $9,000 were not recorded on the statement.
5. A $150 customer's check that Blake Company had deposited was returned with "nonsufficient funds" stamped across the face.
6. The bank erroneously charged someone else's check, $200, against Blake's account.
7. Blake Company was credited on the bank statement with the receipt of $240 from another depositor.
8. A $96 check was erroneously recorded in Blake's check stubs as $69.

SOLUTION

1. (c)   5. (d)
2. (c)   6. (a)
3. (a)   7. (b)
4. (b)   8. (d)

9.11. Of the following transactions involving the bank reconciliation statement, which ones necessitate an adjusting entry on the depositor's books?

1. Outstanding checks of $3,000 did not appear on the bank statement.

2. The last two days' deposited receipts, $2,850, did not appear on the bank statement.

3. The depositor's check for $120 for supplies was written in his records as $210.

4. Bank service charge, $4.

5. A note left at the bank for collection, $822, was paid and credited to the depositor's account.

SOLUTION

3.	Cash	90	
	Supplies		90
4.	Bank Service Charge	4	
	Cash		4
5.	Cash	822	
	Notes Receivable		822

9.12. Using the following data, reconcile the bank account of the Kemper Motor Company.

> Bank balance, $7,780.
>
> Depositor's balance, $6,500.
>
> Note collected by bank, $1,000, plus interest of $30; a collection charge of $10 was made by the bank.
>
> Outstanding checks, $410.
>
> Deposit in transit, $150.

SOLUTION

Balance per Kemper's books		$6,500	Balance per bank statement		$7,780
Add: Note collected by bank			Add: Deposit in transit		150
Note	$1,000				$7,930
Interest	30	1,030	Less:		
		$7,530	Outstanding checks		410
Less: Collection charge		10			
Adjusted balance		$7,520	Adjusted balance		$7,520

9.13.   Correct the following incorrect bank reconciliation proof.

Kaney Company
Bank Reconciliation
December 31, 197–

Balance per depositor's books		$7,250
Add:		
Note collected by bank including interest	515	
Deposit in transit	1,200	
Bank error charging Kane's check to Kaney account	860	
Total		$9,825
Deduct:		
Check from customer of Kaney's deposited and returned by bank as NSF	$ 150	
Service charge	5	
Check for $250 written in Kaney's ledger and checkbook stubs as $150	100	
Outstanding checks	1,100	1,355
		$8,470
Less: Unexplained difference		1,920
Balance per bank statement		$6,550

SOLUTION

Kaney Company
Bank Reconciliation
December 31, 197–

Balance per depositor's books		$7,250	Balance per bank statement		$6,550
Add: Note collected by bank		515	Add: Deposit in transit		1,200
		$7,765	Error		860
Less:					$8,610
NSF	$150				
Bank service charge	5		Less:		
Error	100	255	Outstanding checks		1,100
Adjusted balance		$7,510	Adjusted balance		$7,510

Chapter 10

Receivables

10.1 NOTES RECEIVABLE

A large proportion of all business transactions are credit transactions. One way of extending credit is by the acceptance of a *promissory note*, a contract in which one person (the maker) promises to pay another person (the payee) a specific sum of money at a specific time, with or without interest. In the examples to follow, we will consider interest-bearing notes receivable rather than open accounts (accounts receivable) which carry no interest. A promissory note is used for the following reasons:

1. The holder of a note can usually obtain money by taking the note to the bank and selling it (*discounting* the note).

2. The note is a written acknowledgment of a debt and is better evidence than an open account. It takes precedence over accounts in the event that the debtor becomes bankrupt.

3. It facilitates the sale of merchandise on long-term or installment plans.

EXAMPLE 1.

Assume that James Allen owes A. Bagon $400 and gives him a 90-day, 6% note in settlement. On Mr. Bagon's books the entry is:

Notes Receivable	400	
Accounts Receivable		400

Mr. Allen still owes the debt, but his obligation is now of a different type. Only the principal ($400) is recorded when the note is received, since it represents the amount of the unpaid account. The interest is not due until the date of collection, 90 days later. At that time, the interest earned (income) will be part of the entry recognizing the receipt of the proceeds from the note:

Cash	406	
Notes Receivable		400
Interest Income		6

10.2 METHODS OF COMPUTING INTEREST

For the sake of simplicity, interest is commonly computed on the basis of a 360-day year divided into 12 months of 30 days each. Two widely used methods are (1) the cancellation method and (2) the 6%-60 days method.

EXAMPLE 2. The Cancellation Method.

The basic formula is:

$$\textbf{INTEREST} = \textbf{PRINCIPAL} \times \textbf{RATE} \times \textbf{TIME}$$

Consider a note for $400 at 6% for 90 days. The *principal* is the face amount of the note ($400). The *rate of interest* is written as a fraction: $6\%/100\% = 6/100$. The *time*, if less than a year, is expressed as a fraction by placing the number of days the note runs over the number of days in a year: 90/360. Thus,

$$\text{INTEREST} \quad = \quad \$400 \times \frac{6}{100} \times \frac{90}{360} \quad = \quad \$6$$

EXAMPLE 3. The 6%-60 Days Method.

This is a variation of the cancellation method, based on the fact that 60 days, or $\frac{1}{6}$ year, at 6% is equivalent to 1%, so that the interest is obtained simply by shifting the decimal point of the principal two places to the left. The method also applies to other time periods or other interest rates. For instance:

$400 Note	30 Days	6%
(a) Determine the interest for 60 days		$4.00
(b) Divide the result by 2 (30 days is one-half of 60 days)		*Ans.* $2.00

$400 Note	45 Days	6%
(a) Determine the interest for 30 days		$2.00
(b) Determine the interest for 15 days		$1.00
(c) Add the interest for 30 days and 15 days		*Ans.* $3.00

$400 Note	60 Days	5%
(a) Determine the interest at 6%		$4.00
(b) Determine the interest at 1% by taking one-sixth of the above amount		.67
(c) Multiply the interest at 1% by the rate desired, $.67 \times 5$		*Ans.* $3.35

10.3 DISCOUNTING

Once the interest to be paid has been determined, the procedure for discounting a note is quite simple. We define the *maturity value* of a note by:

(1) MATURITY VALUE = FACE OF NOTE + INTEREST INCOME

where the *face* is the principal and the interest income is computed as in Sec. 10.2. The holder of a note may discount it at the bank *prior to its due date*. He will receive the maturity value, less the *discount,* or interest charge imposed by the bank for holding the note for the unexpired portion of its term. In other words,

(2) DISCOUNT = MATURITY VALUE $\times$ DISCOUNT RATE $\times$ UNEXPIRED TIME

and

(3) NET PROCEEDS = MATURITY VALUE — DISCOUNT

EXAMPLE 4.

Mr. Bagon holds a $400, 90-day, 6% note written on April 10 (see Example 1). It is discounted at 6% on May 10. The interest on the note, as found in Example 2, amounts to $6. Hence,

$$(1) \qquad \text{MATURITY VALUE} \quad = \quad \$400 + \$6 \quad = \quad \$406$$

Since, at the time of discounting, Mr. Bagon has held the note for only 30 days, the bank will have to wait $90 - 30 = 60$ days until it can receive the maturity value. The discount charge is then:

$$(2) \qquad \text{DISCOUNT} \quad = \quad \$406 \times \frac{6}{100} \times \frac{60}{360} \quad = \quad \$4.06$$

and Mr. Bagon receives

$$(3) \qquad \text{NET PROCEEDS} \quad = \quad \$406 - \$4.06 \quad = \quad \$401.94$$

In this example the bank's discount rate happened to be equal to the interest rate of the note; this need not always be the case (see Problem 10.6).

10.4 DISHONORED NOTES RECEIVABLE

If the issuer of a note does not make payment on the due date, the note is said to be *dishonored*. It is no longer negotiable and the amount is charged back to Accounts Receivable. The reasons for transferring the dishonored notes receivable to the accounts receivable account are: (1) the notes receivable account is then limited to current notes that have not yet matured, and (2) the accounts receivable account will then show the dishonoring of the note, giving a better picture of the transaction.

EXAMPLE 5.

A $500, 60-day, 6% note written by A. Black was dishonored on the date of maturity. The entry runs:

Accounts Receivable, A. Black	*505*	
Notes Receivable		*500*
Interest Income		*5*

Observe that the interest income is recorded and is charged to the customer's account.

When a payee discounts a note receivable, he creates a *contingent* (potential) *liability*. This occurs because there is a possibility that the maker may dishonor the note. Bear in mind that the payee has already received payment from the bank in advance of the maturity date. He is, therefore, contingently liable to the bank to make good on the amount (maturity value) in the event of default by the maker. Any *protest fee* arising from the default of the note is charged to the maker of the note and is added to the amount to be charged against his account.

EXAMPLE 6.

An $800, 90-day, 6% note, dated May 1, is discounted on May 31 at 6%. Upon presentation on the due date, the note is dishonored. The entry will be:

Accounts Receivable	*812**	
Cash		*812*
* $800 (Face)		
12 (Interest)		
$812 (Maturity value)		

Had the bank issued a protest fee of $3, the amount charged to the customer would be $815.

10.5 RECORDING OF UNCOLLECTIBLE ACCOUNTS

Businesses must expect to sustain some losses from uncollectible accounts and should therefore show on the balance sheet the *net amount of accounts receivable,* the amount expected to be collected, rather than the gross amount. The difference between the gross and net amounts represents the estimated uncollectible accounts, or bad debts. These expenses are attributed to the year in which the sale is made, though they may be realized at a later date.

There are two methods of recording uncollectible accounts.

1. **Direct write-off method.** In small businesses losses that arise from uncollectible accounts are recognized in the accounts *in the period in which they become uncollectible.* Under this method, when an account is deemed uncollectible, it is written off the books by a debit to the expense account, Uncollectible Accounts Expense, and a credit to the individual customer's account and to the controlling account.

EXAMPLE 7.

If William Anderson's $300 account receivable, dated May 15, 1971, was deemed uncollectible in January of 1973, the entry in 1973 would be:

Uncollectible Accounts Expense	*300*	
Accounts Receivable, William Anderson		*300*

2. **Allowance method.** As has been stated before, one of the fundamentals of accounting is that revenue be matched with expenses in the same year. Under the direct write-off method, in Example 7, the loss was not recorded until two years after the revenue had been recognized. The allowance method does not permit this. The income statement for each period must include all losses and expenses related to the income earned *in that period.* Therefore, losses from uncollectible accounts should be deducted in the year the sale was made. Since it is impossible to predict which particular accounts will not be collected, an adjusting entry is made, usually at the end of the year.

EXAMPLE 8.

Assume that in the first year of operation a firm has estimated that $2,000 of accounts receivable will be uncollectible. The adjusting entry would be:

Uncollectible Accounts Expense	*2,000*	
Allowance for Uncollectible Accounts		*2,000*

The credit balance of Allowance for Uncollectible Accounts appears on the balance sheet as a deduction from the total amount of Accounts Receivable:

Accounts Receivable	*$29,920*	
Less: Allowance for Uncollectible Accounts	*2,000*	*$27,920*

The $27,920 will become the estimated realizable value of the accounts receivable at that date. The uncollectible accounts expense will appear as an operating expense in the income statement.

10.6 COMPUTATION OF UNCOLLECTIBLE ACCOUNTS

There are two generally accepted methods of calculating the amount of uncollectible accounts. One method is to use a flat percentage of the net sales for the year. The other method takes into consideration the ages of the individual accounts at the end of the fiscal year.

1. **Percentage of sales method.** Under this method, a fixed percentage of the total sales on account is taken. For example, if charge sales were $200,000 and experience has shown that approximately 1% of such sales will become uncollectible at a future date, the adjusting entry for the uncollectible accounts would be:

Uncollectible Accounts Expense	*2,000*	
Allowance for Uncollectible Accounts		*2,000*

The same amount is used whether or not there is a balance in Allowance for Uncollectible Accounts. However, if any substantial balance should accumulate in the allowance account, a change in the percentage figure would become appropriate.

2. **Balance sheet method.** Under this method, every account is "aged"; that is, each item in its balance is related to the sale date. The further past due the account, the more probable it is that the customer is unwilling or unable to pay. A typical analysis is shown in Example 9.

EXAMPLE 9.

Age of Account	Accounts Receivable Balance	Estimated % Uncollectible	Amount
1–30 days	$ 8,000	1%	$ 80
31–60 days	12,000	3%	360
61–90 days	6,000	5%	300
91–180 days	3,000	20%	600
Over 180 days	920	50%	460
	$29,920		$1,800

The calculated allowance for uncollectible accounts ($1,800 in Example 9) is reconciled at the end of the year with the actual balance in the allowance account, and an adjusting entry is made.

EXAMPLE 10.

The analysis showed that $1,800 would be required in the Allowance for Uncollectible Accounts at the end of the period. The Allowance for Uncollectible Accounts has a credit balance of $200. The adjusting entry at the end of the year would be:

Uncollectible Accounts Expense	1,600	
Allowance for Uncollectible Accounts		1,600

If, however, there had been a debit balance of $200, a credit to Allowance for Uncollectible Accounts of $2,000 would be necessary to bring the closing balance to $1,800.

When it becomes evident that a customer's account is uncollectible, it is written off the books. This is done by crediting Accounts Receivable and the individual customer's account in the subsidiary ledger for the amount deemed uncollectible and by debiting Allowance for Uncollectible Accounts.

EXAMPLE 11.

John Andrews' account (a) was deemed uncollectible.

GENERAL LEDGER	**ACCOUNTS RECEIVABLE LEDGER**
Allowance for Uncollectible Accounts	*John Andrews*
(a) 600 Bal. 1,800	Bal. 600 (a) 600
Accounts Receivable	
Bal. 29,920 (a) 600	

10.7 RECOVERY OF BAD DEBTS

If a written-off account is later collected in full or in part (a *recovery of bad debts*), the write-off will be reversed for the amount received.

EXAMPLE 12.

At a later date, Mr. Andrews (see Example 11) pays his account in full. The reversing entry (b) to restore his account will be:

> Accounts Receivable, John Andrews   600
>   Allowance for Uncollectible Accounts   600

A separate entry, (c), will then be made in the cash receipts journal to record the collection, debiting Cash $600 and crediting Accounts Receivable, John Andrews. If a partial collection was made, the reversing entry should be made for the amount recovered.

GENERAL LEDGER

Cash

(c) 600	

Accounts Receivable

29,200	(c) 600
(b) 600	

Allowance for Uncollectible Accounts

(a) 600	Bal. 1,800
	(b) 600

ACCOUNTS RECEIVABLE LEDGER

John Andrews

Bal. 600	(a) 600
(b) 600	(c) 600

Summary

(1) The practice of transferring a customer's note to the bank is called _____.

(2) The face of a note plus the interest due is known as _____.

(3) Under the _____ method, uncollectible accounts are charged to expense when they become uncollectible.

(4) Uncollectible Accounts Expense appears in the _____ statement, while Allowance for Uncollectible Accounts appears in the _____.

(5) The method based on the age of the accounts receivable is known as the _____ _____ approach.

(6) Ascertaining the amount and time outstanding for each account is known as _____.

(7) If Bill Henderson issues to Sam Borach a $400 note, Bill Henderson is called the _____ and Sam Borach the _____.

(8) The interest on a $800, 90-day, 6% note would be _____.

(9) Normally, banks will base their discount on the _____ of the note.

(10) What effect does the acceptance of a note receivable have on the total assets of a firm? _____.

Answers: (1) discounting; (2) maturity value; (3) direct write-off; (4) income, balance sheet; (5) balance sheet; (6) aging; (7) maker, payee; (8) $12; (9) maturity value; (10) no effect

Solved Problems

10.1. Below is an example of a note receivable.

> Date: *July 1, 197—*
>
> "*I, Charles Nelson, promise to pay Acme Stores $800, 60 days from date, at 6% interest.*"
>
> *Charles Nelson*

(a) Who is the maker of the note? (b) Who is the payee of the note? (c) What is the maturity date of the note? (d) What is the maturity value of the note?

SOLUTION

(a) Charles Nelson   (b) Acme Stores   (c) August 30   (d) $808

10.2. A note written on August 1 and due on November 15 was discounted on October 15. (a) How many days was the note written for? (b) How many days did the bank charge for in discounting the note?

SOLUTION

(a)			(b)		
August 2–31	30 days		October 16–31	16 days	
September	30 days		November 1–15	15 days	
October	31 days			31 days *Ans.*	
November	15 days				
	106 days *Ans.*				

10.3. Determine the interest on the following notes: (a) $750 principal, 6% interest, 96 days; (b) $800 principal, 4% interest, 90 days.

SOLUTION

(a)	$750	6%	60 days	$ 7.50	(b)	$800	6%	60 days	$ 8.00
		6%	30 days	3.75			6%	30 days	4.00
		6%	6 days	.75			6%	90 days	$12.00
		6%	96 days	$12.00 *Ans.*					

The interest at 4% is then

$$\frac{4\%}{6\%} \times \$12.00 = \$8.00 \; Ans.$$

10.4. A 90-day, 6%, $4,000 note receivable in settlement of an account, dated June 1, is discounted at 6% on July 1. Compute the proceeds of the note.

SOLUTION

$4,000.00	Principal
60.00	Interest income (90 days, 6%)
$4,060.00	Maturity value
40.60	Discount (60 days, 6% of maturity value)
$4,019.40	Proceeds, July 1–August 30 (due date)

10.5. What are the entries needed to record the information in Problem 10.4 (a) on June 1? (b) on July 1?

(a)			
(b)			

SOLUTION

(a)	Notes Receivable	4,000.00	
	Accounts Receivable		4,000.00
(b)	Cash	4,019.40	
	Interest Income		19.40
	Notes Receivable		4,000.00

10.6. Record the following transactions in the books of Robert Ryan Company.

(a) May 1: Received a $6,000, 90-day, 7% note in settlement of the Happy Valley account

(b) May 31: Discounted the note at 6% at the bank

(c) July 30: Happy Valley paid the note in full

(a)			
(b)			
(c)			

SOLUTION

(a)	Notes Receivable	6,000.00	
	Accounts Receivable, Happy Valley		6,000.00
(b)	Cash	6,043.95*	
	Interest Income		43.95
	Notes Receivable		6,000.00

* $6,000.00	Principal
105.00	Interest income
6,105.00	Maturity value
61.05	Discount
$6,043.95	Proceeds

(c) No entry

10.7. If in Problem 10.6 Happy Valley dishonored their obligation on July 30 and a $5 protest fee was imposed by the bank, what entry would be required to record this information?

SOLUTION

Accounts Receivable, Happy Valley	6,110*	
Cash		6,110

* $6,105 (maturity value) + $5 (protest fee)

10.8. Shown are balances for Prurient Press:

Accounts Receivable	Sales	Allowance for Uncollectible Accounts
120,000	350,000	400

What is the adjusting entry needed to record the provision for uncollectible accounts if the uncollectible expense is estimated: (a) as 1% of net sales? (b) by aging the accounts receivable, the allowance balance being estimated as $3,600?

(a)

(b)

SOLUTION

(a)	Uncollectible Accounts Expense	3,500*	
	Allowance for Uncollectible Accounts		3,500
	*1% of $350,000		
(b)	Uncollectible Accounts Expense	3,200**	
	Allowance for Uncollectible Accounts		3,200
	** $3,600 − $400. Balance of $400 in allowance must be taken into consideration.		

10.9. Using the aging schedule below, prepare the adjusting entry providing for the uncollectible accounts expense.

Amount	Age	Estimated % Uncollectible
$24,000	1-30 days	1%
$18,000	31-60 days	3%
$10,000	61-180 days	25%
$6,000	181 days and over	60%

SOLUTION

Uncollectible Accounts Expense	6,880*	
Allowance for Uncollectible Accounts		6,880
* $240 1-30 days		
$540 31-60 days		
$2,500 61-180 days		
$3,600 181 days and over		

10.10. Below are some accounts of the Jay Balding Company, as of January 197–.

GENERAL LEDGER	ACCOUNTS RECEIVABLE LEDGER

Accounts Receivable		D. Grego	
210,000		1,400	

Allowance for Uncollectible Accounts		J. Philips	
	2,600	1,200	

Prepare entries needed to record the following information:

    (a)   March 5:   D. Grego account was determined to be uncollectible

    (b)   April 14:   Wrote off J. Philips account as uncollectible

(a)

(b)

SOLUTION

(a)	Allowance for Uncollectible Accounts	1,400	
	Accounts Receivable, D. Grego		1,400
(b)	Allowance for Uncollectible Accounts	1,200	
	Accounts Receivable, J. Philips		1,200

10.11. If, in Problem 10.10, J. Philips later paid his accounts in full, what entries would be necessary?

SOLUTION

Accounts Receivable, J. Philips	1,200	
Allowance for Uncollectible Accounts		1,200
Cash	1,200	
Accounts Receivable, J. Philips		1,200

Chapter 11

Merchandise Inventory

11.1 INTRODUCTION

In a mercantile business, inventory is merchandise that is held for resale. As such, it will ordinarily be converted into cash in less than a year and is thus a current asset. In a manufacturing business, there will usually be inventories of raw materials and goods in process in addition to an inventory of finished goods.

11.2 PERIODIC AND PERPETUAL METHODS OF INVENTORY

Under the *periodic method,* inventory is physically counted at regular intervals (annually, quarterly, or monthly). When this system is used, credits are made to the inventory account or to Purchases not as each sale is made, but rather in total at the end of the inventory period.

The *perpetual method* is generally used when units are of relatively high value. Running balances by unit and by cost are maintained for units purchased and sold. Individual receipts of goods are debited to the inventory account and individual sales are credited to this account. At the end of the accounting period the cost of goods sold can be determined by adding the costs of the individual items sold.

Of the two methods, the periodic system is the more common in retail businesses such as grocery stores, hardware stores, etc., which sell a wide variety of items of low unit cost. The expense of maintaining records of individual costs for such low-priced items would be prohibitive. The balance of this chapter will be concerned with the periodic system only.

11.3 DETERMINING INVENTORY

When, as is often the case in mercantile businesses, inventory consists of identical articles purchased at different times and at different unit prices, the problem arises as to how to assign a cost to each inventory item. This problem is commonly resolved by use of one or another of five methods, which will be individually described below. In all examples given, the following data will be used:

Date	Type	Units	Unit Cost	Total Amount	
Jan. 1	Inventory	100	$ 6.00		$ 600
Feb. 5	Purchases	150	8.00		1,200
April 10	Purchases	200	9.00		1,800
Sept. 25	Purchases	250	10.00		2,500
		700		Available for Sale	$6,100

It will also be assumed that a physical inventory on December 31 shows 320 units on hand.

Method 1.   First-In-First-Out (FIFO).   Here the assumption is that the goods are sold in the order in which they were received.

EXAMPLE 1.

Under FIFO, goods on hand are considered to be those most lately received. Therefore the 320 units on hand at the end of the year would be costed as follows:

Most recent purchase (Sept. 25):   250 units @ $10.00 = $2,500
Next purchase (April 10):   70 units @   9.00 =   630
                          Total units 320   Total cost $3,130

It should be emphasized that, as a method of assigning *costs*, FIFO may be used regardless of the actual, physical flow of merchandise. Indeed, we might say that FIFO really stands for First-Price-In-First-Price-Out.

Method 2.   Last-In-First-Out (LIFO).   Under this method, it is assumed that goods are sold in reverse order of receipt. Hence, it is the most recent costs which are applied against income.

EXAMPLE 2.

Under LIFO, the inventory at the end of the period is considered to be merchandise purchased in the first part of the period. The cost of the 320 units on hand would be calculated as:

Earliest purchase (Jan.1):   100 units @ $6.00 = $ 600
Next purchase (Feb. 5):   150 units @ 8.00 =   1,200
Next purchase (April 10):   70 units @ 9.00 =   630
                  Total units 320   Total cost $2,430

LIFO has several advantages over FIFO:

1. LIFO matches the most recent costs against current sales. In a rising cost market, net income under LIFO would be smaller, thus producing a smaller tax.

2. LIFO permits a more realistic measurement of realized income because it matches current costs and current revenues. This method is widely used for tax purposes.

Method 3.   Weighted Average.   In this method a weighted average unit cost is obtained by dividing the total cost of goods available for sale during the inventory period by the total number of units of these goods. This average unit price is used for both the inventory and cost of goods sold. An advantage of the weighted average method is that it assigns cost equitably between ending inventory and goods sold.

EXAMPLE 3.

According to the data, the 700 units of available goods cost a total of $6,100. Therefore:

$6,100   ÷   700   = $8.71
(goods)   (units)   (unit cost)

and

$8.71   ×   320   = $2,787
(unit cost) (on hand) (ending inventory)

In Example 4 below, we compare the results of the FIFO, LIFO, and weighted average methods, with regard to both ending inventory and cost of goods sold. Since the two amounts are related through the equation

GOODS AVAILABLE FOR SALE − ENDING INVENTORY   =   COST OF GOODS SOLD it is seen that if the ending inventory is *overstated,* the cost of goods sold will be *understated* and net profit *overstated.* On the other hand, if inventory is *understated,* then cost of goods sold will be *overstated* and net profit *understated.* Clearly, the method chosen for inventory computation can have a marked effect on the profit of the firm. There is no *one* method that is the best for all firms, but careful consideration of the following factors will be helpful in making the decision: (1) the effect upon the income statement and balance sheet, (2) the effect upon taxable income, (3) the effect upon the selling price.

EXAMPLE 4.

	First-In-First-Out	Last-In-First-Out	Weighted Average
Goods Available For Sale	$6,100	$6,100	$6,100
Ending Inventory, Dec. 31	3,130	2,430	2,787
Cost of Goods Sold	$2,970	$3,670	$3,313

Method 4. Specific Identification. If the units of inventory can be traced to invoices, the specific identification method may be used to assign to the ending inventory its actual cost. This method is commonly applied where the value of the units is high.

EXAMPLE 5.

Purchase invoice #2146, April 10:	10 units @ $ 90 =	$ 900
Purchase invoice #2184, Sept. 25:	22 units @ 100 =	2,200
Total units	32 Total cost	$3,100

Method 5. Lower of Cost or Market. A conservative view is that unrealized profit should not be recorded in accounting. If an asset such as inventory increases in value, there should be no formal record of the fact until the actual gain has been realized through sale. When an asset declines in value, it is important to recognize this as an expense or a loss even though the asset has not yet been sold. One way of keeping the inventory valuation conservatively low is to choose as the effective unit cost the *smaller of* (a) the unit cost as computed by FIFO or by weighted average and (b) the market price (i.e., the current unit replacement cost). This is the so-called "cost or market" method; it need not be used when costs are calculated by LIFO.

EXAMPLE 6.

Assume a market price of $9.00 on December 31. If FIFO is used (see Example 1), the unit cost of the inventory is 3,130 ÷ 320 = $9.78. Since this exceeds the market price, the "cost or market" method would assign $9.00 as the unit cost and would produce a valuation of 320 × 9 = $2,880. However, the weighted average unit cost of $8.71 (see Example 3) is lower than the market price, so that "cost or market" would produce the same valuation obtained in Example 3.

One can also apply "cost or market" when inventory consists of separate lots:

Lot	Quantity	Unit Cost	Unit Market Price	Lower of Cost or Market
A	150 units	$ 6.00	$ 6.50	$ 900 (cost)
B	250 units	7.00	9.00	1,750 (cost)
C	400 units	9.00	8.00	3,200 (market)
D	500 units	10.00	12.00	5,000 (cost)
				Inventory $10,850

11.4 COST OF GOODS SOLD

Since we do not reflect purchases or sales of goods in the inventory account during the year (periodic method), we must determine the cost of the inventory remaining on hand at the end of the accounting period and make any adjustments necessary. Ending inventory, or merchandise which has not been sold and is on hand at the end of the period, is an asset which appears on the balance sheet. Cost of Goods Sold appears in the income statement as a reduction from Sales. This cost may be calculated by the following scheme:

(a)	Inventory (beginning), January 1, 1973	$	
(b)	Add: Purchases		_____
(c)	Goods Available for Sale		
(d)	Less: Inventory (ending), December 31, 1973		_____
(e)	Cost of Goods Sold		$ _____

(a) **Inventory (beginning).** The amount to be used will be the same as the ending inventory of 1972 (determined by counting and applying one of the methods of Sec. 11.3).

(b) **Purchases.** This is the total amount of goods bought for resale during 1972, minus any purchases returned to the seller and any discounts given (*net* purchases).

(c) **Goods Available for Sale.** Computed by adding the inventory at the beginning of the year to the net purchases during 1973.

(d) **Inventory (ending).** Determined by taking a physical count of all goods remaining in the business on December 31, 1973, and applying one of the methods of Sec. 11.3.

(e) **Cost of Goods Sold.** This is calculated as the difference between what was available for sale and what is left at the end of the year. The cost of goods sold will then be deducted from net sales to determine the gross profit.

EXAMPLE 7.

Cost of Goods Sold	
Beginning Inventory	$20,000
Add: Purchases	36,000
Goods Available for Sale	$56,000
Less: Ending Inventory	26,000
Cost of Goods Sold	$30,000

Assuming that net sales were $75,000, gross profit from operations would be $45,000:

Sales	$75,000
Cost of Goods Sold	30,000
Gross Profit	$45,000

11.5 INVENTORY ADJUSTMENT AND THE WORKSHEET

Adjusting entries for inventory and the use of the worksheet were treated in detail in Sec. 7.3 (see especially Example 7.2). Example 8 below will serve to review the salient points.

EXAMPLE 8.

Assume that the January 1 (beginning) inventory is $20,000 and the December 31 (ending) inventory is $26,000. Two entries are required to show the replacement of the old by the new inventory:

Entry 1	Expense and Income Summary	20,000	
	Merchandise Inventory		20,000

Entry 2   *Merchandise Inventory*   26,000

                        Expense and Income Summary   26,000

The effect on the inventory and the expense and income balances is as follows:

Merchandise Inventory		*Expense and Income Summary*	
Jan. 1 20,000	Dec. 31 20,000	Dec. 31 20,000	Dec. 31 26,000
Dec. 31 26,000			

On' the worksheet (Fig. 11-1) the $20,000 balance of the inventory account that appears in the trial balance represents the inventory at the beginning of the year. This amount will be transferred to Expense and Income Summary as Entry (*a*).

    (*a*)   *Expense and Income Summary*   20,000

              Merchandise Inventory   20,000

The inventory at the end of the current year, $26,000, is an asset and will be adjusted on the worksheet as (*b*).

    (*b*)   *Merchandise Inventory*   26,000

              Expense and Income Summary   26,000

Unlike the procedure for other accounts, both the debit and the credit amounts for Expense and Income Summary are extended to the income statement in Fig. 11-1. This is done because the amount of the debit adjustment (which represents the beginning inventory of $20,000) and of the credit adjustment (which represents the ending inventory of $26,000) are needed to prepare the income statement. It would not be practical to net the two items, as the single figure would not give enough information regarding the beginning and ending inventories. The merchandise inventory of $26,000 (ending) is extended to the debit column of the balance sheet.

Account Title	Trial Balance		Adjustments		Income Statement		Balance Sheet	
	Dr.	Cr.	Dr.	Cr.	Dr.	Cr.	Dr.	Cr.
Merchandise Inventory	20,000		(b) 26,000	(a) 20,000			26,000	
Expense and Income Summary			(a) 20,000	(b) 26,000	20,000	26,000		

Fig. 11-1

Summary

(1) When inventory is physically counted at the end of a recurrent period, we have the _____ method of inventory.

(2) The inventory method used when units are generally of high value is the _____ method.

(3) The _____ inventory method is most commonly used in retail establishments.

(4) A method of inventory valuation based on the concept that the goods are sold in the order in which received is known as _____.

(5) The valuation of inventory based upon the concept that the most recent costs incurred should be charged against income is known as _____.

(6) In a rising market, net income under _____ would be smaller, thus producing a smaller tax.

(7) The inventory method based on the concept that the unit cost of merchandise sold is the average of all expenditures for inventory is known as the _____ method.

(8) A conservative valuation system which can be used with FIFO or the weighted average method, and is designed to yield the lowest inventory valuation, is known as _____.

(9) Merchandise which has not been sold at the end of the period is known as _____ _____ and appears as an _____ in the balance sheet.

(10) The beginning inventory, plus net purchases during the period, minus ending inventory, is the _____.

Answers: (1) periodic; (2) perpetual; (3) periodic; (4) First-In-First-Out (FIFO); (5) Last-In-First-Out (LIFO); (6) LIFO; (7) Weighted Average; (8) Lower of Cost or Market; (9) ending inventory, asset; (10) cost of goods sold

Solved Problems

11.1. From the following data, prepare a Cost of Goods Sold statement: Merchandise Inventory, Jan. 1, 1973, $62,000; Merchandise Inventory, Dec. 31, 1973, $84,000; Purchases during the year (net), $120,000.

SOLUTION

Cost of Goods Sold		
Inventory, Jan. 1, 1973	$ 62,000	
Purchases (net)	120,000	
Goods Available for Sale	$182,000	
Less: Inventory, Dec. 31, 1973	84,000	
Cost of Goods Sold		$98,000

11.2. In addition to the data of Problem 11.1 we are given:

Purchases	$132,000
Purchase Returns	12,000
Sales Income	146,000
Sales Returns	9,000

What is the gross profit (before expenses) of the firm?

SOLUTION

Sales Income	$146,000	
Less: Sales Returns	9,000	
Net Sales		$137,000
Cost of Goods Sold		
Inventory, Jan. 1, 1973	62,000	
Purchases	$132,000	
Less: Purchase Returns	12,000	
Net Purchases	$120,000	
Goods Available for Sale	$182,000	
Inventory, Dec. 31, 1973	84,000	
Cost of Goods Sold		$ 98,000
Gross Profit		$ 39,000

11.3. On the basis of the inventory data below, journalize the merchandise entries.

Inventory, Jan. 1, 1973	$62,000
Inventory, Dec. 31, 1973	84,000

SOLUTION

Expense and Income Summary	62,000	
Merchandise Inventory		62,000
Merchandise Inventory	84,000	
Expense and Income Summary		84,000

11.4. The inventory information of product A is given below.

Jan. 1	Inventory	12 units	$15.00
Feb. 16	Purchase	8 units	16.00
Mar. 4	Purchase	15 units	18.00
Oct. 15	Purchase	10 units	20.00

After taking a physical count, we discover 14 units on hand. Determine the inventory cost by (a) First-In-First-Out, (b) Last-In-First-Out, (c) Weighted Average.

SOLUTION

(a) Most recent purchase (Oct. 15):   10 units @ $20 = $200

   Next most recent (Mar. 4):   4 units @ 18 = 72

                    Total units   14   Total cost $272

(b) Earliest cost (Inv.):   12 units @ $15 = $180

   Next earliest (Feb. 16):   2 units @ 16 = 32

                    Total units   14   Total cost $212

(c) Jan. 1:   12 units @ $15 = $180

   Feb. 16:   8 units @ 16 = 128

   Oct. 15:   15 units @ 18 = 270

                         10 units @ 20 = 200

                         45 units $778

The weighted average cost per unit is thus $778 ÷ 45 = $17.28, so that the total cost of the 14 units on hand is $17.28 × 14 = $241.92.

11.5. Based upon the data below, determine the value of the inventory at the lower of cost or market by completing the table.

Item	Inventory	Unit Cost	Market Value
A	100	$1.00	$1.50
B	150	4.00	4.50
C	200	6.00	5.00
D	250	8.00	7.00

Item	Inventory	Basis	Lower of Cost or Market
A	100		
B	150		
C	200		
D	250		

Value of Inventory

SOLUTION

Item	Inventory	Basis	Lower of Cost or Market
A	100	$1.00	$ 100
B	150	4.00	600
C	200	5.00	1,000
D	250	7.00	1,750

Value of Inventory $3,450

11.6. Given the accounts below, prepare the income statement for the Blasberg Company as of December 31, 1973.

Sales	$86,400
Sales Returns	1,200
Purchases	59,700
Purchase Returns	650
Sales Salaries	14,700
Advertising Expense	2,100
Depreciation Expense, Delivery Equipment	900
Store Supplies Expense	650
Insurance Expense	3,200
Miscellaneous Selling Expense	590
Tax Expense	2,440
Office Supplies Expense	750
Inventory, January 1, 1973	36,240
Inventory, December 31, 1973	41,630

Blasberg Company		
Income Statement		
for the period ending December 31, 1973		
Sales Income		
Cost of Goods Sold		
Gross Profit		
Operating Expenses		
Selling Expenses		
General Expenses		

SOLUTION

Blasberg Company		
Income Statement		
for the period ending December 31, 1973		
Sales Income	*$86,400*	
Sales Returns	*1,200*	
Net Sales		*$85,200*
Cost of Goods Sold		
Merchandise Inventory, January 1	*$36,240*	
Purchases	*$59,700*	
Purchase Returns	*650*	*59,050*
Goods Available for Sale		*$95,290*
Merchandise Inventory, December 31		*41,630*
Cost of Goods Sold		*53,660*
Gross Profit		*$31,540*
Operating Expenses		
Selling Expenses		
Sales Salaries	*$14,700*	
Advertising Expense	*2,100*	
Depreciation Expense, Delivery Equipment	*900*	
Store Supplies Expense	*650*	
Insurance Expense	*3,200*	
Miscellaneous Selling Expense	*590*	
Total Selling Expenses		*$22,140*
General Expenses		
Tax Expense	*$ 2,440*	
Office Supplies Expense	*750*	
Total Grand Expenses		*3,190*
Total Operating Expenses		*25,330*
Net Profit		*$ 6,210*

11.7. Prepare the annual income statement as of July 31, 1973, using only the accounts that are needed:

Sales	$225,000
Sales Returns	12,600
Inventory, August 1, 1972	16,400
Inventory, July 31, 1973	19,200
Accounts Receivable	6,800
Allowance for Uncollectible Accounts	2,400
Uncollectible Accounts Expense	700
Purchases	106,400
Purchase Returns	8,200
Depreciation Expense, Office Equipment	1,600
Accumulated Depreciation	24,000
Equipment, Office	44,000
Advertising Expense	3,800
Office Salaries	9,200
Salesmen's Salaries	15,600
Rent Expense, Office	4,400
Miscellaneous Expense	1,600
Prepaid Rent	450

SOLUTION

Sales Income		$225,000	
Sales Returns		12,600	
Net Sales			$212,400
Cost of Goods Sold			
Inventory, August 1, 1972		$ 16,400	
Purchases	$106,400		
Purchase Returns	8,200		
Net Purchases		98,200	
Goods Available for Sale		$114,600	
Inventory, July 31, 1973		19,200	
Cost of Goods Sold			95,400
Gross Profit			$117,000
Operating Expenses			
Selling Expenses			
Uncollectible Accounts Expense	$ 700		
Advertising Expense	3,800		
Salesmen's Salaries	15,600		
Miscellaneous Selling Expense	1,600		
Total Selling Expenses		$ 21,700	
General Expenses			
Depreciation Expense, Office Equipment	$ 1,600		
Office Salaries	9,200		
Rent Expense, Office	4,400		
Total General Expenses		15,200	
Total Expenses			36,900
Net Profit			$ 80,100

11.8. From the trial balance of the J. C. Company prepare an eight-column worksheet.

J. C. Company
Trial Balance
June 30, 197–

	Debit	Credit
Cash	$12,300	
Accounts Receivable	16,000	
Merchandise Inventory	2,700	
Supplies	450	
Prepaid Insurance	500	
Accounts Payable		$ 3,200
Notes Payable		7,100
J. C., Capital		14,750
Sales Income		39,800
Purchases	17,200	
Salaries Expense	11,400	
Advertising Expense	2,300	
General Expense	2,000	
	$64,850	$64,850

Use the following data for adjustments: (*a*) Merchandise Inventory, June 30, $1,900; (*b*) Supplies on Hand, $150; (*c*) Expired Insurance, $200.

J. C. Company
Worksheet
June 30, 197–

Account Title	Trial Balance		Adjustments		Income Statement		Balance Sheet	
	Dr.	Cr.	Dr.	Cr.	Dr.	Cr.	Dr.	Cr.
Cash	12,300							
Acct. Rec.	16,000							
Merch. Inv.	2,700							
Supplies	450							
Prepaid Ins.	500							
Acct. Pay.		3,200						
Notes Pay.		7,100						
J. C., Capital		14,750						
Sales Income		39,800						
Purchases	17,200							
Salaries Exp.	11,400							
Adv. Exp.	2,300							
Gen. Exp.	2,000							
	64,850	64,850						
Exp. & Inc. Sum.								
Supplies Exp.								
Ins. Exp.								
Net Income								

SOLUTION

J. C. Company
Worksheet
June 30, 197—

Account Title	Trial Balance		Adjustments		Income Statement		Balance Sheet	
	Dr.	Cr.	Dr.	Cr.	Dr.	Cr.	Dr.	Cr.
Cash	12,300						12,300	
Acct. Rec.	16,000						16,000	
Merch. Inv.	2,700		(a) 1,900	(a) 2,700			1,900	
Supplies	450			(b) 300			150	
Prepaid Ins.	500			(c) 200			300	
Acct. Pay.		3,200						3,200
Notes Pay.		7,100						7,100
J. C., Capital		14,750						14,750
Sales Income		39,800				39,800		
Purchases	17,200				17,200			
Salaries Exp.	11,400				11,400			
Adv. Exp.	2,300				2,300			
Gen. Exp.	2,000				2,000			
	64,850	64,850						
Exp. & Inc. Sum.			(a) 2,700	(a) 1,900	2,700	1,900		
Supplies Exp.			(b) 300		300			
Ins. Exp.			(c) 200		200			
			5,100	5,100	36,100	41,700	30,650	25,050
Net Income					5,600			5,600
					41,700	41,700	30,650	30,650

11.9. The accounts and their balances in the M. Rothfeld Company ledger on December 31, the end of the current year, are as follows:

Cash	$ 4,600
Accounts Receivable	6,900
Merchandise Inventory	28,300
Supplies	750
Prepaid Rent	1,800
Equipment	16,000
Accumulated Depreciation, Equipment	1,900
Accounts Payable	6,110
M. Rothfeld, Capital	48,200
M. Rothfeld, Drawing	12,900
Sales Income	128,000
Purchases	91,000
Advertising Expense	3,200
Salaries Expense	16,600
Miscellaneous Expense	2,160

Prepare an eight-column worksheet, if the adjustments are:

(a)	Merchandise inventory as of December 31	$33,400
(b)	Supplies on hand	250
(c)	Depreciation for the period	600
(d)	Accrued salaries	1,250

Account Title	Trial Balance Dr.	Trial Balance Cr.	Adjustments Dr.	Adjustments Cr.	Income Statement Dr.	Income Statement Cr.	Balance Sheet Dr.	Balance Sheet Cr.
Cash	4,600							
Acct. Rec.	6,900							
Merch. Inv.	28,300							
Supplies	750							
Prepaid Rent	1,800							
Equipment	16,000							
Accum. Deprec.		1,900						
Accounts Pay.		6,110						
M. Rothfeld, Capital		48,200						
M. Rothfeld, Drawing	12,900							
Sales Income		128,000						
Purchases	91,000							
Adv. Exp.	3,200							
Salaries Exp.	16,600							
Misc. Exp.	2,160							
	184,210	184,210						
Exp. & Inc. Sum.								
Supplies Exp.								
Deprec. Exp.								
Salaries Pay.								
Net Income								

SOLUTION

Account Title	Trial Balance Dr.	Trial Balance Cr.	Adjustments Dr.	Adjustments Cr.	Income Statement Dr.	Income Statement Cr.	Balance Sheet Dr.	Balance Sheet Cr.
Cash	4,600						4,600	
Acct. Rec.	6,900						6,900	
Merch. Inv.	28,300		(a) 33,400	(a) 28,300			33,400	
Supplies	750			(b) 500			250	
Prepaid Rent	1,800						1,800	
Equipment	16,000						16,000	
Accum. Deprec.		1,900		(c) 600				2,500
Accounts Pay.		6,110						6,110
M. Rothfeld, Capital		48,200						48,200
M. Rothfeld, Drawing	12,900						12,900	
Sales Income		128,000				128,000		
Purchases	91,000				91,000			
Adv. Exp.	3,200				3,200			
Salaries Exp.	16,600		(d) 1,250		17,850			
Misc. Exp.	2,160				2,160			
	184,210	184,210						
Exp. & Inc. Sum.			(a) 28,300	(a) 33,400	28,300	33,400		
Supplies Exp.			(b) 500		500			
Deprec. Exp.			(c) 600		600			
Salaries Pay.				(d) 1,250				1,250
			64,050	64,050	143,610	161,400	75,850	58,060
Net Income					17,790			17,790
					161,400	161,400	75,850	75,850

11.10. Based on the data in Problem 11.9, prepare:

    (*a*)   an income statement

    (*b*)   a capital statement

    (*c*)   a balance sheet

INCOME STATEMENT

CAPITAL STATEMENT

BALANCE SHEET

SOLUTION

INCOME STATEMENT

Sales Income		$128,000
Cost of Goods Sold		
Merchandise Inventory, January 1, 197–	$ 28,300	
Purchases	91,000	
Goods Available for Sale	119,300	
Merchandise Inventory, December 31, 197–	33,400	
Cost of Goods Sold		85,900
Gross Profit		$ 42,100
Expenses		
Advertising Expense	$ 3,200	
Salaries Expense	17,850	
Supplies Expense	500	
Depreciation Expense	600	
Miscellaneous Expense	2,160	
Total Expenses		24,310
Net Income		$ 17,790

CAPITAL STATEMENT

Capital, January 1, 197–		$ 48,200
Net Income	$ 17,790	
Drawing	12,900	
Increase in Capital		4,890
Capital, December 31, 197–		$ 53,090

BALANCE SHEET

ASSETS		
Current Assets		
Cash	$ 4,600	
Accounts Receivable	6,900	
Merchandise Inventory	33,400	
Supplies	250	
Prepaid Rent	1,800	
		$ 46,950
Fixed Assets		
Equipment	$ 16,000	
Less: Accumulated Depreciation	2,500	13,500
Total Assets		$ 60,450
LIABILITIES AND CAPITAL		
Current Liabilities		
Accounts Payable	$ 6,110	
Salaries Payable	1,250	
Total Liabilities		$ 7,360
Capital		$ 53,090
Total Liabilities and Capital		$ 60,450

Chapter 12

Property, Plant, and Equipment

12.1 FIXED ASSETS

Tangible assets that are relatively permanent and are needed for the production or sale of goods or services are termed *property, plant, and equipment,* or *fixed assets.* These assets are not held for sale in the ordinary course of business. The broad group is usually separated into classes according to the physical characteristics of the items (e.g. land, buildings, machinery and equipment, furniture and fixtures).

The cost of property, plant, and equipment includes all expenditures necessary to put the asset into position and ready for use.

EXAMPLE 1.

For a lathe purchased by AB Optical Company, the data were: invoice price, $11,000; cash discount, $220; freight-in, $300; trucking, $200; electrical connections and installation, $720. The total cost is $11,000 − 220 + 300 + 200 + 720 = $12,000. Therefore, the entry is:

$$Machinery\ and\ Equipment \qquad 12,000$$
$$Cash \qquad\qquad\qquad\qquad\qquad 12,000$$

12.2 DEPRECIATION AND SCRAP VALUE

Though it may be long, the useful life of a fixed asset is limited. Eventually the asset will lose all productive worth and will possess only salvage value (scrap value). The accrual basis of accounting demands a period-by-period matching of costs against derived revenues. Hence, the cost of a fixed asset (over and above its scrap value) is distributed over its entire estimated lifetime. This spreading of the cost over the periods which receive benefits is known as *depreciation.*

Depreciation decreases the fixed asset's book value and also decreases capital. Depreciation is considered an operating expense of the business. It may be recorded by an entry at the end of each month or at the end of the year, usually depending on the frequency of preparing financial statements. Fixed assets are recorded at cost and remain at that figure as long as they are held. The depreciation taken to date is shown as a credit in the offset account Accumulated Depreciation (Sec. 6.2), and is deducted from the asset account on the balance sheet, as shown in Example 2 below.

EXAMPLE 2.

Equipment	10,000	
Less: Accumulated Depreciation	4,000	6,000

The book value of the equipment has gone from $10,000 to $6,000.

There is one exception to the above considerations: land. This fixed asset is non-depreciable; it is usually carried on the books permanently at cost.

12.3 METHODS OF DEPRECIATION

The depreciable amount of a fixed asset — that is, cost minus scrap value — may be written off in different ways. For example, the amount may be spread evenly over the years affected, as in the straight-line method. Two accelerated methods, the double declining balance method and the sum-of-the-years'-digits method, provide for larger amounts of depreciation in the earlier years. The view is that the total cost of depreciation and repairs should be about the same each year. The units of output method bases depreciation each period on the amount of output.

STRAIGHT-LINE METHOD

This is the simplest and most widely used depreciation method. Under this method an equal portion of the cost of the asset is allocated to each period of use. The periodic charge is expressed as:

$$\frac{\text{COST} - \text{SCRAP VALUE}}{\text{USEFUL LIFE (IN YEARS)}} = \text{ANNUAL DEPRECIATION CHARGE}$$

EXAMPLE 3.

Cost of machine, $12,000; scrap value, $2,000; estimated life, 5 years.

$$\frac{\$12,000 - \$2,000}{5} = \$2,000 \text{ per year}$$

The entry to record the depreciation would be:

Depreciation Expense, Machinery	2,000	
Accumulated Depreciation, Machinery		2,000

SUM-OF-THE-YEARS'-DIGITS METHOD

The years of the asset's lifetime are labeled 1, 2, 3, etc., and the depreciation amounts are based on a series of fractions having the sum of the years' digits as the common denominator. The largest digit is used as the numerator for the first year, the next largest digit for the second year, and so forth.

EXAMPLE 4.

Cost of machine, $12,000; scrap value, $2,000; estimated life, 5 years.

The depreciable amount is $12,000 - 2,000 = \$10,000$. To find the fraction of this amount to be written off each year, proceed as follows:

(1)   Label the years 1, 2, 3, 4, and 5.

(2)   Calculate the sum of the years' digits: $S = 1 + 2 + 3 + 4 + 5 = 15$.

(3)   Convert the sum to a sum of fractions: $\frac{1}{15} + \frac{2}{15} + \frac{3}{15} + \frac{4}{15} + \frac{5}{15} = 1$.

(4)   Take the above series of fractions *in reverse order* as the depreciation rates. Thus:

Year	Fraction		Amount		Depreciation
1	5/15	×	$10,000	=	$ 3,333
2	4/15	×	$10,000	=	$ 2,667
3	3/15	×	$10,000	=	$ 2,000
4	2/15	×	$10,000	=	$ 1,333
5	1/15	×	$10,000	=	$ 667
				Total depreciation	$10,000

For a lifetime of N years, it is simplest to use the formula

$$S = 1 + 2 + 3 + \cdots + N = \frac{N(N+1)}{2}$$

in Step (2) above.

DOUBLE DECLINING BALANCE METHOD

The double declining balance method produces the highest amount of depreciation in the earlier years. *It does not recognize scrap value.* Instead, the book value of the asset remaining at the end of the depreciation period becomes the scrap value. Many companies prefer the double declining balance method because of the faster write-off in the earlier years when the asset contributes most to the business and when the expenditure was actually made. The procedure is to apply a *fixed rate* to the declining book value of the asset each year. As the book value declines, the depreciation becomes smaller.

EXAMPLE 5.

A $12,000 asset is to be depreciated over 5 years, the double declining balance rate being 40% per year.

Year	Book Value at Beginning of Year	Rate	Depreciation for Year	Book Value at End of Year
1	$12,000	40%	$4,800	$7,200
2	7,200	40%	2,880	4,320
3	4,320	40%	1,728	2,592
4	2,592	40%	1,037	1,555
5	1,555	40%	622	933

The $933 book value at the end of the fifth year becomes the scrap value.

UNITS OF OUTPUT METHOD

Where the use of equipment varies substantially from year to year, the units of output method is appropriate. For example, in some years logging operations can be carried on for 200 days, in other years for 230 days, in still other years only for 160 days, depending on weather conditions. Under this method depreciation is computed for the appropriate unit of output or production (such as hours, miles, or pounds) by the following formula:

$$\frac{\text{COST} - \text{SALVAGE VALUE}}{\text{ESTIMATED UNITS OF OUTPUT DURING LIFETIME}} = \text{UNIT DEPRECIATION}$$

The total number of units for each year is then multiplied by the unit depreciation to arrive at the depreciation amount for that year.

This method has the advantage of relating more directly the depreciation cost to revenue.

EXAMPLE 6.

Cost of machine, $12,000; scrap value, $2,000; estimated life, 8,000 hours $\left(5 \text{ years} \times 200 \frac{\text{days}}{\text{year}} \times 8 \frac{\text{hours}}{\text{day}}\right)$.

$$\frac{\$12,000 - \$2,000}{8,000} = \$1.25 \text{ depreciation per hour}$$

If during the year in question the machine was operated for 1,800 hours, the depreciation would be:

$$1,800 \text{ hours} \times \$1.25 \text{ per hour} = \$2,250$$

The four principal methods of depreciation are compared in Table 12-1 below. It is assumed that over a five-year lifetime the asset was in operation for the following numbers of hours: 1,800, 1,200, 2,000, 1,400, 1,600. Cost of asset, $12,000; scrap value, $2,000.

Table 12-1. Annual Depreciation Charge

Year	Straight-Line	Sum-of-the-Years'-Digits	Double Declining Balance	Units of Output
1	$2,000	$3,333	$4,800	$2,250
2	2,000	2,667	2,880	1,500
3	2,000	2,000	1,728	2,500
4	2,000	1,333	1,037	1,750
5	2,000	667	622	2,000

12.4 DISPOSING OF FIXED ASSETS

BY DISCARDING OF THE ASSET

When plant assets are no longer needed (and usually are fully depreciated), they may be arbitrarily sold for scrap.

EXAMPLE 7.

An item of equipment bought for $15,000 is fully depreciated at the close of the preceding year and is now deemed to be worthless. The entry to record the disposal of the asset is:

Accumulated Depreciation	15,000	
Equipment		15,000

If the asset has book value (has not been fully depreciated), entries are made (1) to bring the depreciation up to the date of disposal, (2) to record the gain or loss on disposal.

EXAMPLE 8.

A $15,000 asset with accumulated depreciation of $12,600 had been depreciated at the annual rate of 10%. If we decide to discard the asset on April 30, an adjusting entry is needed to record the depreciation for the period January 1–April 30 (4 months), since no entry to record the expense has been made. Therefore, one-third of the annual depreciation of $1,500 ($15,000 × 10%) must be recorded.

Entry 1	*Depreciation Expense*	500	
	Accumulated Depreciation		500

This entry is necessary to bring the accumulated depreciation up to date of disposal. The entry to record the disposal of the asset would be:

Entry 2	*Accumulated Depreciation*	13,100	
	Loss on Disposal of Fixed Asset	1,900	
	Equipment		15,000

The $1,900 loss ($15,000 − $13,100) would appear as a nonoperating item under the heading "Other Expense" in the income statement.

BY SALE OF THE ASSET

Assets that are no longer useful to a business may be sold. The sale requires entries (1) to bring the depreciation (and hence the book value) up to date, (2) to record the sale at either a gain (if the selling price exceeds the updated book value) or a loss (if the selling price is below the updated book value).

EXAMPLE 9.

A $15,000 asset with accumulated depreciation of $12,600 as of December 31, and an estimated life of 10 years, is sold on the following April 30 for $2,300.

Entry 1	*Depreciation Expense*	500*	
	Accumulated Depreciation		500
	1/3 × $1,500		

Entry 2	*Cash*	2,300	
	Accumulated Depreciation	13,100	
	Equipment		15,000
	Gain on Sale of Fixed Asset		400
	Sale of equipment		

Proof of Gain	*Sale of Equipment*	$2,300	
	Book Value	1,900	(15,000 − 13,100)
	Gain on Disposal of Fixed Asset	$ 400	

Gain on disposal of a fixed asset would be treated as nonoperating income in the income statement, under the heading "Other Income."

BY TRADE-IN WITH RECOGNITION OF GAIN OR LOSS

Old equipment may be traded in for new equipment. The trade-in allowance is deducted from the price of the new equipment and the balance is paid in accordance with the agreement. If the allowance is greater than the carrying value of the asset, a gain results; conversely, a loss is recognized if the allowance is less than the carrying value.

Again entries are required (1) to bring the depreciation up to date, (2) to record the trade-in.

EXAMPLE 10.

DATA:	Cost of equipment	$15,000
	Accumulated depreciation as of	
	December 31, previous year	12,600
	Depreciation for the current year	500
	Book value at date of exchange	1,900
	Price of new equipment	20,000
	Trade-in allowance	2,500
	Cash to be paid	17,500

Entry 1	*Depreciation Expense*	500	
	Accumulated Depreciation		500

Entry 2	*Accumulated Depreciation*	13,100*	
	Equipment (new)	20,000	
	Equipment (old)		15,000
	Cash		17,500
	Gain on Disposal of Fixed Asset		600
	* $12,600 + $500		

Proof of Gain	Trade-In	$2,500
	Book Value	1,900
	Gain	$ 600

BY TRADE-IN WITHOUT RECOGNITION OF GAIN OR LOSS

This method is also called the *tax method*. The entry to bring the depreciation up to date (Entry 1) is the same as in Example 10. However, Entry 2 is different because the new equipment will not be recorded at cost. Rather, the gain (if any) is subtracted from the cost of the new equipment, or the loss (if any) is added to the cost.

EXAMPLE 11.

Using the same data as in Example 10, we have:

Entry 1	Depreciation Expense	500	
	Accumulated Depreciation		500
Entry 2	Accumulated Depreciation	13,100	
	Equipment (new)	19,400**	
	Equipment (old)		15,000
	Cash		17,500
Proof of Gain	Trade-In	$2,500	
	Less: Book Value	1,900	
	Gain	$ 600	

The unrecognized gain at the time of the exchange will be matched later on by a reduction of the carrying value of the equipment:

**Cost	$20,000
Gain on Disposal	600
New Equipment	$19,400

Summary

(1)   The main reason for depreciation is _____.

(2)   Accumulated Depreciation is an example of an _____ account, since the fixed asset remains at cost while the offset builds up.

(3)   The market value of a fixed asset at the end of its service is known as _____.

(4)   The uniform distribution of depreciation over the life of the asset is known as the _____ method.

(5)   The _____ method is used to write off the asset based upon a series of fractions.

(6)   The method that produces the largest amount of depreciation in the earlier years, then rapidly declines, is known as the _____ method.

(7)   Loss on disposal of fixed assets is _____ in a journal entry.

(8)   Gain on disposal of fixed assets appears on the income statement as _____ and is added to Net Income.

(9) A new machine costing $24,000, with a gain on trade-in of $2,000, will be recorded at $ _____ .

Answers: (1) aging; (2) offset or valuation; (3) scrap value; (4) straight-line; (5) sum-of-the-years'-digits; (6) double declining balance; (7) debited; (8) Other Income; (9) 22,000

Solved Problems

12.1. Hacol Company acquired an asset on January 1, 197–, at a cost of $38,000, with an estimated useful life of 8 years and a salvage value of $2,000. What is the annual depreciation based upon the straight-line method?

SOLUTION

Cost	$38,000
Scrap value	2,000
Amount to be depreciated	$36,000

$36,000 ÷ 8 years = $4,500 depreciation per year

12.2. For the asset of Problem 12.1, compute the depreciation for the first two years by the sum-of-the-years'-digits method.

SOLUTION

$$S = 8\left(\frac{8+1}{2}\right) = 36$$

Year 1: $\frac{8}{36} \times \$36,000 = \$8,000$

Year 2: $\frac{7}{36} \times \$36,000 = \$7,000$

12.3. Repeat Problem 12.2, but using the double declining balance method.

SOLUTION

For the depreciation rate we take twice the straight-line rate; i.e.,

$$2 \times \frac{100\%}{8 \text{ years}} = 25\% \text{ per year}$$

Therefore,

Year 1: $38,000 × 25% = $9,500

Year 2:   ($38,000 − $9,500) × 25% = $7,125

12.4. A truck was purchased on January 1, 1972, for $8,500, with an estimated scrap value of $500. It will be depreciated for 8 years using the straight-line method. Show how the truck account and the related accumulated depreciation account would appear on the balance sheet on (*a*) December 31, 1972; (*b*) December 31, 1973.

(*a*)

(*b*)

SOLUTION

(a)

Truck	$8,500			
Less: Accumulated Depreciation	1,000*	$7,500		

(b)

Truck	$8,500			
Less: Accumulated Depreciation	2,000*	$6,500		

$$* \frac{\$8,500 - \$500}{8 \ years} = \$1,000 \ per \ year$$

12.5. What amount will appear in the income statement for Depreciation Expense, Truck (a) on December 31, 1972?   (b) on December 31, 1973?

SOLUTION

(a) $1,000   (1 year's depreciation)

(b) $1,000   (1 year's depreciation)

12.6. Equipment costing $9,600, with an estimated scrap value of $1,600, was bought on July 1, 1972.   The equipment is to be depreciated by the straight-line method for a period of 10 years.   The company's fiscal year is January through December.   Show how the equipment account and the related accumulated depreciation account would appear in the balance sheet on (a) December 31, 1972; (b) December 31, 1973.

(a)

(b)

SOLUTION

(a)

Equipment	$9,600			
Less: Accumulated Depreciation	400*	$9,200		

$$* \frac{\$9,600 - \$1,600}{10 \ years} = \$800 \ depreciation \ per \ year$$

$\frac{1}{2}$ year (July 1 to Dec. 31) $\times$ $800 per year $=$ $400

(b)

Equipment	$9,600			
Less: Accumulated Depreciation	1,200*	$8,400		

* $1\frac{1}{2}$ year $\times$ $800 per year $=$ $1,200

12.7. What amount will appear in the income statement for Depreciation Expense, Equipment (Problem 12.6) (a) on December 31, 1972? (b) on December 31, 1973?

SOLUTION

(a) $400 ($\frac{1}{2}$ year's depreciation)   (b) $800 (1 year's depreciation)

12.8. As of December 31, 197–, accumulated depreciation of $9,000 has been recorded on equipment which originally cost $14,000. What is the entry to record the disposal of the asset if the equipment was discarded with no salvage value?

SOLUTION

Accumulated Depreciation, Equipment	9,000	
Loss on Disposal of Fixed Asset	5,000	
Equipment		14,000

The book value of $5,000 is considered a loss because there is no salvage value.

12.9. For Problem 12.8, what entry would be recorded if the equipment were sold for $6,000?

SOLUTION

Accumulated Depreciation, Equipment	9,000	
Cash	6,000	
Equipment		14,000
Gain on Disposal of Fixed Asset		1,000*

* Cost	$14,000	Cash Sale	$6,000
Accumulated Depreciation	9,000	Book Value	5,000
Book Value	$ 5,000	Gain	$1,000

12.10. S. Altman Company traded in a cutting machine for a new one priced at $2,600, receiving a trade-in allowance of $600 and paying the balance in cash. The old machine cost $1,800 and had an accumulated depreciation of $1,400. What is the entry to record the acquisition of the new machine if gain or loss is to be recognized?

SOLUTION

Accumulated Depreciation, Machine	1,400	
Machine (new)	2,600	
Machine (old)		1,800
Cash		2,000
Gain on Disposal of Fixed Asset		200*

* Cost of Old Machine	$1,800	Cash Sale	$600
Accumulated Depreciation	1,400	Book Value	400
Book Value	$ 400	Gain	$200

12.11. What would be the entry in Problem 12.10 if gain or loss were not recognized?

SOLUTION

Accumulated Depreciation, Machine	1,400	
Machine (new)	2,400*	
Machine (old)		1,800
Cash		2,000

* Price of New Machine   \$2,600
Less: Unrecognized Gain   200
Cost of New Machine   \$2,400

12.12. A fixed asset costing \$60,000, with an estimated salvage value of \$5,000, has a life expectancy of 10 years. Compare the results of the various depreciation methods by filling in the tables below. Take twice the straight-line rate as the rate in the double declining balance method.

STRAIGHT-LINE METHOD

Year	Depreciation Expense	Accumulated Depreciation	Book Value at End of Year
1			
2			
3			
4			

SUM-OF-THE-YEARS'-DIGITS METHOD

Year	Depreciation Expense	Accumulated Depreciation	Book Value at End of Year
1			
2			
3			
4			

DOUBLE DECLINING BALANCE METHOD

Year	Depreciation Expense	Accumulated Depreciation	Book Value at End of Year
1			
2			
3			
4			

SOLUTION

STRAIGHT-LINE METHOD

Year	Depreciation Expense	Accumulated Depreciation	Book Value at End of Year
1	\$5,500*	\$ 5,500	\$54,500**
2	5,500	11,000	49,000
3	5,500	16,500	43,500
4	5,500	22,000	38,000

* (60,000 − 5,000) ÷ 10 = 5,500   ** 60,000 − 5,500 = 54,500

SUM-OF-THE-YEARS'-DIGITS METHOD

Year	Depreciation Expense	Accumulated Depreciation	Book Value at End of Year
1	$10,000*	$10,000	$50,000
2	9,000	19,000	41,000
3	8,000	27,000	33,000
4	7,000	34,000	26,000

$$*S = \frac{10(10+1)}{2} = 55$$

$$\frac{10}{55} \times 55,000 = 10,000$$

DOUBLE DECLINING BALANCE METHOD

Year	Depreciation Expense	Accumulated Depreciation	Book Value at End of Year
1	$12,000*	$12,000	$48,000
2	9,600**	21,600	38,400
3	7,680	29,280	30,720
4	6,144	35,424	24,576

$* (2 \times 10\%) \times 60,000 = 12,000$

$** 20\% \times (60,000 - 12,000) = 9,600$

12.13. The four transactions below were selected from the ledger of J. B. Adam regarding the disposal of some of his fixed assets. Depreciation is considered to be recorded only at the end of the prior year. Present journal entries for each transaction. (*Note*: If an item is disposed of before the 15th, do not count the month.)

(*a*) March 3: Discarded four typewriters, realizing no scrap value. Total cost, $3,000; accumulated depreciation as of Dec. 31, $2,000; annual depreciation, $360.

(*b*) March 29: Sold office furniture for cash, $1,600. Total cost, $8,000; accumulated depreciation through Dec. 31, $6,800; annual depreciation, $600.

(*c*) May 2: Traded in an old automobile for a new one priced at $4,000, receiving a trade-in allowance of $1,400 and paying the balance in cash. Data on the old automobile:

Cost	$3,900
Accumulated Depreciation	2,700
Annual Depreciation	960

Gain or loss to be recognized.

(*d*) May 5: Traded in dictating equipment costing $1,000, with $800 accumulated depreciation as of Dec. 31. The annual depreciation is $240. We received a trade-in allowance of $100, paying the balance in cash for a new dictating unit at $1,400. Gain or loss not to be recognized.

(*a*) **(1)**

(2)

(b) **(1)**

     (2)

(c) **(1)**

     (2)

(d) **(1)**

     (2)

SOLUTION

(a) **(1)** Depreciation Expense   60
              Accumulated Depreciation   60
              [2 months × $30 per month = $60]
     (2) Accumulated Depreciation   2,060
              Loss on Disposal of Fixed Assets   940
                  Typewriters   3,000

(b) **(1)** Depreciation Expense   150
              Accumulated Depreciation   150
              [3 months × $50 per month = $150]
     (2) Accumulated Depreciation   6,950
              Cash   1,600
                  Office Equipment   8,000
                  Gain on Disposal of Fixed Assets   550

(c) **(1)** Depreciation Expense   320
              Accumulated Depreciation   320
              [4 months × $80 per month = $320]

(cont. next page)

(2)	Accumulated Depreciation		3,020	
	Automobile (new)		4,000	
	Cash			2,600
	Automobile (old)			3,900
	Gain on Disposal of Fixed Asset			520*
	* Trade-In	$1,400		
	Gain	880		
	Book Value	$ 520		

(d)

(1)	Depreciation Expense		80	
	Accumulated Depreciation			80
	[4 months × $20 per month = $80]			
(2)	Equipment (new)		1,420**	
	Accumulated Depreciation		880	
	Equipment (old)			1,000
	Cash			1,300
	** Book Value	$120　(1000 − 880)		
	Trade-In	100		
	Loss (to be added			
	to fixed asset)	$ 20		

Examination III

Chapters 8-12

1. Define (a) revenue, (b) net income, (c) expenses.

2. What is a contingent liability? Give an example of one.

3. Contrast the periodic and perpetual methods of inventory calculation.

4. For the week ending May 31, the total amount of earnings was $20,000. Of that amount, earnings subject to FICA was $15,000. The amount subject to unemployment compensation tax was $8,000. Present the general journal entry to record the employer's payroll tax for the week, assuming the following rates: FICA, 5%; State Unemployment, 2%; Federal Unemployment, 0.4%.

5. Below is the payroll information for three of the employees of the Ernst Company.

Employee	Amount Earned to Date	Gross Pay for Week
A	$2,500	$100
B	$2,800	$250
C	$5,000	$200

The company is located in a state that imposes an unemployment insurance tax of 2% on the first $3,000. Federal unemployment tax is 0.4%; FICA tax, 5%. Present the journal entry necessary to record the employer's payroll tax expenses.

6. Transactions for the Blaky Company for the month of January, pertaining to the establishment of a petty cash fund, were as follows.

> January 1: Established an imprest petty cash fund for $75
>
> January 31: Examination of the petty cash box showed: Office Supplies, $10; Transportation, $20; Freight, $15; Charity, $6; Miscellaneous Expense, $15

What are the journal entries necessary to record the petty cash information?

7. A 60-day, 6%, $3,000 note receivable in settlement of an account, dated June 1, is discounted at 6% on July 1. What are the entries needed to record the information (a) on June 1? (b) on July 1?

8.

Accounts Receivable		Sales	
100,000			400,000

Allowance for Uncollectible Accounts	
	300

For the balances given above, what is the adjusting entry to record the provision for uncollectible accounts, if the uncollectible expense is estimated as:

(a) 1% of sales?

(b) $3,600, by the balance sheet method?

9. (a) The following information was taken from selected accounts of the Agin Supply Company. What is the gross profit (before expenses) of the firm?

Merchandise Inventory, July 1, 1972 $ 38,000
Merchandise Inventory, June 30, 1973   46,000
Purchases   133,000
Purchase Returns   9,000
Sales Income   178,000
Sales Returns   6,000

(b) Present the entries necessary to adjust the inventory accounts.

10. Determine the value of the inventory at the lower of cost or market, by completing the second table below.

Item	Inventory	Unit Cost	Market Value
A	200	$ 6.00	$ 8.50
B	150	4.25	4.00
C	300	3.50	3.80
D	1,000	12.00	14.00

Item	Inventory	Basis	Total Value
A	200		
B	150		
C	300		
D	1,000		

11. Journalize the necessary adjusting entries as of July 31, the close of the current fiscal year.

(a) Merchandise Inventory, August 1 $58,200
Merchandise Inventory, July 31 $70,400

(b) Prepaid Insurance has a balance of $1,800 before adjustments. Analysis of the policies indicates that 1/3 of the amount has expired.

(c) The physical inventory of supplies shows that of the beginning balance of $640, only $60 remains.

12. The merchandise inventory in June 197– of the Altwong Company consisted of 200 units with a unit price of $1.50. Purchases during the period were:

Date	Quantity	Unit Cost
July	300	$2.00
October	400	3.00
November	200	4.00
December	100	5.00

At the end of the year, 300 units were on hand. Compute the ending inventory under (a) FIFO, (b) LIFO, (c) weighted average.

13. Based upon the information below, prepare an income statement.

Inventory, September 1 $ 48,000
Inventory, August 31   28,000
Purchases during the year   126,000
Sales Income   182,000
Salaries Expense   29,000
Rent Expense   12,000
General Expense   3,000

14. Jeffrey Steinberg Company acquired an asset on January 1, 197–, at a cost of $28,000, with an estimated useful life of 10 years and a salvage value of $500. Find the annual depreciation for the first two years, using the (a) straight-line method, (b) sum-of-the-years'-digits method, (c) double declining balance method.

15. As of December 31, 197–, accumulated depreciation of $10,000 has been recorded on equipment which originally cost $15,000. What is the entry to record the disposal of the assets (a) if the equipment was discarded and no funds received for it? (b) if it was sold for $8,000?

16. Saltman Company traded in an electric motor for a new one priced at $5,200, receiving a trade-in allowance of $800 and paying the balance in cash. For the old motor the cost and accumulated depreciation were $3,800 and $3,400 respectively. What is the entry needed to record the acquisition, (a) if gain or loss is to be recognized? (b) if gain or loss is not to be recognized?

Answers to Examination III

1. (a) Revenue is the inflow of resources resulting from delivery of goods or services in the effort to produce a profit.
   (b) Net income is the excess of the earned inflow of resources over the consumption of resources used in earning that inflow. Thus it is gross sales, less sales reductions and all expenses incurred in earning the sales.
   (c) Expenses are the consumption of resources in the effort to produce income. Every expense must be matched with the revenue to which it relates.

2. A contingent liability is a potential liability. Whether or not it will actually be incurred depends on future events. An example is the liability that may arise from the discounting of a note receivable.

3. All units are lumped together under the periodic method. Inventory is physically counted at the end of the period and credits are then made to the inventory account in total. On the other hand, the perpetual method calls for a separate, running record for each unit.

4.
Payroll Tax Expense	942	
FICA Taxes Payable		750
State Unemployment Insurance Payable		160
Federal Unemployment Insurance Payable		32

5.
Payroll Tax Expense	34.70	
FICA Taxes Payable		27.50
State Unemployment Insurance Payable		6.00
Federal Unemployment Insurance Payable		1.20

The calculations are as follows:

Employee	FICA	State	Federal
A	$ 5.00 (5% × $100)	$2.00 (2% × $100)	.40 (.004 × $100)
B	$12.50 (5% × $250)	$4.00 (2% × $200)	.80 (.004 × $200)
C	$10.00 (5% × $200)	—	—
	$27.50	$6.00	$1.20

6.
Petty Cash	75	
Cash		75
Transportation Expense	20	
Freight Expense	15	
Charity Expense	6	
Office Supplies Expense	10	
Miscellaneous Expense	15	
Cash		66

7.
$3,000.00	Principal	
30.00	Interest income	
$3,030.00	Maturity value	
15.15	Discount	
$3,014.85	Net proceeds	

(a)   Notes Receivable   3,000.00

        Accounts Receivable   3,000.00

(b)   Cash   3,014.85

        Interest Income   14.85

        Notes Receivable   3,000.00

8.   (a)   Uncollectible Accounts Expense   4,000

        Allowance for Uncollectible Accounts   4,000

(b)   Uncollectible Accounts Expense   3,300*

        Allowance for Uncollectible Accounts   3,300

* 3,600 − 300 = 3,300; the balance in the allowance account must be taken into consideration

9.   (a)

Sales Income	$178,000	
Sales Returns	6,000	
Net Sales		$172,000
Cost of Goods Sold		
Inventory, July 1, 1972	$ 38,000	
Purchases	$133,000	
Purchase Returns	9,000 124,000	
Goods Available for Sale	$162,000	
Inventory, June 30, 1973	46,000	
Cost of Goods Sold		116,000
Gross Profit		$ 56,000

(b)   Expense and Income Summary   38,000

        Merchandise Inventory   38,000

    Merchandise Inventory   46,000

        Expense and Income Summary   46,000

10.

Item	Inventory	Basis	Total Value
A	200	$ 6.00 (cost)	$ 1,200
B	150	4.00 (market)	600
C	300	3.50 (cost)	1,050
D	1,000	12.00 (cost)	12,000
			$14,850

11.   (a)   Expense and Income Summary   58,200

        Merchandise Inventory   58,200

    Merchandise Inventory   70,400

        Expense and Income Summary   70,400

(b)   Insurance Expense   600

        Prepaid Insurance   600

(c)   Supplies Expense   580

        Supplies   580

12.   (a) $1,300   (b) $500   (c) $849

13.

Sales Income		$182,000
Cost of Goods Sold		
Inventory, September 1	$ 48,000	
Purchases	126,000	
Goods Available for Sale	$174,000	
Inventory, August 31	28,000	
Cost of Goods Sold		146,000
Gross Profit		$ 36,000
Expenses		
Salaries Expense	$ 29,000	
Rent Expense	12,000	
General Expense	3,000	
Total Expenses		44,000
Net Loss		($ 8,000)

14.

	First Year	Second Year
(a)	$2,750	$2,750
(b)	5,000	4,500
(c)	5,600	4,480

15. (a)

Accumulated Depreciation, Equipment	10,000	
Loss on Disposal of Fixed Asset	5,000	
Equipment		15,000

(b)

Accumulated Depreciation, Equipment	10,000	
Cash	8,000	
Equipment		15,000
Gain on Disposal of Fixed Asset		3,000

16. (a)

Accumulated Depreciation	3,400	
Equipment (new)	5,200	
Equipment (old)		3,800
Cash		4,400
Gain on Disposal of Fixed Asset		400*

* Cost	$3,800		Trade-In	$800
Less: Accum. Deprec.	3,400		Less: Value	400
Value	$ 400		Gain	$400

(b)

Accumulated Depreciation	3,400	
Equipment (new)	4,800*	
Equipment (old)		3,800
Cash		4,400

* Price of New Machine	$5,200
Less: Unrecognized Gain	400
New Machine	$4,800

Chapter 13

Investments, Intangibles, Deferred and Other Assets

13.1 INTRODUCTION

The past four chapters have dealt with cash, receivables, and inventory – all current assets, intended to be liquidated in the short run – and property, plant, and equipment – a noncurrent asset. There remain a number of asset items that do not wholly fit into one category or the other. These items, which may or may not be of sufficient dollar value to warrant separate captions on the balance sheet, form the topic of the present chapter.

13.2 INVESTMENTS

By *investments* we mean funds which a company does not put into working capital or tangible assets, but applies in various other ways. The purpose of the investment, rather than the type of security involved, determines whether the investment is short-term, and therefore a current asset, or long-term, and thus a noncurrent asset.

SHORT-TERM INVESTMENTS

Many companies, particularly those in seasonal businesses, have idle cash during certain times of the year, which they can profitably invest in corporate stocks, bonds, or notes, or in government securities. The important thing is that the asset be readily convertible back into cash.

LONG-TERM INVESTMENTS

These generally serve one of the following purposes: (1) to achieve control of another company, (2) to diversify products, (3) to meet contractual requirements. In the case of (1), it is not essential to acquire 50% of the voting stock; a considerable influence over the other company can be presumed if 20% or more of its stock is owned. The motive in (2) is to enable a supplier or subsidiary to bring out additional products, or to diversify the investor's own product line. As regards (3), the terms of an issue of bonds may require that funds be set aside in a special account called a *sinking fund* to pay off the principal or interest. Often these funds may be invested in bonds or stocks of other companies to earn income for the fund. Likewise there are thousands of pension funds, many over a million dollars, which must be maintained in accordance with the terms of the pension plan.

In view of the above purposes, the following assets constitute long-term investments:

- marketable securities which are to be held for long periods
- stocks of, and advances to, subsidiaries or affiliates
- bonds, notes, mortgages, etc., not traded in open markets
- cash surrender value of life insurance
- nonoperating real estate
- bond sinking funds
- other interests held for income or appreciation in value

13.3 ACCOUNTING FOR INVESTMENTS

Investments in stocks, whether short-term or long-term, are recorded at total cost; that is, the cost of the stock plus commissions.

EXAMPLE 1.

On July 1, 1,000 shares of Whyte Metal Company common stock were purchased as an investment at $15\frac{1}{2}$, plus $200 broker's commission. The entry is as follows:

July 1	Whyte Metal Company Stock	15,700	
	Cash		15,700

On October 1, dividends of $1 per share were received and recorded as follows:

October 1	Cash	1,000	
	Dividend Income		1,000

On December 15, the 1,000 shares of Whyte Metal Company stock were sold at $17\frac{1}{2}$, less commission and taxes of $300. The transaction is recorded as follows:

December 15	Cash	17,200	
	Whyte Metal Company Stock		15,700
	Gain on Sale of Investment		1,500

Investments in bonds, like those in stocks, are recorded at total cost. Bonds, however, pay interest, and this interest accrues; whereas stock dividends are earned only as they are declared.

EXAMPLE 2.

On July 1, ten Blacke Metal Company 6%, $1,000 bonds were purchased at $93\frac{1}{2}$, plus commissions of $100 and accrued interest of $150, 10 years before maturity. Interest is payable April 1 and October 1. The entry is as follows:

July 1	Investment in Bonds	9,450	
	Bond Interest Receivable	150	
	Cash		9,600

On October 1, interest of $300 was received and recorded:

October 1	Cash	300	
	Bond Interest Receivable		150
	Bond Interest Income		150

As of December 31, the close of the fiscal year, the interest earned since the last interest received should be recorded. The amount would be $150 for the 3 months ($10,000 × 6% per year × 3/12 year).

December 31	Accrued Bond Interest	150	
	Bond Interest Income		150

Another feature of accounting for bond investments is amortization. When bonds are bought as a long-term investment (and, usually, only then), any discount or premium is treated as an interest adjustment and amortized over the remaining life of the bonds.

EXAMPLE 3.

In Example 2, the ten $1,000 face value, 6%, 10-year bonds were purchased for $9,450, a discount of $550. During each year, then, a portion of the $550 is to be recorded as additional interest. On the straight-line method the additional interest would be $55 per year. Since the bonds were purchased July 1, the prepaid interest would be $27.50.

Investment in Bonds	*27.50*	
Bond Interest Income		*27.50*

As stated in Sec. 14.2, stocks, bonds, etc., when held as short-term investments, appear on the balance sheet under "Current Assets." When held as long-term investments, they appear below the current asset section—either in a classification of their own, "Investments," or under a heading such as "Other Assets."

EXAMPLE 4.

Current Assets

Cash	$15,000
Marketable Securities (market value $13,000)	*12,500*
Accounts Receivable	*3,000*

Investments

Securities	*$20,000*
Real Estate Not Used in Business	*25,000*

Other Assets

Bond Sinking Fund	*$100,000*
Deposit on Lease	*10,000*
Securities Held	*5,000*

13.4 INTANGIBLES

Intangible assets are those which benefit the business through special rights and privileges, as distinguished from the physical characteristics of tangible assets. Intangible assets may be either acquired or developed internally. The following are the principal types:

Patents
Copyrights
Franchises
Leaseholds
Trademarks
Leasehold Improvements
Organization Costs
Goodwill
Research and Development Costs

13.5 ACCOUNTING FOR INTANGIBLES

Significant changes in accounting for intangible assets were specified in APB Opinion 17, the main directives of which are given in the following paragraphs.

Acquired intangibles should be recorded as assets at cost. This includes goodwill acquired in a business combination. If an intangible is acquired for consideration other than cash, then cost is determined by either the market value of the consideration or by the fair market value of the right acquired, whichever is the more evident. It is seen that arbitrary write-offs of intangibles, once the practice, are not allowed under this directive.

Internally developed intangibles which are identifiable should be recorded as assets, those which are not specifically identifiable should be recorded as expenses.

Identifiable intangibles, whether acquired or developed internally, should be recorded at cost, except certain research and development costs and preoperating costs not covered by APB Opinion 17. Examples of intangibles which may be identified are patents, franchises, and trademarks. *Unidentifiable intangibles,* where acquired, should be recorded at cost and shown as assets; where such items are internally developed, they should be recorded as expenses when incurred. The most common unidentifiable intangible is goodwill, representing the excess of cost of an acquired company over the sum of identifiable intangibles. Such intangibles cannot be acquired singly but must be part of a group of assets or an entire enterprise.

All intangible assets should have their cost amortized over a limited service life of at most 40 years. Previous to this directive it was held that certain intangibles had unlimited life and were thus not subject to amortization. Intangibles should be amortized by systematic charges against income over the estimated periods of useful life. They are normally amortized by a debit to expense and a credit directly to the asset account.

Depending on their characteristics, the various intangibles may be shown in the accounts and classified on the balance sheet as current assets, investments, fixed assets, deferred charges, or other assets. The latter two categories will be discussed in the two Sections to follow.

13.6 DEFERRED CHARGES

Prepaid expenses and deferred charges are similar in that they are to be charged to expense in a subsequent period. *However, prepaid expenses are recurring expenses, of short duration, and limited to one or two future periods. Deferred charges are seldom recurring, of longer duration, and are allocated to a number of future periods.* Typical deferred charges are: (1) bond issue costs, (2) organization and reorganization costs, (3) plant rearrangements.

Deferred charges are classified as noncurrent assets on the balance sheet. They usually do not have significant dollar value in relation to total assets and are ordinarily shown as the last asset classification. Sometimes they may be shown as a separate item under Other Assets. Unamortized bond discount is sometimes shown as a deferred charge, but it is preferable to show it as a contra item to the bond liability.

13.7 OTHER ASSETS

This classification includes noncurrent items which cannot reasonably be included under any of the classifications discussed above. The conditions will vary by kind of item and by amount. If the dollar amounts are not large, there may be only one amount for the caption. Generally it is desirable to try to put items in other classifications before including them in Other Assets.

EXAMPLE 5.

Other Assets

Fixed Assets Held for Resale	*$2,100*
Cash in Closed Bank	*750*
Miscellaneous Other Assets	*120*

Summary

(1) The Whitecavage Company has excess cash and buys 5,000 shares of the readily marketable stock of the Petersen Company. The Compton Company obtains most of its raw material from the Petersen Company and buys stock in the latter company to guarantee its source of supply. The securities would be shown on the Whitecavage Company's balance sheet under _____ and on the Petersen Company's balance sheet under _____.

(2) The Oken Company purchases, as a marketable security, $10,000 in bonds of the Barclay Company at 104, plus accrued interest of $200 and brokerage commission of $50. The investment amount should be recorded as $_____.

(3) The bonds described in the preceding question were sold for 107, less broker's commission and tax of $150. The gain on the sale was $_____.

(4) Assets which are long-term and useful in the operation of a business but are not held for sale and have no physical attributes are termed _____.

(5) A patent which has 12 years of legal life remaining was purchased for $15,000. Because of possible obsolescence the economic life was estimated at 10 years. The amount of the annual amortization is $_____.

(6) In the course of forming a corporation there are legal fees, accounting fees, incorporation fees, expenses for meetings, etc. These expenditures are considered to be _____ under the account title _____.

(7) The Witt Company has a checking account at the Cheatum National Bank, with a balance at the end of the year of $9,500. On January 2, the company was notified that because of a large defalcation the bank will have to close. The company should then debit _____ and credit _____.

(8) Among (a) marketable securities held temporarily, (b) savings accounts, (c) cash surrender value of life insurance, (d) bond sinking funds, (e) franchises, (f) goodwill, (g) research and development costs, _____ are current assets, whereas _____ are noncurrent assets.

Answers: (1) Current Assets, Other Assets (or a separate caption); (2) 10,450; (3) 100; (4) intangible assets; (5) 1,500; (6) assets, Organization Costs; (7) Cash in Closed Bank, Cash in Bank; (8) (a) and (b), (c) through (g)

Solved Problems

13.1. The John Shavelson Company has products which are highly seasonal and consequently at certain times of the year excess funds are available for investment. Heretofore such investments have been made in short-term Government securities, but management has decided to purchase AT&T common stock. How should these latter securities be reported on the balance sheet?

SOLUTION

Since AT&T securities are readily marketable, they should be shown as current assets. Ordinarily they would be shown at cost, with the current market value cited parenthetically.

13.2. The E. R. Serotta Company management has decided to purchase stock of the Richmond Corporation, a small manufacturer, in order to provide a guaranteed source of raw materials. How should these securities be reported on the balance sheet?

SOLUTION

Since the purpose of the investment is to influence or exert control over another company, it would not be an investment primarily of idle funds but one of longer duration. The stock would ordinarily not be readily marketable and would thus be a noncurrent asset. The stock would be valued at cost.

13.3. The Brown Company on January 1 purchased 100 shares of the Green Company at $101, plus commission of $100. On July 1, a dividend of $5 per share was received. The stock was sold on October 1 for $105, less commission of $125. Prepare the necessary journal entries.

SOLUTION

January 1	Marketable Securities	10,200	
	Cash		10,200
July 1	Cash	500	
	Dividend Income		500
October 1	Cash	10,375	
	Marketable Securities		10,200
	Gain on Sale of Securities		175

13.4. The Murray Company purchased $100,000 of 6% bonds of the Enright Corporation at 94. The bonds are due 10 years from date of purchase. Assuming that the bonds are temporary investments, compute (1) the annual income, (2) the gain or loss if the bonds are sold at 97 two years from date of purchase.

SOLUTION

(1) $6,000   (2) $3,000 gain

13.5. The Stroble Company has net assets of $1,200,000, which includes intangibles of $200,000. Another firm has agreed to buy the business, paying book value for the net assets and for goodwill to be capitalized at 20%. Goodwill is to be based on excess earnings over 10%. The earnings per year have averaged 13% of net tangible assets. What is the amount of goodwill?

SOLUTION

Average annual earnings ($1,000,000 × 13%)	$130,000
Normal earnings ($1,000,000 × 10%)	100,000
Excess earnings per year	$ 30,000
Goodwill, capitalized at 20% (30,000 ÷ .20)	$150,000

13.6. The Folk Company has net assets of $400,000 and average net earnings of 5% on sales of $600,000 per year. An investor offers to pay for the net assets and to compute goodwill based on excess earnings over 6% of net assets, capitalized at 10%. What is the amount of goodwill?

SOLUTION

Average annual earnings ($600,000 × 5%)	$30,000
Normal earnings ($400,000 × 6%)	24,000
Excess earnings per year	$ 6,000
Goodwill, capitalized at 10% (6,000 ÷ .10)	$60,000

13.7. The Wilkinson Company leases a building for a 10-year period at an annual rental of $4,800 payable on January 1 each year. At the end of the fourth year of the lease, special display shelves were installed at a cost of $3,600, with no salvage value. (a) Give the journal entry to record the cost of the display shelves. (b) Give the journal entry to record the monthly occupancy cost during the last year of the lease.

(a)

(b)

SOLUTION

(a)	Leasehold Improvements	3,600	
	Accounts Payable (or Cash)		3,600
(b)	Occupancy Expense	450	
	Prepaid Rent		400
	Leasehold Improvements		50

In (b) the amortization of the leasehold improvements, which is included in the monthly occupancy cost, is calculated as $3,600 ÷ 6 years = $600 per year = $50 per month.

13.8. The Weag Company purchased a patent from the inventor for $24,000 after 5 years of the 17-year legal life had expired. The company estimates that the useful life will be 15 years. Prepare the journal entries to record (a) the original purchase and (b) the annual amortization.

(a)

(b)

SOLUTION

(a)	*Patents*	*24,000*	
	Cash (or Accounts Payable)		*24,000*
(b)	*Amortization Expense, Patents*	*2,000**	
	Patents		*2,000*

* $24,000 ÷ 12 unexpired years = $2,000 per year

13.9. The Kelso Company has been informed by the local chapter of the Ecology Council that a complaint is being issued against its disposal of waste material. Equipment needed to meet antipollution standards will cost $100,000. Ordinarily, that general classification of fixed assets would be depreciated over a 15-year period. However, to encourage the installation of such equipment the Internal Revenue Service has allowed the cost to be amortized over a 5-year period. Write (a) the journal entry for the cost of the equipment, (b) the journal entry for the annual write-off, and (c) the presentation on the balance sheet after one year's amortization.

(a)			
(b)			
(c)			

SOLUTION

(a)	*Deferred Charges, Antipollution Equipment*	*100,000*	
	Cash (or Accounts Receivable)		*100,000*
(b)	*Amortization, Antipollution Equipment*	*20,000*	
	Deferred Charges, Antipollution Equipment		*20,000*
(c)	*Deferred Charges*		
	Antipollution Equipment	*$ 80,000*	

13.10. The Krautwurst Company has decided to purchase an insurance policy for $50,000 on the life of its president. The company will pay the insurance cost, which will be offset by the cash surrender value of the policy, which increases each year. The annual premium is $2,000, and the cash surrender value is: at the end of year 2, $850; at the end of year 3, $1,350. Prepare the journal entries for (a) the first year, (b) the second year, and (c) the third year; and (d) give the balance sheet presentation at the end of the third year.

(a)			
(b)			
(c)			
(d)			

SOLUTION

Each year the company's insurance expense is the annual premium, less the appreciation of the policy's cash surrender value during that year.   Therefore:

(a)	Insurance Expense	2,000	
	Cash		2,000
(b)	Insurance Expense	1,150	
	Cash Surrender Value, Life Insurance	850	
	Cash		2,000
(c)	Insurance Expense	1,500	
	Cash Surrender Value, Life Insurance	500	
	Cash		2,000
(d)	Other Assets:		
	Cash Surrender Value, Life Insurance		$1,350

Chapter 14

Liabilities

14.1 GENERAL DESCRIPTION

Liabilities are claims which require the payment or consumption of business resources. Most liabilities of a business are based on *commitments* or *contracts* and are legally enforceable by the creditor. Examples are accounts payable, notes payable, salaries, and interest. Some liabilities are due to provisions of law, such as various taxes imposed on the company which are legally enforceable.

The complexities of business operations and tax regulations in recent years have caused the recognition of liabilities based on economic considerations rather than strictly on legal enforcement. Examples are various kinds of performance obligations, such as product warranties and guarantees, and deferred income taxes, which arise when deductions are taken on tax returns earlier than on company books.

Liabilities are classified into two general groups: current liabilities and long-term liabilities.

14.2 CURRENT LIABILITIES

These are liabilities that are due for payment within the operating cycle or one year, whichever is longer. The settlement of a current liability usually requires the use of current assets. The ratio of current assets to current liabilities, or *current ratio,* is a useful index of a company's debt-paying capacity. It tells how many times over current liabilities could be paid with current assets.

EXAMPLE 1.

Current Assets $70,000
Current Liabilities   32,000

$$\text{CURRENT RATIO} = \frac{\text{CURRENT ASSETS}}{\text{CURRENT LIABILITIES}} = \frac{70,000}{32,000} = 2.19 : 1$$

Thus, $2.19 of current assets is available for every $1 of current liabilities.

Following are the seven principal types of current liabilities.

(1) *Notes payable.* Liabilities evidenced by written promise to pay at a later date.

(2) *Accounts payable.* Liabilities for goods or services purchased on account, trade payables, and also nontrade obligations.

(3) *Accrued liabilities.* Liabilities that have accumulated but are not yet due, as payment does not coincide with the end of the period. These are *expenses* of the company and are shown on the income statement under:

Salaries and Wages	Payroll Taxes
Commissions	Sales Taxes
Insurance	Income Taxes
Interest	Pensions
Property Taxes	Royalties

(4) **Withholdings.** Amounts which have been withheld from employees' pay and are to be turned over to governmental agencies, insurance companies, etc. These are *not* expenses of the company but must be properly safeguarded until transmitted to the specified agency. These include:

- income taxes
- Social Security taxes
- unemployment taxes
- hospitalization
- group insurance
- pension

(5) **Dividends payable.** Dividends become payable only as declared by the Board of Directors of the company. They do not accrue, or accumulate, as does interest on bonds.

(6) **Unearned revenues.** Sometimes revenue is received in advance, such as magazine subscriptions or rent. These are liabilities, as they represent claims against the company. Generally they are settled by delivery of goods or services in the next accounting period. Where these are long-term advances extending well beyond the next period, they should be classed on the balance sheet as noncurrent.

(7) **Portion of long-term debt.** The portion of long-term debt payable in the next twelve months should be included in the current liabilities category. This includes such amounts due on bonds, mortgages, or long-term notes.

14.3 ACCOUNTING FOR CURRENT LIABILITIES

Entries to current liabilities very often result from accrual entries made at the end of the month. Many others, especially the tax withholding entries, accompany payrolls. Still others result from regular payables. The usual adjusting entries were described and illustrated in some detail in Secs. 6.2 and 6.3 We give here a few additional examples.

Regular payables. At the end of the month there will usually be invoices from suppliers and others that are not yet paid. It is essential that every effort be made to record all unpaid items, lest the income amount for the month be distorted.

EXAMPLE 2.

At the end of the month it was found that an invoice of $150 for material received and an invoice of $75 for supplies received had not been recorded.

Material	150	
Supplies	75	
Accounts Payable		225

Accrued expenses. For expenses which have accrued or accumulated, but have not been recorded at the end of the month, adjusting entries have to be made.

EXAMPLE 3.

At the end of February it was found that there were accrued salaries and wages of $500 and accrued insurance of $200. The adjusting entry would be:

Salaries and Wages Expense	500	
Insurance Expense	200	
Salaries and Wages Payable		500
Insurance Payable		200

Payroll deductions. As explained in Sec. 14.2, these represent amounts owed to others, and thus are current liabilities rather than current expenses.

EXAMPLE 4.

The payroll totals for the pay period ending February 15 were: salaries, $2,000; withholdings for income taxes, $300; social security, $100; state unemployment, $75; hospitalization insurance, $50; and a net amount payable of $1,475.

Salaries and Wages	2,000	
Income Taxes Payable		300
Social Security Taxes Payable		100
State Unemployment Taxes Payable		75
Hospitalization Insurance Payable		50
Accrued Payroll		1,475

When employees' checks for the net amounts are issued in a few days, the entry is:

Accrued Payroll	1,475	
Cash		1,475

As for the balance sheet presentation, the degree of detail shown in current liabilities will depend on the amounts involved and the desires of management. Generally these amounts, other than accounts payable, are not large in relation to other balance sheet items and may be combined as desired.

EXAMPLE 5.

Notes Payable	$10,000
Accounts Payable	12,000
Income Taxes Payable	5,000
Accrued Expenses	2,000
Other Liabilities	1,500
Total Current Liabilities	$30,500

14.4 LONG-TERM LIABILITIES

Where funds are needed for a long-term purpose such as construction of a building, a long-term liability account would be used. Presumably, increased earnings will be used to retire the debt. Almost always, long-term liabilities are interest-bearing and have a fixed due date.

(1) *Long-term notes payable.* The company may be able to obtain the needed amount from one lender rather than by issuing bonds for sale to the public. Sometimes notes may be issued to await better terms for issuing bonds.

(2) *Mortgages payable.* The terms of a mortgage generally pledge the property of the company as security. The mortgage involves a lien on the property, not a transfer of title.

(3) *Bonds payable.* If the amount of funds needed is larger than a single lender can supply, bonds may be sold to the investing public, splitting the loan into thousands of units. A bond is a written promise to pay the face amount, generally $1,000, at a future date and to make interest payments semiannually at a stipulated rate of interest. Interest payments on bonds are deductible as expense for income tax purposes, but dividends paid on preferred or common stock are not. This is an important consideration in deciding whether to use stocks or bonds for long-term financing.

EXAMPLE 6.   Bonds versus Stock.

Let us assume that a company needs $5 million to finance new buildings and equipment.   The company is considering whether to issue 6% bonds or 7% preferred stock.   Presently the company has $3 million common stock outstanding, $100 par value (30,000 shares).   After the new plant and equipment are operating, the annual earnings will be $1,500,000 before interest expense and income taxes.   The following schedule shows the net earnings per share for each financing method.

	Bonds, 6%	Preferred Stock, 7%
Earnings before interest and income taxes	$1,500,000	$1,500,000
Less: Interest on bonds	300,000	
Net earnings before taxes	$1,200,000	$1,500,000
Less: Income taxes (50%)	600,000	750,000
Net income	$ 600,000	$ 750,000
Less: Preferred stock dividends		350,000
Available for common stock dividends	$ 600,000	$ 400,000
Net earnings per common share	$ 20.00	$ 13.33

In this example the use of bonds provides an annual saving of $200,000, or $6.67 per share.   The saving comes from two factors:

Deductibility of bond interest (50% of $300,000)	$150,000	
Marketing cost (preferred stock, $350,000; bonds, $300,000)	50,000	
	$200,000	

14.5 ACCOUNTING FOR LONG-TERM LIABILITIES

We shall illustrate the accounting entries for long-term liabilities by considering a single bond issue.

Bonds may be issued (1) at par, (2) at a discount, or (3) at a premium.   When the interest rate of the bonds is less than the prevailing market rate, the bonds will have to be sold at a discount to bring the yield to the investors up to the market rate.   If the interest rate offered is greater than the market rate, investors may pay a premium.   *The discount or premium is part of the cost of borrowing and becomes part of the net cost to the company.*

EXAMPLE 7.   Bonds Issued at Par.

Bonds of $100,000 face value, 6% interest, 10 years, were sold at par.

Cash	*100,000*	
Bonds Payable		*100,000*

EXAMPLE 8.   Bonds Issued at a Discount.

Bonds of $100,000 face value, 6% interest, 10 years, were sold at 96.

Cash	*96,000*	
Discount on Bonds	*4,000*	
Bonds Payable		*100,000*

The actual interest expense per year would be $6,000 *plus* $400 ($4,000 ÷ 10), as shown by the following computation:

Face value at maturity	$100,000
Interest: 6% a year, 10 years	60,000
Total to be paid	$160,000
Less: Amount received	96,000
Excess to be paid	$ 64,000
Yearly interest expense ($64,000 ÷ 10)	$ 6,400

EXAMPLE 9.   Bonds Issued at a Premium.

Bonds of $100,000 face value, 6% interest, 10 years, were sold at 103.

Cash	*103,000*	
Bonds Payable		*100,000*
Premium on Bonds		*3,000*

The actual interest expense per year would be $6,000 *minus* $300 ($3,000 ÷ 10), as shown by the following computation:

Face value at maturity	$100,000
Interest: 6% a year, 10 years	60,000
Total to be paid	$160,000
Less: Amount received	103,000
Excess to be paid	$ 57,000
Yearly interest expense	$ 5,700

As can be seen from Examples 8 and 9, the interest expense each year consists of two parts: (1) the cash paid to the investors and (2) the amortization of the discount or premium made by the company.   The entries are as follows:

Interest Expense	*6,000*	
Cash		*6,000*
Interest payment		
Interest Expense	*400*	
Discount on Bonds		*400*
Amortization of discount		
Premium on Bonds	*300*	
Interest Expense		*300*
Amortization of premium		

14.6 YEAR-END ADJUSTMENTS AND BALANCE SHEET PRESENTATION

It is rarely the case that a payment of interest coincides with the end of the fiscal year.   Therefore, accruals have to be set up for (1) accrued interest and (2) amortization of discount or premium.

EXAMPLE 10.

In Example 9 if the interest was payable April 1 and October 1, there would be, at the close of a calendar year, accrued interest and amortization for 3 months, or 1/4 of a year.

Interest Expense (6,000 × 1/4)	*1,500*	
Accrued Interest Payable		*1,500*
Interest Expense (400 × 1/4)	*100*	
Discount on Bonds		*100*

On the balance sheet, preferred treatment is to show the discount as a deduction from the face amount.

Long-Term Liabilities
6% Bonds Payable, due Oct. 1, 197— $100,000
  Less: Bond Discount   4,000 $96,000

When a portion of the discount ($400) has been amortized, as illustrated in Example 8, the presentation a year later will be as follows:

Long-Term Liabilities
6% Bonds Payable, due Oct. 1, 197— $100,000
  Less: Bond Discount   3,600 $96,400

The premium would be shown as an addition to the face amount.

Long-Term Liabilities
6% Bonds Payable, due Oct. 1, 197— $100,000
  Plus: Premium on Bonds   3,000 $103,000

A year later, after a portion of the premium ($300) has been amortized, the presentation will be as follows:

Long-Term Liabilities
6% Bonds Payable, due Oct. 1, 197— $100,000
  Plus: Premium on Bonds   2,700 $102,700

14.7 CONTINGENT LIABILITY

A contingent liability may be defined as a potential liability arising from past events. When, for example, a note receivable is endorsed and transferred to another person, no liability is created. However, there is a possibility that a liability in the future could exist, because the maker of the note might not honor it. In that event, the business which endorsed the note would be required to make payment. Some other examples of contingent liabilities are: additional tax assessments, product guarantees, pending lawsuits, discount of notes receivable, litigation.

It is not necessary to prepare an entry before the potential liability becomes an actuality. However, it cannot be ignored. Therefore, a contingent liability should be reflected in the balance sheet as a footnote describing the possibility of the loss. This will give the reader a more accurate picture of the total credit rating and financial position of the firm.

Summary

(1) Liabilities are classified into _____ liabilities and _____ liabilities.

(2) Current liabilities are those liabilities that are due for payment within the operating cycle or _____, whichever is longer.

(3) Liabilities that have accumulated but are not yet due are known as _____ liabilities.

(4) When the amount of funds needed is larger than a single lender can supply, then _____ are offered for sale to the investing public.

(5) The face amount of bonds is generally $ _____, and interest is paid _____ at a fixed rate.

(6) A thousand-dollar bond sold at 96 is said to be sold at a _____, while one sold at 102 would be said to be sold at a _____.

(7) The treatment for the disclosure of a discount on the balance sheet would be a deduction from the _____ amount of the bond.

(8) If the current assets of a firm are $80,000 and the current liabilities are $20,000, the current ratio is _____.

(9) Contingent liabilities are defined as _____ liabilities arising from past events.

(10) A contingent liability should be reflected in the balance sheet as a _____ describing the possibility of the loss.

Answers: (1) current, long-term;   (2) one year;   (3) accrued;   (4) bonds;   (5) 1,000, semiannually;   (6) discount, premium;   (7) face;   (8) 4 : 1;   (9) potential;   (10) footnote

Solved Problems

14.1. A summary of the balance sheet of the Alden Company appears below.

ASSETS

Current	*$40,000*
Fixed	*26,000*
Total Assets	*$66,000*

LIABILITIES AND CAPITAL

Current Liabilities	*$15,000*
Long-Term Liabilities	*28,000*
Total Liabilities	*$43,000*
Capital	*23,000*
Total Liabilities and Capital	*$66,000*

Determine the current ratio.

SOLUTION

$$\frac{\text{CURRENT ASSETS}}{\text{CURRENT LIABILITIES}} = \frac{40,000}{15,000} = 2.67 : 1$$

14.2. Match the item in Column I with the appropriate description in Column II. (Use the letter adjacent to the description.)

COLUMN I	COLUMN II
1. Notes receivable	(a) Liabilities for goods or services purchased on account
2. Accounts payable	
3. Accrued liabilities	(b) Income received but not yet earned
4. Withholding	(c) A lien on property
5. Dividends payable	(d) Written promise to pay at future date
6. Unearned revenue	(e) Written promise to pay face amount at future date and to make interest payments semiannually
7. Mortgage payable	
8. Bonds payable	
	(f) Amount withheld from employees' salaries
	(g) Amount payable arising from distribution of earnings
	(h) Liabilities accumulated but not yet due for payment

SOLUTION

1. (d)   2. (a)   3. (h)   4. (f)   5. (g)   6. (b)   7. (c)   8. (e)

14.3. Salary expense of $1,000 represents $200 a day for a 5-day week. If the last day of the calendar year (December 31) falls on a Wednesday, what is the entry to record the accrued liability for the year?

SOLUTION

Salary Expense	600*	
Salary Payable		600
* 3 days × $200 per day = $600		

14.4. Wages paid for the week total $12,400, from which the following items were withheld: Income taxes, $1,400; Social Security, $650; Hospitalization, $450; Union dues, $560. Present the entry necessary to record (a) the accrued payroll, (b) the payment of the payroll.

(a)

(b)

SOLUTION

(a)

Wages Expense	12,400	
Withholding Taxes Payable		1,400
Social Security Taxes Payable		650
Hospitalization Payable		450
Union Dues Payable		560
Accrued Wages Payable		9,340

(b)

Accrued Wages Payable	9,340	
Cash		9,340

14.5. (a) The rent income account has a credit balance of $14,400 which includes $1,200 of rental income that will not be earned until the new calendar year. What entry is necessary to record this unearned revenue?

(b) What classification is given to Unearned Rent Income?

SOLUTION

(a)	Rent Income	1,200	
	Unearned Rent Income		1,200

(b) It is a current liability.

14.6. Two different plans for financing a $4,000,000 acquisition are being considered: Method 1 — issue of 5% bonds; Method 2 — issue of 6% preferred stock. The following information is available:

> Common stock — $100 par, 40,000 shares
>
> Estimated net earnings after acquisition — $2,000,000
>
> Income tax — 50%

Determine the better method by finding the net earnings per common share under both methods.

	Bonds, 5%	Preferred Stock, 6%
Earnings before interest and taxes		
Less: Interest on bonds		
Net earnings before taxes		
Less: Income tax (50%)		
Net income		
Less: Dividends on preferred stock		
Available for common stock dividends		
Net earnings per common share (40,000 shares)		

SOLUTION

	Bonds, 5%	Preferred Stock, 6%
Earnings before interest and taxes	$2,000,000	$2,000,000
Less: Interest on bonds	100,000	
Net earnings before taxes	$1,900,000	$2,000,000
Less: Income taxes (50%)	950,000	1,000,000
Net income	$ 950,000	$1,000,000
Less: Dividends on preferred stock		240,000*
Available for common stock dividends	$ 950,000	$ 760,000
Net earnings per common share (40,000 shares)	$23.75	$19.00

*6% × 4,000,000

It is seen that the bond issue is superior in that it would produce savings of $4.75 per share, or total annual savings of $4.75 × 40,000 = $190,000.

14.7. Record the issuing of $200,000 worth of 5%, 10-year bonds, if the bonds are sold (a) at par, (b) at 98, (c) at 102.

(a)

(b)

(c)

SOLUTION

(a)	Cash	200,000	
	Bonds Payable		200,000
(b)	Cash	196,000	
	Discount on Bonds	4,000	
	Bonds Payable		200,000
(c)	Cash	204,000	
	Premium on Bonds		4,000
	Bonds Payable		200,000

14.8. Bonds valued at $1,000,000, with 4% interest to be paid on January 1, are sold on April 1.

    (a)   What is the entry to record the sale?

    (b)   What entry is made for the annual payment of interest?

    (c)   What will be the *net* amount of interest expense for the year?

(a)

(b)

(c)   Interest Expense

SOLUTION

(a)	Cash	1,010,000	
	Bonds Payable		1,000,000
	Interest Expense		10,000*
	* 1/4 × $40,000 interest		
(b)	Interest Expense	40,000	
	Cash		40,000

(c)   Interest Expense

Dec. 40,000	Jan. 10,000
Bal. 30,000	

14.9. W. Schneider Company issues $100,000, 6%, 10-year bonds at 99 on January 1, the first day of the fiscal year. Present the entry to record (a) the sale of the bonds, (b) the payment of the interest, (c) the amortization of the discount.

(a)

(b)

(c)

SOLUTION

(a)	Cash	99,000	
	Discount on Bonds Payable	1,000	
	Bonds Payable		100,000
(b)	Interest Expense	6,000	
	Cash		6,000
(c)	Interest Expense	100	
	Discount on Bonds Payable		100*

    * (1% × $100,000) ÷ 10 years = $100 per year

14.10. If, in Problem 14.9, the payments of interest were semiannual, made on April 1 and October 1, determine the entries needed to record (a) the interest accrued on December 31, (b) the amortization accrued on December 31. (c) How is the discount treated on the balance sheet?

(a)

(b)

(c)

SOLUTION

(a)	Interest Expense		1,500	
	Accrued Interest Payable			1,500*
	* 1/4 year × $6,000 per year = $1,500			
(b)	Interest Expense		25	
	Discount on Bonds Payable			25**
	** 1/4 year × $100 per year = $25			
(c)	Long-Term Liabilities			
	6% Bonds Payable	$100,000		
	Less: Discount on Bonds	1,500	$98,500	

Chapter 15

Owners' Equity

15.1 INTRODUCTION

The terms *owners' equity*, *capital*, and *proprietorship* are used interchangeably in accounting. Another less desirable term, *net worth*, is sometimes used, though less frequently than in the past. The term is not desirable because readers may get the impression that *net worth* is the exact worth, or value, of the equity. Assets are recorded at cost, and their worth or market value may have changed considerably since acquisition.

While the principles of accounting apply generally to all economic units, the equity aspects and types of accounts vary significantly. On the one hand, there are profit-making enterprises; on the other hand, nonprofit entities, such as states, cities, churches, hospitals, etc. In this chapter we will be concerned primarily with profit-making enterprises, which comprise most of the business units, and which are grouped into sole proprietorships, partnerships, and corporations. Emphasis in the Solved Problems will be on corporations, as the equity for sole propriortorships and partnerships was illustrated earlier.

15.2 SOLE PROPRIETORSHIP

A sole proprietorship is a business owned by one individual. It is a separate business entity but it is not a separate *legal entity*. The proprietor owns the assets and owes the creditors personally, not as a business, as in the case of a corporation.

The equity of the sole proprietor consists of three accounts: a capital account, a drawing account, and an expense and income summary account. These accounts are described and illustrated below.

Capital account. The proprietor's capital account reflects the changes in his equity during the year. Examples 1 through 3 follow the sequence of events in the business of Aaron Baker.

EXAMPLE 1.

On January 1, Aaron Baker invested $20,000 in his business. The entry is as follows:

Jan. 1	Cash	20,000	
	Aaron Baker, Capital		20,000

The account Aaron Baker, Capital will appear as follows:

Aaron Baker, Capital
Jan. 1 Investment 20,000

Drawing account. Before earnings are made, the proprietor usually has to draw compensation for his living expenses. He is not an employee; therefore, he does not earn a salary; his earnings result from profits of the company. Such drawings reduce his equity and reduce cash.

EXAMPLE 2.

Aaron Baker decided that he would withdraw $500 a month for personal expenses. He expects this equity reduction to be more than offset by earnings which will be determined at the end of the year. The entry to be made each month is:

> Aaron Baker, Drawing   500
>> Cash   500

The account Aaron Baker, Drawing is used to accumulate the details of the drawings so that only one figure, the total, is transferred to the capital account at the end of the year. The drawing account will appear as follows:

Aaron Baker, Drawing

Jan.	31	500			
Feb.	28	500			
Mar.	31	500			
April	30	500			
May	31	500			
June	30	500			
July	31	500			
Aug.	31	500			
Sept.	30	500			
Oct.	31	500			
Nov.	30	500			
Dec.	31	500	Dec. 31	6,000	
		6,000		6,000	

When the drawings of $6,000 for the year are transferred, the entry is as follows:

> Dec. 31   Aaron Baker, Capital   6,000
>> Aaron Baker, Drawing   6,000

Expense and income summary account. When the accounts are summarized and closed, the various expenses are debited in total to Expense and Income Summary and the individual expense accounts are credited. The income is credited in total to Expense and Income Summary and debited to the individual income accounts. The net difference, a profit or a loss, is transferred to the capital account. This process was treated in Chapter 6 (see, in particular, Sec. 6.4).

EXAMPLE 3.

The business of Aaron Baker had income from fees of $20,000 and expenses for: rent, $5,000; salary, $2,000; and supplies, $2,000. The account will appear as follows:

Expense and Income Summary

Dec. 31	Rent	5,000	Dec. 31	Income	20,000
Dec. 31	Salary	2,000			
Dec. 31	Supplies	2,000			
Dec. 31	To Capital	11,000			
		20,000			20,000

The income of $20,000, less total expenses of $9,000, results in net income of $11,000. The account is closed out and the balance transferred to the capital account with the following entry:

> Dec. 31   Expense and Income Summary   11,000
>> Aaron Baker, Capital   11,000

The account Aaron Baker, Capital will now reflect the proprietor's investment, drawings, and income:

Aaron Baker, Capital

Dec. 31	Drawings	6,000	Jan. 1	Investment	20,000
31	Balance	25,000		Net Income	11,000
		31,000			31,000
			Jan. 1	Balance	25,000

Instead of showing the capital as a single item on the balance sheet, as above, and in order to have a separate schedule showing the increases and decreases for the period, the data can be presented on the balance sheet as follows:

OWNER'S EQUITY

Aaron Baker, Capital

Balance, January 1, 197—		$20,000
Net Income for 197—	$11,000	
Drawing for 197—	6,000	5,000
Balance, December 31, 197—		$25,000

15.3 PARTNERSHIP

A partnership is a business owned by two or more persons in accordance with a partnership arrangement. Such an arrangement should preferably be expressed in a partnership agreement. Profits may be shared equally, according to invested capital, or on any other basis. A partner's share is called his *interest* in the business.

The partnership capital accounts consist of a capital account for each partner, a drawing account for each partner, and an expense and income summary account. These accounts are described and illustrated below.

Capital accounts. Like the sole proprietor's account (Example 1), each partner's account reflects the changes in his equity during the year.

EXAMPLE 4.

On January 1, Joseph Kelso invested $15,000 and James Murray invested $10,000 to begin a retail hardware business. The entry is as follows:

Jan. 1	Cash	25,000	
	Joseph Kelso, Capital		15,000
	James Murray, Capital		10,000

Drawing accounts. The individual drawing accounts will also be similar to the sole proprietor's drawing account.

EXAMPLE 5.

It was agreed that Joseph Kelso would draw $400 a month and James Murray $300 a month. The entry each month will be as follows:

Joseph Kelso, Drawing	400	
James Murray, Drawing	300	
Cash		700

The monthly amounts will be accumulated in each partner's drawing accounts as in Example 2. At the end of the year, the totals for the year will be transferred to the partners' accounts as follows:

Dec. 31	Joseph Kelso, Capital	4,800	
	James Murray, Capital	3,600	
	Joseph Kelso, Drawing		4,800
	James Murray, Drawing		3,600

Expense and income summary account.   The expense and income accounts are closed into Expense and Income Summary as described for a single proprietor (Example 3). However, the profit or loss will be transferred to two or more accounts rather than a single account.   The Expense and Income Summary, like the drawing accounts, will be closed out for the period.

EXAMPLE 6.

At the end of the year the partnership showed net income of $15,000.   Profits are shared as follows: Kelso, 60%; Murray, 40%.   The closing entry would be:

Dec. 31	Expense and Income Summary	15,000	
	Joseph Kelso, Capital		9,000
	James Murray, Capital		6,000

Each partnership account will show the partner's investment, drawings, and income as follows:

Joseph Kelso, Capital

Dec. 31	Drawings	4,800	Jan. 1	Investment	15,000
Dec. 31	Balance	19,200	Dec. 31	Net Income	9,000
		24,000			24,000
			Jan. 1	Balance	19,200

James Murray, Capital

Dec. 31	Drawings	3,600	Jan. 1	Investment	10,000
Dec. 31	Balance	12,400	Dec. 31	Net Income	6,000
		16,000			16,000
			Jan. 1	Balance	12,400

The partners' equities would be shown on the balance sheet as follows:

Partners' Equities		
Kelso, Capital	$19,200	
Murray, Capital	12,400	$31,600

While the amounts for net income and drawings may be shown on the balance sheet for a sole proprietorship, such detail is cumbersome where two or more partners are involved.   It is preferable to have a separate statement, called Statement of Partners' Equities or Statement of Partners' Capital or simply Capital Statement.   A form is shown below.

Kelso and Murray
Statement of Partners' Capital
year ended December 31, 197–

	Total	Kelso	Murray
Investment, Jan. 1, 197–	$25,000	$15,000	$10,000
Net Income for the Year	15,000	9,000	6,000
	$40,000	$24,000	$16,000
Less: Drawings	8,400	4,800	3,600
Balance, December 31, 197–	$31,600	$19,200	$12,400

Further details on the nature of partnerships and their formation and dissolution are discussed in the sequel to this volume, *Accounting II*.

15.4 CORPORATION

A corporation is a separate legal entity organized in accordance with state or federal laws, with ownership represented by shares of stock. The applicable laws require that a distinction be made between the amount invested in a corporation by its owners (stockholders) and the subsequent changes due to profits or losses. Because of these requirements, the stockholders' equity is shown in at least two parts. If there is more than one class of stock, such as preferred and common, there may be more parts in the Stockholders' Equity section.

STOCKHOLDERS' EQUITY

Capital Stock	*$100,000*	
Retained Earnings	*25,000*	*$125,000*

The principal corporation equity accounts are those for capital stock, dividends, and retained earnings. (There may be additional, more specialized accounts in some companies, but the above types will serve for purposes of illustration.)

Capital stock. The corporate capital stock is evidenced by stock certificates. There are a specified number of shares of stock authorized by the state, generally at a specified par value. No-par stock also can be issued in most states. When stock is issued at a price above par, the amount above par is termed a *premium*. If stock is issued below par, the difference is termed a *discount*. If only one type of stock is issued, it may be termed *capital stock* or, specifically, *common stock*. Sometimes, when there is a future possibility of issuing preferred stock, the first issue may be termed common stock. In large companies there may be more than one class of common stock and more than one class of preferred stock. Capital stock that has been issued, fully paid, and reacquired by the company, but not canceled, is called *treasury stock*.

EXAMPLE 7.

The ABC Corporation issued on January 1, 1970, 5,000 shares of capital stock at $100 par value. The entry is as follows:

Cash	*500,000*	
Capital Stock		*500,000*

Dividends. A dividend is a distribution to stockholders. It is on a pro rata basis and generally represents a distribution from retained earnings (see below). Most commonly, dividends are paid in cash, but there may also be dividends in the stock of the paying, or of another, company. Less frequently, dividends may be paid in scrip or in property (particularly, liquidating dividends).

EXAMPLE 8.

On December 1, 1973, the board of directors declares a quarterly cash dividend of $1 per share on the 5,000 shares of capital stock outstanding. The dividend is payable to stockholders of record as of December 10, and will be paid January 15, 1974. The dividend becomes a current liability when declared and would be included as a current liability on the balance sheet of December 31.

Dec. 1	*Retained Earnings*	*5,000*	
	Dividends Payable		*5,000*

Retained earnings. Retained earnings represent stockholders' equity that has accumulated from profitable operation of the business. Generally they represent total net income less dividends declared. Retained earnings result only from operations of the business, and no entries from transactions in company stock are to be made to the account. The account is to be debited for dividends declared and credited for net income for the period. At the end of the year, Expense and Income Summary is debited and Retained Earnings credited for net income.

EXAMPLE 9.

The net income for the year ended December 31, 197–, was determined to be $20,000. The entry is:

Expense and Income Summary	*20,000*	
Retained Earnings		*20,000*

Some companies distinguish between appropriated and unappropriated retained earnings in order to indicate to stockholders and others that a specified amount ("appropriated") is not available for dividends. The stockholders' equity section for most companies would appear as follows:

STOCKHOLDERS' EQUITY

Capital stock, $100 par value, 500 shares	*$500,000*
Retained Earnings	*15,000**
Total Stockholders' Equity	*$515,000*

* Net income	*$ 20,000*
Less: Dividend declared	*5,000*
	$ 15,000

Summary

(1) The principal types of profit-making enterprises are the _____, the _____, and the _____.

(2) When the proprietor invests $10,000 cash in the business, the debit is to Cash and the credit is to _____ .

(3) If there is a credit balance in the Expense and Income Summary after closing the accounts, then a _____ has been made for the period.

(4) The shares of stock of a corporation must be authorized by the _____.

(5) When the proceeds exceed the par value of stock, it is said to sell at a _____ .

(6) A person may become a partner by making an investment or buying an _____ .

(7) When capital stock has been issued and later reacquired, it is called _____ .

(8) The price at which the stock of a corporation is selling on the stock exchange is the _____ of the stock.

(9) The two principal sections of the stockholders' equity section are _____ and _____ .

(10) Retained earnings are classified as either _____ or _____ .

Answers: (1) sole proprietorship, partnership, corporation; (2) Capital; (3) profit; (4) state; (5) premium; (6) interest; (7) treasury stock; (8) market value; (9) paid-in capital, retained earnings; (10) appropriated, unappropriated

Solved Problems

15.1. The St. Charles Recreation Institute was incorporated January 1, 1973, to take over the business of the partnership of Bona and Fide, whose balance sheet is as follows:

Bona and Fide
Balance Sheet
December 31, 1972

ASSETS		LIABILITIES AND CAPITAL	
Various Assets	$150,000	*Accounts Payable*	$ 25,000
		Bona, Capital	50,000
		Fide, Capital	75,000
	$150,000		$150,000

The authorized capital of the corporation is 1,000 shares of $25 par value, 6% cumulative preferred stock and 10,000 shares of $10 par value common stock. Each partner was issued capital stock at par for his interest, one-half in preferred stock, one-half in common stock. During the year 1973 the income was $45,000 before income taxes. Accounts payable increased by $30,000 during the year and income taxes payable amounted to $15,000 at year end. Dividends of $10,000 were paid on common stock. Prepare the balance sheet of the St. Charles Recreation Institute as of December 31, 1973.

St. Charles Recreation Institute		
Balance Sheet		
December 31, 1973		
ASSETS		
LIABILITIES AND STOCKHOLDERS' EQUITY		

SOLUTION

St. Charles Recreation Institute		
Balance Sheet		
December 31, 1973		
ASSETS		
Various Assets		$215,000*

* $150,000 + $45,000 + $30,000 − $10,000

LIABILITIES AND STOCKHOLDERS' EQUITY		
Liabilities		
Accounts Payable	$ 55,000	
Income Taxes Payable	15,000	$ 70,000
Stockholders' Equity		
Preferred Stock, 6%, $25 par value		
(cumulative; 3,000 shares authorized,		
1,000 shares issued)	$ 25,000	
Common Stock, $10 par (25,000 shares		
authorized, 10,000 shares issued)	100,000	
Retained Earnings	20,000**	145,000
		$215,000

**Income before Income Taxes*		$45,000
Less: Income Taxes Payable	$15,000	
Dividends	10,000	25,000
Retained Earnings		$20,000

15.2. The XYZ Corporation has the following balances in the stockholders' equity section of the balance sheet as of December 31: Preferred Stock, 6%, $100 par, $100,000; Common Stock, $25 par, $250,000; Premium on Preferred Stock, $8,000; Premium on Common Stock, $20,000; Retained Earnings, $100,000. On January 1, because of expected losses, the corporation was dissolved. (*a*) What is the equity of each class of stock at December 31? (*b*) If, after liquidation, $396,000 remained, what would be the distribution per share for each class of stock, if preferred stock is callable at 110%, plus dividends for the current year?

SOLUTION

		Preferred	Common
(*a*)	Par value	$100,000	$250,000
	Premium	8,000	20,000
	Retained earnings		100,000
	Total	108,000	370,000
	Number of shares	÷ 1,000	÷ 10,000
	Equity per share	$108.00	$37.00
(*b*)	Cash available for distribution		$396,000
	Preferred stock priority		
	Distribution at $110	$110,000	
	Dividends — one year	6,000	116,000
	Remainder to common stock		$280,000

The distributions per share are then:

Preferred stock: $116,000 ÷ 1,000 = $116.00

Common stock: $280,000 ÷ 10,000 = $ 28.00

15.3. Total dividends amounting to $40,000, including dividends in arrears for two prior years, are to be divided between preferred stock (6%, $100 par value, $100,000) and common stock ($100 par value, $300,000). Find the amount paid to each class of stock if the preferred stock is (*a*) cumulative, nonparticipating; (*b*) cumulative, fully participating; (*c*) noncumulative, fully participating; (*d*) noncumulative, participating up to 8%.

SOLUTION

		Preferred	Common
(a)	Arrears on preferred	$12,000	
	Preferred, current year	6,000	
	Common, current year		$22,000
		$18,000	$22,000
(b)	Arrears on preferred	$12,000	
	Preferred, current year	6,000	
	Common, current year (to match preferred)		$18,000
	Balance (ratably with shares)	1,000	3,000
		$19,000	$21,000
(c)	Preferred, current year	$ 6,000	
	Common, current year (to match preferred) ($3,000 × 6)		$18,000
	Balance (ratably with shares)	4,000	12,000
		$10,000	$30,000
(d)	Preferred, current year	$ 6,000	
	Common, current year (to match preferred) ($3,000 × 6)		$18,000
	Preferred, additional 2%	2,000	
	Common, balance		14,000
		$ 8,000	$32,000

15.4. The Vincent C. Devane Company was organized at the beginning of the current fiscal year with an authorization of 1,000 shares of cumulative preferred 6% stock, $25 par, and 10,000 shares of common stock, $5 par.

(a) Prepare journal entries for the current year's transactions.

Jan. 5: Sold 3,000 shares of common stock for cash, at par

Jan. 10: Issued 200 shares of common stock to the attorney who helped organize the company

July 1: Issued 4,000 shares of common stock in exchange for land and buildings with fair market values of $5,000 and $20,000

July 2: Issued 1,000 shares of common stock in exchange for machinery and equipment with a fair market value of $6,000

Sept. 30: Sold 800 shares of preferred stock at $22, for cash

Jan. 5		
Jan. 10		
July 1		

(Form continued next page.)

July 2		
Sept. 30		

(b) Prepare the stockholders' equity section of the balance sheet as of December 31 of the current year. The net income for the year was $4,000.

SOLUTION

(a)

Jan. 5	Cash	15,000	
	Common Stock		15,000
Jan. 10	Organization Expenses	1,000	
	Common Stock		1,000
July 1	Land	5,000	
	Building	20,000	
	Common Stock		20,000
	Premium on Common Stock		5,000
July 2	Machinery and Equipment	6,000	
	Common Stock		5,000
	Premium on Common Stock		1,000
Sept. 30	Cash	17,600	
	Discount on Preferred Stock	2,400	
	Preferred Stock		20,000

(b)

Paid-In Capital		
Preferred Stock, 6%, cumulative, $25 par		
(1,000 shares authorized, 800 shares issued)	$20,000	
Less: Discount on Preferred Stock	2,400	$17,600
Common Stock, $5 par (10,000 shares		
authorized, 8,200 shares issued)	41,000	
Premium on Common Stock	6,000	47,000
Total Paid-In Capital		$64,600
Retained Earnings		4,000
Total Stockholders' Equity		$68,000

15.5. The Kerry Brenner Company has the following capital accounts: Preferred Stock, 6%, cumulative, $50 par, $500,000; Common Stock, $15 par, $3,000,000; Premium on Common Stock, $200,000; Retained Earnings, $800,000. (*a*) What is the equity of each class of stock if the preferred stock is to receive $60 on liquidation? (*b*) What is the equity of each class of stock if the preferred stock is to receive $65 on liquidation and one year's dividends are in arrears?

SOLUTION

(*a*)   Total equity $4,500,000

        Allocated to preferred stock

            Liquidation price (10,000 shares at $60)   600,000

        Common stock equity $3,900,000

            Preferred stock equity: $600,000 ÷ 10,000 shares = $60.00 per share

            Common stock equity: $3,900,000 ÷ 200,000 shares = $19.50 per share

(*b*)   Total equity $4,500,000

        Allocated to preferred stock

            Liquidation price (10,000 shares at $65) $650,000

            Dividends in arrears   30,000   680,000

        Common stock equity $3,820,000

            Preferred stock equity: $680,000 ÷ 10,000 shares = $68.00 per share

            Common stock equity: $3,820,000 ÷ 200,000 shares = $19.10 per share

15.6. Compute the amount to be received per share, upon dissolution of the Dan M. Cooper Corporation, in the four cases below. Preferred stock has prior claim on liquidation to the extent of par or above, where indicated.

		Preferred Stock, 6%	Common Stock
(*a*)	Capital stock amount	$600,000	$2,000,000
	Par value	100	50
	Premium or (discount)	30,000	(50,000)
	Retained earnings		120,000
(*b*)	Capital stock amount	$500,000	$1,500,000
	Par value	50	100
	Premium or (discount)	(25,000)	35,000
	Deficit		80,000
	Preferred % on liquidation	110%	
(*c*)	Capital stock amount	$125,000	$500,000
	Par value	25	50
	Premium or (discount)	20,000	
	Retained earnings		75,000
	Years preferred dividends in arrears, including current year	4	
(*d*)	Capital stock amount	$100,000	$200,000
	Par value	25	25
	Premium or (discount)	—	(20,000)
	Deficit		30,000
	Years preferred dividends in arrears, including current year	5	

		Total Equity	Number of Shares	Equity per Share
(a)	Preferred			
	Common			
(b)	Preferred			
	Common			
(c)	Preferred			
	Common			
(d)	Preferred			
	Common			

SOLUTION

		Total Equity	Number of Shares	Equity per Share
(a)	Preferred	$ 600,000	6,000	$100.00
	Common	2,100,000	40,000	52.50
(b)	Preferred	550,000	10,000	55.00
	Common	1,380,000	15,000	92.00
(c)	Preferred	155,000	5,000	31.00
	Common	565,000	10,000	56.50
(d)	Preferred	130,000	4,000	32.50
	Common	120,000	8,000	15.00

15.7. The Rudolph S. Guy Company has the following stockholders' equity and related accounts on January 1, the start of the fiscal year.

Subscriptions Receivable, Preferred Stock	$ 150,000
Preferred Stock, 6%, $100 par (15,000 shares authorized, 10,000 shares issued)	1,000,000
Preferred Stock Subscribed (3,000 shares)	300,000
Common Stock, $25 par (250,000 shares authorized, 100,000 shares issued)	2,500,000
Premium on Common Stock	200,000
Retained Earnings	2,000,000

Prepare journal entries to reflect the following transactions affecting stockholders' equity accounts.

(a) Received the balance due on preferred stock subscribed; issued certificates.

(b) Subscriptions were received for 2,000 shares of preferred stock at $105; 50% of subscription price was collected.

(c) Bought 5,000 shares of treasury common stock for $150,000.

(d) Sold 2,000 shares of treasury stock for $64,000.

(e) Issued 10,000 shares of common stock for cash, at $28.

(a)

(b)

(c)

(d)

(e)

SOLUTION

(a)	Cash	150,000	
	Subscriptions Receivable, Preferred Stock		150,000
	Preferred Stock Subscribed	300,000	
	Preferred Stock		300,000
(b)	Subscriptions Receivable, Preferred Stock	210,000	
	Preferred Stock Subscribed		200,000
	Premium on Preferred Stock		10,000
	Cash	105,000	
	Subscriptions Receivable, Preferred Stock		105,000
(c)	Treasury Common Stock	150,000	
	Cash		150,000
(d)	Cash	64,000	
	Treasury Common Stock		60,000
	Paid-In Capital from Sale of		
	Treasury Stock		4,000
(e)	Cash	280,000	
	Common Stock		250,000
	Premium on Common Stock		30,000

15.8. The controller of the Joseph E. Lindbeck Corporation has prepared the following statement of stockholders' equity at the end of the current year.

Stockholders' Equity

Preferred Stock, 6% cumulative (8,000 shares)	$ 200,000
Common Stock (50,000 shares)	445,000
Surplus	615,000
	$1,260,000

The authorized stock consists of 10,000 shares of preferred, $25 par value, and 100,000 shares of common, $10 par value. The preferred stock was issued for the following prices: 5,000 at par, 3,000 at $28. The 50,000 common stock shares shown were issued at an average price of $13 per share. Treasury common stock of 5,000 shares reacquired at a cost of $55,000 was deducted from the Common Stock balance. From the foregoing information, prepare a revised form of the stockholders' equity section.

SOLUTION

Joseph E. Lindbeck Corporation
Stockholders' Equity
December 31, 197–

Capital Stock		
Preferred Stock, 6% cumulative, $25 par value (10,000 shares authorized, 8,000 shares issued)		*$ 200,000*
Common Stock, $10 par value (100,000 shares authorized; 50,000 shares issued, of which 5,000 are held in treasury)		*500,000*
		$ 700,000
Additional Paid-In Capital		
Excess of Par Value on Preferred	*$ 9,000*	
Excess of Par Value on Common	*150,000*	*159,000*
Total Paid-In Capital		*$ 859,000*
Retained Earnings ($55,000 restricted due to treasury stock transactions)		*456,000*
		$1,315,000
Less: Cost of Treasury Common Stock		*55,000*
Total Stockholders' Equity		*$1,260,000*

15.9. The stockholders' equity accounts of the Richard E. Mori Company as of the beginning of the current fiscal year are shown below:

Common Stock, stated value $15 (100,000 shares authorized, 50,000 shares issued)	$750,000
Paid-In Capital in Excess of Stated Value	150,000
Appropriation for Treasury Stock	42,000
Retained Earnings	210,000
Treasury Stock (2,000 shares at cost)	42,000

Transactions related to the above accounts occurred during the year as follows:

(a) Issued 10,000 shares of stock for $250,000.

(b) Declared a 4% stock dividend, market price $29 per share.

(c) Sold 1,000 shares of treasury stock for $25,000.

(d) Issued stock certificates on dividend declared.

(e) Declared a dividend of 50 cents per share.

(f) Bought 3,000 shares of treasury stock for $69,000.

(g) Land with $20,000 market value received as a donation.

(h) The appropriation for treasury stock was increased as required.

(i) The credit balance in the expense and income summary is $125,500.

(1) Prepare journal entries.

(a)

(b)

(c)

(d)

(e)

(f)

(g)

(h)

(i)

(2) Post journal entries and opening balances to "T" accounts.

(3) Prepare stockholders' equity section of the balance sheet at year end.

SOLUTION

(1)

(a)	Cash	250,000	
	Common Stock		150,000
	Paid-In Capital in Excess of Stated Value		100,000
(b)	Cash	25,000	
	Treasury Stock		21,000
	Paid-In Capital from Sale of Treasury Stock		4,000
(c)	Retained Earnings	69,600	
	Stock Dividend Distributable		36,000
	Paid-In Capital in Excess of Stated Value		33,600
(d)	Stock Dividend Distributable	36,000	
	Common Stock		36,000

(e)	Retained Earnings	30,700	
	Cash Dividends Payable		30,700
(f)	Treasury Stock	69,000	
	Cash		69,000
(g)	Land	20,000	
	Donated Capital		20,000
(h)	Retained Earnings	48,000	
	Appropriation for Treasury Stock	21,000	
	Appropriation for Treasury Stock		69,000
(i)	Expense and Income Summary	125,500	
	Retained Earnings		125,500

(2)

Common Stock

	Bal. 750,000
	(a) 150,000
	(d) 36,000

Paid-In Capital from Sale of Treasury Stock

	(b) 4,000

Paid-In Capital in Excess of Stated Value

	Bal. 150,000
	(a) 100,000
	(c) 33,600

Retained Earnings

(c) 69,600	Bal. 210,000
(e) 30,700	(i) 125,500
(h) 48,000	

Donated Capital

	(g) 20,000

Appropriation for Treasury Stock

(h) 21,000	Bal. 42,000
	(h) 69,000

Treasury Stock

Bal. 42,000	(b) 21,000
(f) 69,000	

Stock Dividends Distributable

(d) 36,000	(c) 36,000

(3)   Paid-In Capital

Common Stock, stated value $15		
(100,000 shares authorized, 62,400 shares issued)	$936,000	
Paid-In Capital in Excess of Stated Value	283,600	
Donation	20,000	
Sale of Treasury Stock	4,000	
Total Paid-In Capital		$1,243,600
Retained Earnings		
Appropriated: Treasury Stock	$ 90,000	
Unappropriated	187,200	
Total Retained Earnings		277,200
Total		$1,520,800
Deduct: Treasury Stock (4,000 shares at cost)		90,000
Total Stockholders' Equity		$1,430,800

15.10. The controller of the James W. Pitre Corporation has prepared the income statement for the year 197–, as shown at the top of page 235. The retained earnings balance at the beginning of the year was $115,000. Prepare an acceptable income statement and a statement of retained earnings, based on the all-inclusive concept of income.

James W. Pitre Corporation
Income Statement
year ended December 31, 197–

Net Sales		$350,000
Gain on Sale of Treasury Stock		16,000
		$366,000
Less:		
Cost of Goods Sold	$170,000	
Operating Expenses	75,000	
Loss on Disposal of Equipment	13,000	
Reserve for Contingencies	20,000	
Dividends on Common Stock	15,000	
Provision for Income Taxes	50,000	343,000
Net Income for the Year		$ 23,000

SOLUTION

James W. Pitre Corporation
Income Statement
year ended December 31, 197–

Sales	$350,000
Cost of Goods Sold	170,000
Gross Profit on Sales	$180,000
Operating Expenses	75,000
Income from Operations	$105,000
Extraordinary Item	
Loss on Disposal of Equipment	13,000
	$ 92,000
Provision for Income Taxes	50,000
Net Income	$ 42,000

James W. Pitre Corporation
Statement of Unappropriated Retained Earnings
December 31, 197–

Balance, January 1, 197–		$115,000
Net Income		42,000
Total		$157,000
Dividends Declared on Common Stock	$15,000	
Appropriation to Reserve for		
Contingencies	20,000	35,000
Balance, December 31, 197–		$122,000

Examination IV

Chapters 13-15

Part I. *Circle the letter identifying the best answer.*

1. Which of the following is a short-term investment?
   a. marketable securities of affiliated company
   b. sinking funds
   c. cash surrender value of life insurance
   d. marketable securities held temporarily

2. Which of the following is a long-term investment?
   a. savings accounts
   b. checking accounts
   c. nonoperating real estate
   d. marketable securities

3. Intangible assets benefit the business through
   a. physical characteristics
   b. special rights and privileges
   c. easy storage
   d. low cost

4. Liabilities require
   a. payment of cash
   b. receipt of materials
   c. consumption of resources
   d. proper recording

5. Current liabilities are
   a. mortgage payables
   b. those requiring the use of current assets
   c. those liable to you
   d. currently receivable

6. Long-term liabilities are
   a. payroll withholdings
   b. bonds payable
   c. interest-bearing
   d. issued at a premium

7. Owners' equity section includes
   a. long-term liabilities
   b. current assets
   c. capital stock
   d. merchandise

8. Sole proprietorships are
   a. separate legal entities
   b. permanent
   c. efficient
   d. individually owned

9. Partnerships are

   a. separate legal entities

   b. owned by two or more persons

   c. individually owned

   d. temporary

10. Corporations are

    a. separate legal entities

    b. individually owned

    c. domestic or federal

    d. profit-making

Part II. *Using the code letters given, indicate the accounts to be debited and credited in recording the tabulated transactions. State the amounts involved in units of $1,000.*

A = Cash		H = Capital Stock	
B = Marketable Securities		I = Premium on Capital Stock	
C = Interest Receivable		J = Expense and Income Summary	
D = Long-Term Investment		K = Rental Income	
E = Salaries Payable		L = Interest Income	
F = Unearned Rent		M = Salaries Expense	
G = C. Folk, Capital		N = Gain on Securities	

	Transaction	Acct. Dr. (M $)	Acct. Cr. (M $)
1.	Temporary purchase of 100M, 10-year, 6% bonds at $93\frac{1}{2}$ and $500 commission		
2.	Interest received on above bonds, $6,000		
3.	Sold above bonds at $97\frac{1}{2}$ and $500 commission at end of 3 years		
4.	Long-term investment of 100M, 5-year, 5% bonds at $94\frac{1}{2}$ and $500 commission		
5.	Interest for year on above bonds, $5,000		
6.	Amortization for year ($5,500 discount, less $500 commission), $1,000		
7.	Sold bonds at $99\frac{1}{2}$ and $500 commission, at end of 2 years		
8.	Interest accrued on notes receivable, $2,000		
9.	Salaries accrued, $1,000		
10.	Unearned rent, previously recorded as rental income, $3,000		
11.	C. Folk invested $15,000 cash in his business		
12.	The CL Company issued 10,000 shares of capital stock (par $10) at $13		

Part III. *Circle T for true, F for false.*

1. T F The following assets are classed as intangibles: patents, copyrights, marketable securities, and leaseholds.

2. T F Unidentifiable intangibles should be shown as assets and recorded at market value.

3. T F Antipollution expenditures for capital assets should be amortized over 5 years or less.

4. T F Generally the settlement of current liabilities does not require the use of current assets.

5. T F Accrued expenses include salaries and wages, insurance, taxes, dividends, interest, and commissions.

6. T F The rent income account should be debited for unearned rent.

7. T F To compute the current ratio, the current assets are divided into the current liabilities.

8. T F A sole proprietorship does not have a capital stock account.

9. T F The capital investment of a partnership is the total amount of money in the partnership bank account.

10. T F Retained Earnings represents the balance that has accumulated from the operation of the business.

Answers to Examination IV

Part I

1. d   2. c   3. b   4. c   5. b   6. b   7. c   8. d   9. b   10. a

Part II

	Acct. Dr. (M $)	Acct. Cr. (M $)
1.	B 94	A 94
2.	A 6	L 6
3.	A 97	B 94 N 3
4.	D 95	A 95
5.	A 5	L 5
6.	D 1	L 1
7.	A 99	D 97 N 2
8.	C 2	L 2
9.	M 1	E 1
10.	K 3	F 3
11.	A 15	G 15
12.	A 130	H 100 I 30

Part III

1. F   2. F   3. T   4. F   5. F   6. T   7. F   8. T   9. F   10. T

Appendix

Mechanical and Electronic Data Processing

Introduction

From a theoretical point of view the operations of accounting may be analyzed into:

Handling of source documents. Issuing sales invoices, vouching purchase invoices, issuing checks, etc.

Input. Insertion of data into the accounting system.

Processing. Arithmetical calculations, sorting and classification of data.

Storage. Maintenance of records.

Output. Results of processing.

In illustrating the principles of accounting in Chapters 1-7, we supposed the above basic operations to be carried out by hand — as indeed they might be. However, they can be — and to a large extent actually are — performed by means of mechanical or electronic devices.

Mechanical Data Processing

There is hardly a business today that does not use a machine in some part of its data processing. As transactions increase in number, the proportion of machine processing also increases to reduce costs and speed the data processing. For our purpose we will divide machines into four groups.

REGISTERS

Common forms of registers are cash registers and invoice registers. Today's cash registers do far more than help make change. They accumulate cash sales, credit sales, sales taxes, and cash received on account. They can segregate sales into groups, such as hardware, apparel, etc. There are also registers which issue invoices for credit sales or receipt of cash sales but which do not make change.

KEY-DRIVEN MACHINES

Under this head come typewriters, adding machines, calculators, and comptometers. These machines are simple to operate and are familiar to most office employees. Thus, sales invoices may be prepared by typewriter, the extensions made and checked by calculator or comptometer, the items totaled by adding machine, and sales statistics also prepared by adding machine. Attachments to key-driven machines allow, along with the primary document, the simultaneous preparation of perforated tapes or cards which can be directly processed on electronic equipment.

ACCOUNTING MACHINES

Though normally provided with keyboards and accumulating counters, these machines are more sophisticated and more costly than typewriters or adding machines. They are capable of processing a number of documents at once. To illustrate the scope of such devices we consider the operation of a typical billing machine.

EXAMPLE

A customer's invoice is to be prepared for goods shipped. The following steps are performed by the machine operator:

1. Sales journal form is placed in the machine and each sales transaction is typed on a line of the sales journal.
2. The following forms are placed in the machine:
    (a) Blank invoice form. Includes customer's copy and carbon and carbon copies for the office.
    (b) Customer's account from the subsidiary ledger.
    (c) Statement to be mailed to customer at the end of the month.
3. The previous balance is picked up from the customer's account.
4. The customer's name, address, terms, etc., are typed on the invoice.
5. For each item sold, the description, number of units, and unit price are typed on the invoice.
6. After the units and unit prices are typed, the operator punches a key and the machine automatically multiplies the units times the price and prints the extension for each item.
7. After all items are listed, the operator presses another key and the machine totals the invoice, prints the total on the invoice, and makes the entry in the sales journal. Also, it enters the new balance on the customer's account and on the customer's statement.

PUNCHED CARD DATA PROCESSING

Large-scale mechanization began with punched card machines, which introduced a new concept in data processing. In manual processing, the same information is repeatedly transcribed, but in punched card processing all the data is inserted at the start, in the form of patterns of holes. Later the cards are processed to derive the specific information needed. The principal machines used are as follows:

(1) *Key punch.* The first step is the input of data, which is accomplished by a machine with a keyboard similar to a typewriter. As the keys are depressed, holes are punched in the cards for later processing. Where desired, information can be automatically transferred to other cards by means of a reproducer.

(2) *Sorter.* The next step is to sort the cards according to the information desired. This is done by successive "passes" through the sorter. Cards can be grouped alphabetically, numerically, or otherwise. Thus, sales for a period can be run through once to arrive at the amount of sales by each salesman. The cards can then be run through again to find the amount of sales by product; then, by territory; etc. Cards can be sorted at the rate of up to 2,000 per minute. A collator is used to insert new cards into an existing group or to merge two separate groups.

(3) *Calculator.* Arithmetical operations of addition, subtraction, multiplication, and division are performed by the calculator. The computation is made almost instantaneously and the answer automatically punched in the same card.

(4) *Tabulator.* Generally the final stage is performed by the tabulator, which converts the punched data to printed matter. The data can be printed on special report forms with appropriate subtotals by group. The tabulator can ordinarily print about 150 lines per minute.

Electronic Data Processing

Electronics, in reference to electronic data processing (EDP), means the flow of electrons, acting as signals in the circuitry of electronic equipment. In mechanical processing the speed of the equipment is limited by the movement of mechanical parts that are subject to friction. The electronic impulses used in EDP are not so limited and are many thousands of times faster; some computers can add 250,000 sixteen-digit numbers in one second, or can record the equivalent of 50,000 words in one second. Another important fact is that the electronic computer has a memory or storage bank which makes possible an enormous saving of time in retrieving data.

MACHINE LANGUAGE

The evolution from manual to punched card processing, while resulting in increased speed, did not require the notion of a new language. The various devices accepted and operated upon ("understood") data expressed in decimal numbers and the letters of (say) the English alphabet. Electronic computers, however, "understand" only two values, which we may call "current-off" and "current-on", or simply, "off" and "on". The natural language of these machines is then the *binary number system*, which uses only the two digits 0 ("off") and 1 ("on"). Binary numbers are built up by giving these digits place-values. If, for example, the digit 1 is at the extreme right, as in 0001, it has the value 1. If it is moved one position to the left, as in 0010, its value is doubled, becoming 2. If it is moved one more place to the left, making 0100, it doubles again to become 4. If moved still another place, making 1000, it doubles again to become 8. The number which in the decimal system is represented by 5, is represented by 0101 in the binary system.

To bridge the gap between human languages and machine language, a number of intermediary languages, called *programming languages*, have been developed. These sufficiently resemble human languages to make instructing the machine a not too difficult task. At the same time, they are close enough to machine language to permit direct translation into that language by the computer itself. Two programming languages which have been widely used in data processing are FORTRAN (for FORmula TRANslation) and COBOL (for COmmon Business Oriented Language). Now, simpler languages are being developed and some are already available.

COMPONENTS

An electronic data processing system includes the computer and a number of other machines called *peripheral equipment*. The machines are collectively known as *hardware*; *software* includes computer programs, feasibility studies, manuals, etc. The computer may itself be broken down into the following functional units.

(1) *Control unit.* The control unit directs the operations of all the computer components in accordance with the particular *program*. The program is stored within the computer and guides the flow of processing from the input at the beginning until the output at the end of processing.

(2) *Input unit.* Generally data will be put into the computer by means of punched cards, paper tape, or magnetic tape. The last is by far the fastest method and is the most economical of storage space.

(3) *Arithmetic unit.* The arithmetic unit can do more than merely add, subtract, multiply, and divide. It follows the established program and accepts new data or can recall any needed data from the *memory* of the computer. It also makes yes-or-no decisions such as: Are two numbers equal? Has sufficient accuracy been achieved?

(4) *Output unit.* When the processing is completed the results are made available as desired. The output may be via electric typewriter, line printer, tape, cards, or visual display. The typewriter will produce 10 characters per second, the line printer up to 800 lines a minute, with 120 characters per line.

Accounting Applications of EDP

Electronic data processing can be used for practically every accounting operation, but it becomes most profitable where there is a large mass of data to be processed, as in payroll preparation, billing customers, and maintaining balances for inventories, accounts receivable, and accounts payable. There are various other applications that are concerned more with control and analysis than with detailed processing.

PAYROLL

The payroll operation has become more time-consuming in recent years because of a wide variety of withholdings, such as those for income tax, social security, unemployment insurance, hospitalization, pension, and disability. Also, in many manufacturing plants there are premium rates for the night shift, overtime computations, different rates when an employee does different jobs, etc. When there are hundreds or thousands of employees paid on a weekly basis, the preparation of the payroll can indeed be a major undertaking.

EDP is well-suited to payroll preparation since the repetitive data — the employee's name, address, identification number, pay rate, number of exemptions, types of withholdings — are written only once, and thereafter automatically printed when needed. With manual processing this data generally has to be written each week for each employee. With EDP the only new input is the data that will vary, such as hours worked and the job serial number. The computer calculates all the necessary results, not only what was formerly generated manually by the payroll department, but also such things as the payroll bank reconciliation, many reports to government agencies, and various kinds of management control data. And all this, of course, at a fraction of the time required for manual processing.

BILLING

Much of the information needed for preparing bills to customers is repetitive and is readily performed by the computer. For example, the customer's name, address, and identification number are first stored in the machine. Then the description of the product and price can be stored. As deliveries are made, the sales information can be fed into the machine. Automatically the computer will list the items and summarize all shipments to the customer, calculate prices, print a shipment document, and make out a bill to the customer.

The computer system stores a vast amount of sales information from which summaries can be printed out, showing total sales by customer, by period, by product, by salesman, by territory, or by profitability. These sales statistics are essential to good management and would require a great amount of time if summarized manually.

MAINTAINING BALANCES

In order to manage a company efficiently it is necessary to control the balances of key functions of the business, particularly inventory, accounts receivable, and accounts payable. If a sufficient quantity of various inventory components is not maintained, production may be disrupted; if too much is invested in inventory, then working capital will be insufficient and accounts payable cannot be settled. By the same token, if accounts receivable become too large, working capital is also adversely affected. Many firms maintain all inventory items on the computer: each time goods are received or shipped, punched cards are prepared and a new balance automatically computed. From time to time reports are printed out, showing purchases, usage, stock levels, and inventory value. Comparable data can be prepared for increases and decreases in the accounts for individual customers and individual vendors.

OTHER APPLICATIONS

There are many types of accounting applications besides those described above. The general ledger and all other accounting records can be put on the computer. That is generally the next step after the more repetitive functions have been computerized and are operating satisfactorily. Many companies also have their cost systems and budget systems on the computer.

It should be mentioned that important nonaccounting functions may be computerized in a large company. Purchasing, production, or engineering functions may make continuous or periodic use of the computer, which also allows solution of complex business and management problems that were not previously feasible.

INDEX

Catalog

If you are interested in a list of SCHAUM'S
OUTLINE SERIES in Science, Mathematics,
Engineering and other subjects, send your name
and address, requesting your free catalog, to:

'S OUTLINE SERIES, Dept. C
ILL BOOK COMPANY
Americas
0020